MIGRATION ITALY

The Art of Talking Back in a Destination Culture

In terms of migration, Italy is often thought of as a source country – a place from which people came rather than one to which people go. However, in the past few decades, Italy has become a destination for many people from poor or war-torn countries seeking a better life in a stable environment. Graziella Parati's *Migration Italy* examines immigration to Italy in recent decades and the cultural hybridization that has occurred as a result.

Working from a cultural studies viewpoint, Parati constructs a theoretical framework for discussing Italy as a country of immigration. She gives special attention to immigrant literature, positing that it functions as an act of resistance, a means of 'talking back' to the laws and customs that regulate the lives of migrants. Parati also looks at examples from Italian cinema, demonstrating how native and non-native filmmakers compare and distinguish between old and new migrations.

An appreciation of the complexities inherent in the different cultural, legal, and political positions of Italy's people is at the heart of *Migration Italy*, a work of key importance for understanding society in modern-day Italy and, indeed, the entire European continent.

(Toronto Italian Studies)

GRAZIELLA PARATI is a professor in the Department of French and Italian, the Comparative Literature Program, and the Women's and Gender Studies Program at Dartmouth College.

GRAZIELLA PARATI

Migration Italy: The Art of Talking Back in a Destination Culture

UNIVERSITY OF TORONTO PRESS
Toronto Buffalo London

Toronto Buffalo London
www.utppublishing.com
Printed in the U.S.A.

Reprinted in paperback 2014

ISBN 978-0-8020-3924-8 (cloth)
ISBN 978-1-4426-2672-0 (paper)

Printed on acid-free paper

Toronto Italian Studies

Library and Archives Canada Cataloguing in Publication

Parati, Graziella, author
Migration Italy : the art of talking back in a destination culture / Graziella Parati.

(Toronto Italian studies)
Includes bibliographical references and index.
ISBN 978-0-8020-3924-8 (bound.) – ISBN 978-1-4426-2672-0 (pbk.)

1. Italian literature – History and criticism. 2. Immigrants' writings, Italian – History and criticism. 3. Immigrants in literature. 4. Motion pictures – Italy – History and criticism. 5. Immigrants – In motion pictures. 6. Emigration and immigration law – Italy. I. Title. II. Series.

PQ4049.P37 2005 850.9'3552 C2005-902191-8

Publication of this book was made possible by grants from the Dickey Centre and the Guthrie Fund at Dartmouth College.

University of Toronto Press acknowledges the financial assistance to its publishing program of the Canada Council for the Arts and the Ontario Arts Council.

Canada Council for the Arts Conseil des Arts du Canada

ONTARIO ARTS COUNCIL
CONSEIL DES ARTS DE L'ONTARIO
50 YEARS OF ONTARIO GOVERNMENT SUPPORT OF THE ARTS
50 ANS DE SOUTIEN DU GOUVERNEMENT DE L'ONTARIO AUX ARTS

University of Toronto Press acknowledges the financial support for the publishing activities of the Government of Canada through the Book Publishing Industry Development Program (BPIDP).

Per Pia

Contents

Acknowledgments

This book would not exist without the help of friends and colleagues. Mary Jean Green and Marie Orton have had the arduous job of reading first versions of each chapter. Marie, in particular, has been very generous in correcting grammar mistakes that still plague my life in English. I owe much gratitude to Lynn Higgins, Keala Jewell, Marianne Hirsch, and Barbara Spackman, who read and commented on the manuscript. I want to thank Alec Hargreaves, Nathalie Hester, and Gabriella Romani for their friendship, support, and encouragement when writing becomes a challenge. I am particularly grateful to Rebecca West for her help on this book and for teaching me what mentoring is all about. At Dartmouth College, Michael Mastanduno, director of the Dicky Center, and the Guthrie Fund of the French and Italian Department provided financial support, for which I am very grateful. I warmly thank Beppe Cavatorta, Anna Minardi, Emanuel Rota, and Nora Stoppino for great conversations over Italian food and wine. Without them my life in the Upper Connecticut Valley would be much more isolated and unhappy. I have presented my work on migration issues at Notre Dame, the University of Oregon, New York University, Cornell, Duke, Yale, Georgetown, Columbia, the University of Warwick, UK, Monash University, Melbourne, the Universities of Chicago and Miami Ohio, the University of Bologna, and the University of Rome, La Sapienza; my thanks to colleagues who invited me to speak and to audiences for listening. Ron Schoeffel at the University of Toronto Press was unfailingly encouraging and supportive. I thank him greatly. Deborah Starewich supplied valuable help on the manuscript, which would not have been sent to the publisher without her help.

MIGRATION ITALY

The Art of Talking Back in a Destination Culture

Introduction

It is always curious to note to what extent our critical interests are tied to, or emanate from, our autobiographies.

Susanne Zantop[1]

One of the first sentences I ever pronounced was 'Nona, cüna, nona,' because I wanted my grandmother to rock the cradle in which I was supposed to nap. 'Nona' stayed with my family until I was seven, so I learned to understand her native Occitan, which was also my mother's native tongue. My older sister did not get along with our grandmother and therefore never articulated a sound in her language.[2] My sister firmly embraced standard Italian, the language we siblings spoke to each other. Standard Italian was also the language my mother used in talking to her daughters; she was the only one in the family who could master it, although she learned it when she went to school in 1930. Her mother tongue was Occitan. Even now I am surprised by the fact that she makes mistakes in Italian: her 's' and 'c' are at times interchangeable, her prepositions at times are not correct. She was aware that in the 1960s (I was born in 1960) in Italy social mobility was firmly grounded in the ability to speak standard Italian. When I went to first grade, I realized that children who could only speak the local dialect carried connotations of inferiority, and very little was expected from them.

I grew up in Lombardy. The local language was a variation of Milanese. My mother in fact had migrated from the province of Cuneo and had settled in Melegnano, south of Milan. She had also learned the local dialect, 'Meregnanin,' because speaking it helped her establish a friendly relationship with her customers, who would buy her goods at the market. 'Meregnanin' is a language that has transformed the aristocratic 'o' in Milanese dialect into 'u' or 'ü.' In my family 'Meregnanin' had been subjected to another transformation. My father, who originated from the province of Cremona, hybridized his native 'Cremonese' dialect with 'Meregnanin' and spoke his particular brand of local language. He was born in 1911, and belonged to a generation and a social class that was little exposed to standard Italian. I remember the quarrels between my maternal grandmother and my father: they did not understand each other, had no language in common. It was thoroughly fascinating for me: I could understand what they were both saying, but they could not, and their verbal exchanges made no sense whatsoever.

My father's tongue was never my first or even second language. We spoke very little to each other and I always responded to his questions asked in dialect with answers in standard Italian, which he understood. However, even today, some family sayings remain in the paternal language, some in my mother's Occitan. My father's term 'sghei' (money) and his warning 'Te vegnarà a cu' ('it will hurt you') still remain tongue-in-cheek sayings in our family conversations although my father died a few years ago. I also know how to say 'Siu la fja d'Lena di Brun' ('I am the daughter of Lena of the Brun') in my mother's language, and so I can say whose daughter I am when I go back to the *val Maira*, where she grew up. That's my way of stating that I belong, but in reality although I understand the general topic of a conversation, I could never handle a conversation in Occitan myself. My father's language, that particular brand of 'Meregnanin,' is more familiar to me and I can speak it, but not fluently.

I grew up in a domestic sphere that was a cultural crossroads because languages coexisted in the same house. However, if languages overlapped in my mother's linguistic ability, all the other members rejected dialectal imbrications and embraced a specific identification with one language and one culture. More than Italian, my father was a man from the Cremonese region; my illiterate grandmother migrated to Milan but remained an Occitan woman; my sister and myself embraced Italian, the language of social mobility. Italian was for us also a special link with our mother; it was a maternal language grounded in the betrayal of her own maternal dialect.

The constitutive languages of my familial sphere are at the same time familiar and unfamiliar to me. Local people in Melegnano realize that their 'o' is for me too often an 'ö' in my attempt to overcorrect what I don't know (i.e., correct 'Meregnanin'). I always thought that Meregnanin was a language I could understand, a language with which I was familiar enough to feel comfortable. Once I was riding my bicycle in the countryside near Melegnano and my bicycle broke. A farmer stopped and asked me what the problem was. He told me that to repair it I would need a 'menera.' In my awkward 'Meregnanin' I answered: 'Mi su minga cusa l'è la "menera"' ('I don't know what a "menera" is'). He responded: 'La "menera" a l'è la "menera"' ('A "menera" is a "menera"'). My reaction was exactly the same as the reaction that readers of this text are experiencing: total incomprehension. The farmer loaded my bike and me on his tractor and took us to look for the infamous 'menera', which turned out to be a *chiave inglese* (a wrench). I had previously had the experience of not understanding words that my father had said, but only then, right in the middle of nowhere, did I realize how unfamiliar the familiar was and how inadequate my knowledge of the local languages had always been. I still do not know 'Meregnanin,' or Occitan, as I am a native speaker of standard Italian. Instead of learning the dialects, I chose to learn English, and then Swedish, and then a bit of German. Then I moved to England, and later to the United States. Like my mother, I live in a second language. I also write in a second language.

Both my parents were migrants themselves. Their geographical dislocation is small if measured in kilometres, but considerable if calculated in cultural miles. Italy in the 1930s and 1940s was still linguistically and culturally a very fragmented country. Italian had been chosen in the nineteenth century to become the national language. It had been a decision made by a political force that wanted a national language and culture for the newly constructed Italy. The educational programs implemented since the unification of Italy in the 1860s had not, however, yielded the desired results. My father studied Italian in school for a few years, starting in 1917, and my mother did the same in 1930. It is because of migration that Italian became important for my mother. That was the language that allowed a person to hide a hydrid identity. Nonetheless, that hybrid identity was purloined in plain view because accents in Italian betray one's regional origin. Italian was also the language that allowed one to cross internal cultural borders that were also lines of separation between social classes. Together with wealth, Italian became the acquisition that defined success in the Italian economic boom of the late 1950s and early 1960s.

Television and mandatory schooling became the tools to translate a political agenda of cultural unification orchestrated almost a hundred years earlier. My parents' migration created a familial space in which borders between languages and cultures had to be crossed daily. In my family, identities were inevitably hybrid and talked back to the national plan for a belated cultural unification.

Once I started questioning my own educational race toward a standard Italian acculturation based on homogeneity, I had to go back and reread my life in order to develop an interpretation of Italianness that has also marked my work on the otherness of contemporary migrants to Italy. In particular, this book deals with what is minor in contemporary Italian culture and on migrants who author their stories in a second or third language. Focusing on migrants' writings in Italian is my indirect way of returning to explore the multiple linguistic planes in my own culture in order to understand its multicultural future.

Susanne Zantop has reminded critics who write about alterity that it is necessary to define the location from and the context in which the critic himself or herself articulates his/her theories on otherness. Zantop's invitation to disclose the position from which one is speaking is particularly relevant in this book on migration issues and on processes of cultural hybridization. In recent years Italy has become a country of migrants, with a resulting fundamental redefinition of Italian cultural and ethnic identities. Italy has also gradually adopted rigid positions against immigration, joining the effort of constructing a 'fortress Europe,' a term developed to describe the political agenda of conservative forces vis-à-vis immigration. A 'fortress Europe' is a political entity that wants to protect itself from hordes of migrants, perceived as people who threaten national cultures. Seen as a global phenomenon, however, migration defies any attempt to reclaim national identities and create rhetorical discourses as protection against external contaminations. The agents of migration – the people who perform the difficult journey of migration – are at the centre of this book. My interest in them started while I was writing on autobiographical writing and gender issues. The problem of identity construction in women's autobiography brought me to explore layers of otherness that uncovered the autobiographical writing of women migrants in Italy. As it was a new field and very little had been written about these women, I created an ad-hoc way of researching their writings by collecting oral histories and interviewing the migrants themselves.

Maria Viarengo, one of the women interviewed, agreed to meet with me because, she said, I was a migrant myself and I could understand her story. I was flattered, but also worried that it was not me as a scholar, professor, critic who was meeting her, but another me she had decided to privilege and drag into my academic approach to migration. She was right of course; working on migration was also a way to come to terms with having migrated myself, even if my cultural and geographical displacement was privileged. However, being asked to bring my experience into the articulation of my approach to migration studies and contemporary Italian culture has made writing this book a rather complex operation.

Migrating is never easy. My statement sounds rather simple, but I speak from my position as a privileged migrant who has experienced the complexity of deterritorialization. I left Italy for another European country and later for the United States because I wanted to study and to leave Italy. The country of origin is an artificial construct. The context from which I originated became an uncomfortable location of belonging. Finding unfamiliar the familiar context in which a person is born is the experience of many people who have chosen another place to live. It does not mean that the new location is an ideal place. The new location is only outside one's past. Migrating is easier for me because I can always transmigrate, that is, I can easily live in two places, Italy and the United States. Nomadism replaces migration. My nomadism is a privilege. It is often very difficult, but is part of my inability to belong anywhere, because only a partial belonging is possible.

The difficulty lies in the need to explain myself anywhere I am. My identity needs explanation because, although not uncommon, it is often questioned and people ask for a narrative that can make it familiar. In England, I started the never-ending narrative of explaining myself. The questions are always the same: Why did you leave? Is it better 'here' or 'there'? Do you miss 'your culture'? Are you going 'back'? These are simple questions with no answer: there are many reasons why I left, but the same reasons made other people stay. There is no 'here' or 'there' in migration, even less in transmigration. 'There' will not stay there and follows the migrant constantly. 'Here' changes and is inseparable from 'there.' I have been asked if I prefer to speak or write in Italian or in English, but there cannot be a preference. Italian serves to sustain part of who I am, and gives voice to my right of being different; English feeds the thoughts of the part of myself who functions as a citizen of the American culture for most of the year. The result is neither in-betweenness nor fragmentation, but rather a different way to live and embody an identity that braids cultural borders together. Anything else feels constricting and claustrophobic. The right not to belong is, again, a very privileged condition.

The complexity of the identity of a migrant, of myself, collapses when the language of bureaucracy determines who I am. Moving to the United States, I experienced the agonizing process of documentation that impacted my perspective of both the act of migrating and my identity. Asphalt was never greyer and more ominous-looking than around the consulate where I went to obtain my visas. That asphalt functioned as a mirror of my wide-ranging preoccupations. I never knew if I had all the documentation needed, I never knew how rude the person in charge of my case would be, I never knew how much I would be searched before I could gain access to the consulate, or how long the line would be, or how many people before me would be crying. Consulates are a peculiar place filled with people with guns, people with power over other people's lives, people who cry because they have no control of their future, and people who triumphantly walk out of the building with the necessary visa. I mainly remember the grey asphalt and the bureaucratic challenge of leaving Italy. I also remember the euphoria of leaving to reinvent myself. But then I was in my twenties, and a university was sponsoring my migration.

After almost twenty years, I am tired of justifying my presence outside of what others think is my country. So I say I am from New Hampshire, I just have a speech problem. Or I say that I am from New York and being from New York seems to justify having an accent for most people who interrogate me. Yet, when I went to Australia, people could not hear my non-American accent and they assigned one identity to me and articulated heart-felt affinities between Australians and Americans. I could not help feeling resentment for that mutilation. I am now so accustomed to being two that I could not accept one homogeneous and coherent identity. In the end, not being a migrant seemed to be a much more boring narrative, and one in which I could not recognize myself.

The problem lies with the facile labelling of indefinable identities that fails to articulate identity constructions outside old stereotypes. Whenever a narrative is allowed, then identity can be voiced, even if only in part. However, when bureaucracy is involved, narratives are less important than identities defined in an administrative game of multiple choice. The forms many others and I had to fill out in order to apply for a green card asked for name, birthplace, and profession.

After answering that my profession was 'assistant professor,' I had to mark 'yes' or 'no' in response to questions concerning my possible 'mental retardation,' a vaguely defined 'moral turpitude,' and 'sexual deviance.' In addition, I was required to state that I had never committed a crime for which I had not been caught, and I was not a communist (even though the Berlin Wall had already fallen four years earlier). I had to be tested for all venereal diseases, tuberculosis, and I do not remember what else. When I had the test for my naturalization, the state representative asked me once to name the capital of the United States, but asked me three times if I had ever been a prostitute.

'Naturalizing' a migrant requires decontaminating him or her through a bureaucratic process that employs a medical vocabulary in order to create a legal narrative about identity formation in a new culture. Such a narrative only loses its dehumanizing edge if it is experienced as a text created by the migrant himself or herself and at a distance, articulated through the act of telling a story. Telling the experience of my 'naturalization,' I have entertained friends and acquaintances around the dinner table, but it was nevertheless a process filled with anxiety and loss of control over my own life.

Now I reject distance from both the country of my e-migration and that of my im-migration. In fact, I keep re-migrating in an endless cycle that at times places Italian policemen as my antagonists. As director of foreign programs in Italy, I frequently need to regularize American students in Italy. Again I stand in line. As representative of my students I become again a protagonist, deprived of agency, in the text of the laws that regulate my right to be or not to be on a national soil. In Italy immigration laws and their discretionary interpretations have also supplied new entertaining narratives at dinners with friends. Until a couple of years ago, Siena's immigration office had a rather peculiar ritual. Before even considering attaining the privilege of standing in line, I would have to go to the immigration office around seven in the morning (but not too late after seven). On the side of the medieval well in front of the office, I would find a sheet of paper under a heavy rock, write my name on the paper, then walk around until eight-thirty when the office opened so I could stand in line and then collect the forms that my students would fill out. Then I would go back and, theoretically, start the process again. One year they abruptly changed the way the process worked, as well as the mornings when the office would be open. I stood alone in front of the locked wooden door of the immigration office that still posted the old, obsolete procedure, and looked for a rock that was not there any more, until I asked for help from a passing policeman. I felt like a new migrant. Of course, as a native speaker with a white skin and a professional title, I often did not have to stand in line a second time. I could hand in the completed forms at a police station. I felt guilty about using my privilege, but knew that the following year I would be standing in the same line with the same demands.

I had the questionable privilege of being in Italy in September/October 2002 when the Bossi-Fini immigration law was enacted. It took me about two weeks to understand what kind of documentation was necessary. The extraordinary thing about Italy is that a study-visa obtained at an Italian consulate in the United States guarantees a person's right only to enter Italy but not to stay in Italy. Once on the national territory, my students had to apply for a stay-permit, that is, supply the same documentation already presented at the Italian consulate and stand in the inevitable line. I had to take all my students to the main immigration office in Rome, stand in line with them, and fill out the forms that cannot be collected beforehand any more. Once my privileged private-college students entered the office, they started to worry. The policemen / immigration officers wore white coats and looked like doctors. Some officials who walked around holding piles of folders looked like nurses carrying medical records. The students feared that they would have to give blood. On the counter, there was a book entitled *SOS Aids*, lying face up. It looked like a staged performance of the desire of bureaucracy to heal the body of a country from the disease of migration. The immigration office turned into an institutional theatre hosting a well-rehearsed performance of power relations that both define control over migrants and betray the anxiety that other cultures create in Italy. The book reminded me of the medical tests I had to pass to acquire a green card, but also embodied in a tangible way the anxiety that migrants are potential carriers of disease into a destination culture.

I did not say anything. I did not ask the official there to place the book out of sight. I have learned the lesson that any migrant knows: when asking for stay permits one should not question anything and should accept the authority emanating from a uniform, or a doctor's gown. At the police station, the faces were familiar: some people cried, some triumphantly held a stay-permit in their hands, some looked resigned to standing in another line. There are still guns, as Italian immigration officers are also policemen. I am sure those migrants noticed how grey the asphalt is outside any immigration office. I still see its colour, but my story is another story and the asphalt-grey is losing its ominous connotations.

Of course privilege steps in. My students were loud and oblivious to the silent people standing in line, and they did not have to come back to bring missing documents, or to collect their stay-permits. They were white and American and representatives of their college; as the program director, I could deal with the process for them. In turn, I found a helpful officer who accelerated the process for me because I was the 'same' and not different. Actually, I was exotically 'same' as I was an Italian who had gone to 'America,' and he was curious about my migration.

This book originated from standing in line, waiting for visas, and therefore it often displays a polemical tone. My own experience of migration is the autobiographical context from which my theoretical approach to migration studies began. The purpose of the book is to focus on the specific case of migration to Italy and on the unique case of Italian contemporary multiculturalism. Migration from Italy characterized the end of the nineteenth and most of the twentieth century, but in the 1970s and 1980s Italy became the destination for people migrating from poorer countries. Italy's transformation from a country from which people departed to a country that attracted immigration invited an investigation about the cultural changes that had complemented the changes in the nation's economic status. After taking into consideration studies on global migration, and in particular on francophone culture, I also wanted to address the processes of constructing Italianness at different junctures in time, that is, when Italians e-migrated and when people im-migrated to Italy. Doing so would help me to articulate the language I wanted to employ to write about contemporary Italian multiculturalism. Literature and migrants' writing became the starting points of my research because I wanted to find the voices of the silent people I saw standing in immigration lines. Their narratives about migration tell first hand the (hi)story of contemporary migrations to Italy and interpret the cultural changes in Italian culture.

This book is an interdisciplinary project that belongs to the field of cultural studies. It deals with literature, film, the law, and the relationship between literature and the text of Italian immigration laws. Qualitative and quantitative analysis of contemporary Italian culture is fundamental for describing contemporary Italy as a country that has experienced both migration and immigration. My purpose is to create a theoretical framework for approaching the specific case of immigration culture in Italy vis-à-vis the cultural impact that (e)migratory movements from Italy have had in shaping contemporary Italian culture.

The first chapter, 'Strategies of "Talking Back"' develops the concept of the 'recolouring' of Italian culture. I term 'recolouring' the process of uncovering deliberate efforts to whiten Italian culture and create a European (Northern and white) identity for a culture that lies at a cultural and geographical crossroads in the middle of the Mediterranean Sea. 'Recolouring' becomes a strategic process that uncovers the multicultural identity of Italy, whose monoculturalism is an artificial construct. In fact, before focusing on contemporary migrants to Italy it is necessary to uncover the artificiality of the concept of Italian culture as a homogeneous entity. This monolithically uniform construct has been orchestrated in order to create a national unity, justified in turn by a long linguistic and cultural history. The circularity on which national and cultural unity has been constructed needs contextualization. By questioning the concepts of the 'whiteness' and 'Europeanness' of Italian culture, this chapter theorizes the possibility of 'talking back' to normative narratives that constitute the dominant construction of Italy as part of an economic and cultural North. Strategies of 'talking back' constitute the unassembled skeleton of resistance to prescriptive paradigms that regulate what Italian culture is, but remain weak acts of resistance because of their fragmented nature. By exploring cultural products, often popular literature, I trace the evolution of the process of 'recolouring' and of acts of 'talking back' in texts written by both migrants and native Italians.

Chapter 1 creates the theoretical framework that sustains the following chapters. Grounded on the work on multiculturalism, difference, otherness, and migration authored by Homi Bhabha, Julia Kristeva, Rosi Braidotti, and Alec Hargreaves, to name a few, this chapter discusses the location of Italian multiculturalism in relation to other migratory contexts such as the French. In addition, the work of Fred Gardaphé, Anthony Tamburri, and other scholars of Italian American culture have created the fundamental work without which my discourse on Italian multiculturalism throughout the centuries could not be discussed. The first chapter is particularly indebted to their work on the evolution of Italian American narratives and their discussion of the gradual whitening of the Italian identity in the United States.

'Minor Literature, Minor Italy' is the title of the second chapter. It builds on the concept of 'talking back' in order to challenge the separation between external and internal, and other dichotomies that sustain stereotypes of belonging and unbelonging. Migrants' writings are the focus of chapter 2 because they are texts that dialogue with other narratives that have described Italian migration to northern Europe and the United States. From 1990 until the present migrants have written and published texts that tell of their acculturation into Italian society and portray the context into which they want to inscribe themselves as agents of cultural change. They dialogue with an Italian past grounded in migration and articulate the possibility of constructing what I have termed a 'destination culture,' in which narratives of sameness and difference intersect and articulate possible developments in contemporary Italian culture. Processes of cultural hybridization connect Italian otherness (filtered through the Italian experience of migration) with migrants' difference.

Literature occupies a privileged position in this context. Interpreted as minor literature, intended in a Deleuzian sense, migrants' literature appropriates a major language, Italian in this case, and turns it into a new system of signification that describes complex lives grounded in cultural displacement. In earlier articles, I called 'Italophone' literature that system of texts written by migrants in Italian at the beginning of the 1990s.[3] The emphasis was on the use of the Italian language to narrate life stories of migration and the creation of texts that speak to native Italians. Italian is also the unifying language that allows writers to speak to other migrants. Authored by Africans, eastern Europeans, and South Americans, as well as other nationalities, who write in Italian, Italophone literature included a complex system of narratives that gradually become less autobiographical, experiment with different genres, and dialogue with the Italian literary tradition. Inevitably, these literary and linguistic experimentations are influenced by other Western and non-Western cultures and languages that the migrants speak and by the colonial cultures that have been part of their education. At times Italy becomes a chosen destination in migration in order to interrupt the linear connections between a former colony and a 'mother'-land. This is the case for authors such as the Senegalese Pap Khouma and Saidou Moussa Ba, who preferred to inscribe their lives in Italy and script their life stories in Italian. Their acquisition of Italian was facilitated by their knowledge of French. 'Italophone' authors used the colonial heritage to betray it deliberately by privileging Italian. In fact, a Western colonial language is often the mediating tool for learning Italian, and Italian (which could also be considered another

Western colonial language) in turn becomes the elective language in which migrant authors write their identities.

Defining the word migrant is a complex operation that is, however, necessary to unpack the meaning of 'migrant writer.' According to Deleuze and Guattari: 'The nomad is not at all the same as the migrant; for the migrant goes principally from one point to another, even if the second point is uncertain, unforeseen or not well localized. But the nomad only goes from point to point as a consequence and a factual necessity: in principle, points for him are relays along a trajectory. Nomads and migrants can mix in many ways, or form a common aggregate.'[4] Geographically linear migrations are not often possible. It is therefore impossible to use the words 'immigrant' and 'emigrant' to underline a one-way linear movement. When I use the word 'immigrant' in my discussion, I will in fact intend a rather prescriptive concept that eloquently defines the concept of the migrant in the press, the laws, the institutions. Immigrant is also a term that can be frequently found in sociological texts as an attempt to define the global phenomenon of people moving from one location to another country. Although never just a neutral term, thanks to its Latin prefix 'in' the word immigrant is at times useful in defining a phenomenon that has marked Italy in recent decades as much as e-migration did in the nineteenth and twentieth centuries. In talking about writers and the processes of self-identification in literature, I will always define the subjects as migrants, and often as nomads. Privileging the word 'migrant' allows for a more articulated, multidirectional translation into disparate geographical and cultural contexts. Migrant writers often document their wanderings in Europe before settling in one country where, again, they do not live in one place, but continue their peripatetic acculturation that turns migration into transmigration, often describing the impossibility of settling in one specific place. The different points that mark a migrant's journey are often not only relays, but complex experiences of places where a long-term migration is not possible because of regulations, the economic conditions of the area, or the demands of seasonal work. Transmigration is at times dictated by contingent needs, but in their narratives, migrants also talk about their nomadism, a concept that, borrowing from Rosi Braidotti's work, weakens any limiting sense of belonging to one specific national context or culture. Both transmigration and nomadism are constitutive of migration, and any attempt to clearly separate the terms creates restrictive and problematic categories. However, nomadism can acquire connotations linked to the idea of 'free movement,' which is not often the experience of the migrant who has to cross borders strictly regulated by laws that rigidly define the concepts of belonging and unbelonging.

Nomadism could be interpreted as the translation into writing of the experience of migration. The institutional and cultural limitations imposed on migrants are deliberately challenged in the act of authoring one's life. Writing becomes therefore the tool of self-transformation from migrant to nomad. This nomadism in writing has the function of deterritorializing one's experience by scripting it in another language. The migrant writer deterritorializes Western cultures into a text, becoming the agent in an interpretative process. Writing becomes a means to assert a migrant's position as interpretative subject and to reject the essentializing definition of migrants presented in political rhetoric. Writing in Italian also involves an act of territorial appropriation, as the result is a book that enters into the published, and therefore public, texts about a culture. By becoming writers, migrants as carriers of different cultures destabilize the local cultures in which they settle. In migration, a person inevitably interacts with and changes the destination culture in which he/she has settled. All protectionist discourses on the part of Western countries attempt to ignore or completely demonize the changes brought by migration. By contrast, a migrant writer creates a cultural synthesis that articulates the tensions inherent in all migrations and acts of deterritorialization. In fact, migrant writers are the authors of discourses in which the processes of changing and being changed conflate. Their narratives document the impact that migrants have on local host cultures and the processes through which local cultures reshape the already heterogeneous culture of migrants.

Terms are always subject to revision because they often reveal their inadequacy in translating the complex process of migration and of writing in migration. For instance, my use of 'Italophone literature' and 'migrants' writing' arises from the need to create a terminology that is adequate in discussing the context of contemporary Italian multiculturalism. I am, however, aware of the fluid nature of such definitions. The texts themselves offer various and evolving self-definitions that resist rigid categories, however useful they may be. The neologism 'Italophone' is useful since it emphasizes the acquisition of Italian as a new language in which to inscribe one's life, and was particularly necessary for defining migrants' literature at the beginning of the 1990s. It proves, inevitably, inadequate to describe the complexity that characterizes other texts. Marked by collaboration with a linguistic expert, what I called 'Italophone' texts (such as the first migrants' texts to be published, those authored by Salah Methnani, Saidou Moussa Ba, and Pap Khouma) are quickly replaced by other narratives that articulate wide-ranging issues concerning migration. Even Nassera Chohra's *Volevo diventare bianca* (1993), written in collaboration with a linguistic expert, documents a very complex process of migration that cannot be contained in the label 'Italophone.' In fact, Chohra's text tells of trans-migration across generations. Born in France of Algerian parents, she decided to move to Italy and write in Italian. Her narrative in Italian describes concerns that are typical of a second generation as she narrates her life in France as a daughter of Algerian parents. The linear evolution of narratives that is defined according to first-generation and then second-generation concerns in francophone culture cannot be sustained in an Italian context. In fact, issues across generations appear in a first generation of migrants' writings in Italian that end up talking back to any rigidly scripted definition of post-colonial traditions.

The concept of 'Italophone' writings is complicated by texts that belong to a 'post-migration' and 'post-ethnic' context. In his books, Jadelin Mabiala Gangbo, born in Congo but raised in Italy by native Italians, investigates the complexity of looking different but being familiar with the Western culture in which one is raised. His texts dialogue with an Italian literary tradition and different genres that collapse the separation between high and low culture. In particular, his *Rometta and Giulieo* (2001) is a pulp-fiction novel narrated by using both obsolete nineteenth-century Italian and a contemporary metalanguage borrowed from the youth oral culture. He eloquently intertwines language borrowed from the century that promoted national and cultural unification, and linguistic codification, with the transgressive language of contemporary young Italians. In his post-migrant and post-ethnic text, a Chinese delivery boy delivers the international and stereotypical sign of Italian culture (pizza), but speaks in a rarefied and literary language. Post-migration and post-ethnic writings conflate characteristics that took generations to develop in other national and linguistic milieus and further complicate the issue of naming.

In fact, describing migrants' writings vis-à-vis post-migrant or post-ethnic texts is complicated by the fact that outside forces tend to define them in categories or genres that are not determined by form, but by content, or, even more problematically, by the author's identity. Accepting from the beginning that these texts are expressions of Italian literature, or that the very concept of Italian literature should be dismantled in order to talk about global culture, is not a viable solution because it ignores the problems inherent in such an operation and the difference that these texts embody. The narratives that I analyse in the second chapter embody a transitional complexity that deserves particular attention. It is only by focusing on the in-betweenness of migrants' texts, and on the problematic articulations of post-migration and post-ethnic narratives, that more global theorizations on contemporary literature and culture can be performed. It is the difficulty in naming categories of literary belonging or unbelonging that uncovers the innovations inherent in multicultural literary experimentations. These texts revolutionize categories and reject the possibility of ghettoizing a genre that borrows from many traditions and dialogues with the many traditions in Italian culture.[5]

Grounded in a non-separatist agenda, chapter 2 also includes those novels by native Italian writers who make migrants the protagonists of their texts. These narratives focus on constitutive elements of marginal identities and dialogue (at times with success) with the processes of identity construction in migrants' life stories. Authors such as Giulio Angioni, Marco Lodoli, Giorgio Saponaro, and Emilio Tadini have constructed weak attempts to talk back to a dominant rhetoric about migrants' difference in order to connect internal and external differences. For instance, Angioni's *Una ignota compagnia* (*An Unknown Company,* 1992) revolves around the experiences of two friends: an internal migrant from Sardinia to Milan and a migrant from Kenya to Italy. Lodoli explores points of contact between differences; he writes about a black migrant and an elderly native Italian who inhabit the margins of society. However, these texts are at times guilty of recycling old stereotypes and of being trapped in a normative process they have tried to question.

Still, native Italian writers' work is fundamental for exploring the possibility of a 'destination culture' that is not only the culture of the country toward which people migrate. In the context of my work, a destination culture is the result of a process of hybridization between local and incoming culture, and is therefore a destination culture for native Italians as well. An Italian destination culture is also the context in which terms such as migrant writer, post-migrant literature, and post-ethnic identity will be part of a more complex discourse on cultural hybridity. In a destination culture the emphasis will be on differences rather then on the construction of cultural majorities that create artificial homogeneities.

In the heterogeneity of a destination culture *in fieri*, it is particularly relevant to investigate gender issues. Male writers, like male migrants, tend to be more visible. In fact, their texts have similarly been more readily visible. Women writers such as Shirin Ramzanali Fazel and Viola Chandra remind us of the issues, and of the added layers of otherness, that they had to confront as women and as others. In *Lontano da Mogadiscio* (*Far Away from Mogadishu*, 1994), Shirin Ramzanali Fazel describes her migration from Somalia and her difficult inscription within a culture that she had studied in school in Somalia. She tells of her privileged migration that allowed her to publish one of the first texts by a migrant woman in Italian. Chandra's *Media chiara e noccioline* (*Medium Light with Nuts*, 2001) is a narrative that focuses on the female body as a location of conflict. She describes her problems with eating disorders as part of her quest for an identity. Chandra is the daughter of a native Italian woman and an Indian man who came to Italy for his studies and then remained. She is torn between passing for Italian, because her dark skin is not dissimilar from that of native Italians, and reclaiming a troubled Indian identity by dealing with the conflictual relationship she has with her father. Her post-ethnic identity is claimed through elective affiliations with other migrants and other cultures, and is articulated at a distance from her biological identity.

In their novels and short stories, women writers such as Christiana de Caldas Brito, have eloquently documented the differences that characterize men's and women's migrations. Often isolated in domestic spaces as caretakers who have replaced native Italian women in their domestic chores, migrant women learn the local language more slowly. Their access to public spaces and to visibility is marked by difficulties that are very different from those that men, employed as street vendors or factory workers, experience. Of course, migrant women's employments change, and any clear separation between men's and women's experiences is directly challenged in migrant women's literature.

The existence of migrant women's texts highlights a problematic and disconcerting lack of interest in migration issues that marks current Italian feminist thought. The feminist philosopher Adriana Cavarero remains an exception to the absent feminist voice in Italian migration studies with her articulation of the concepts of 'whoness' and 'whatness.' 'Whoness' is the unrepeatable individuality of a 'self' that has little space in philosophy and finds its ideal location in narratives, in the process of telling a story. 'Whatness' is the definition of what one person is: documented migrant, undocumented migrant, native, non-native, definitions often trapped in dichotomies. Cavarero privileges the uniqueness of whoness and elaborates a theoretical approach to texts that I apply to telling migration stories in film. Therefore, it is film, instead of literature, that is the focus of chapter 3, entitled 'Cinema and Migration: "What" and "Who" Is a Migrant.' It develops the arguments of the previous chapter by discussing the importance of cinematic narratives in the process of talking back to dominant discourses that claim the need to defend a unitary Italian culture against incoming hybridizations. Film that places the story of individual migrants at the centre of a visual narrative talks back to convenient representations, currently at the centre of political discourses, of migrants as an invading mass. In fact, in film migrant characters and their voices embody that uniqueness that allows transforming whatness into whoness. For example, chapter 3 explores how Rachid Benhadj's *L'albero dei destini sospesi* (*The Tree of Pending Destinies*, 1997) portrays a Moroccan man who claims for himself the right to transmigration, that is, the right to live in both Italy and his native country in order to revise an anachronistic concept of migration as a linear process. Mohamed Soudani and Saidou Moussa Ba made a film in Wolof and Pulaar, *Waalo Fendo* (1997), for a Western audience in order to create a cinematographic space that places the audience in the position of confronting difference inscribed in a Western landscape. The film is cross-national in many ways: its plurilinguism exposes a Western audience to unfamiliar language in a familiar landscape and invites viewers to explore the unfamiliar in the comfortably familiar. It is also created for a general Western audience rather than for one national cultural context. What unifies the different audiences is linguistic incomprehension that places the viewers in the role of strangers in their own country. In fact the film is shot in a Western urban context.

Films complement the literary texts that migrants have created to claim the right to self-representation in art. However, making a film is more expensive medium than writing a book. Native Italians, who have easier access to financing films, have created a number of complex representations of otherness that dialogue with the filmic creations by migrants. There are, of course, several films that recycle old stereotypes and have been broadcast on national television channels, as is the case with Gigi Proietti's *Un nero per casa* (*Black and Underfoot*, 1998). Proietti constructs the happy ending in his film on the expendability of an African character and the failure of the love relationship between an African man and a native Italian woman. Most of the films

I analyse are not well known, except Gianni Amelio's *Lamerica* (1994) and Bernardo Bertolucci's *L'assedio* (*Besieged*, 1998). *Lamerica* and *L'assedio* document migration issues and reach larger audiences than do other migrant and native directors. Bertolucci's film is particularly relevant to my discussion because it bridges two parts central to my book: film and literature. Inspired by James Lasdun's eponymous novel, Bertolucci unravels a plot of falling in love with difference, outside any institutional imposition of roles and of whatness.

The fourth chapter, 'The Laws of Migration,' further develops the concepts of 'whatness' and 'whoness' by exploring the relationship between literature and law. The chapter traces the history of Italian immigration laws from 1931 to the present. I argue that literature is a privileged context that can talk back to the text of the immigration laws, created to regulate the lives, and the bodies, of migrants. Immigration laws deprive migrants of that uniqueness fundamental in Cavarero's argument, the uniqueness that finds in narratives and films its translation into practice. Artistic representations become, in fact, one of the few means for under-represented people to respond to laws that regulate their daily lives. Even if they cannot vote, and therefore their opinion does not count and literally cannot be counted, migrants have used literature and film to dialogue with that 'whatness' that dominates the language of the law. Migrants' literature and film talk back to the essentializing power of the law and set up alternative paradigms for identity construction. If such a dialogue can be established, the law becomes a text to which the rules of literary criticism can apply. Privileging literary and filmic interpretations of the effect that laws have on migrants involves giving particular relevance to migrants' interpretation of the texts of the law. In fact, seeing law through the lens of literature and filmic narratives means emphasizing a specific kind of interpretation in which migrants appropriate the role of agents in understanding the rules that regulate their lives. Literature and filmic narratives therefore create a destabilizing effect that talks back and sets up the possibility to construct resistance. Of course the emphasis here is on agency and transgression, which still inhabit just the margins of Italian culture. In fact, minor publishing companies often publish books by migrants, and any film on migration issues is randomly distributed and cannot reach a wide audience. The effectiveness of literature and film in talking back to the text of the law that allows and forbids is limited, but I argue that literature and film remain unerasable forms of cultural representation.

Migrants' cultural productions still remain outside of any canonical discipline in Italian culture. This book seeks to create the critical language that theorizes the innovative charge of texts that 'talk back' to the history and the identities of Italians, uncover repressed narratives, and articulate possible future developments in Italian culture. It also contributes to discussions on global migrations by presenting the particular case of contemporary migrations to Italy that cannot be interpreted without taking into consideration the uninterrupted tradition on e-migration that has characterized Italy in the last century. In fact, Italy at the beginning of the third millennium is a country that is still experiencing both migration and immigration. Italians continue to leave the peninsula to find qualified jobs. Migrants accept those positions that native Italians refuse and thus help to sustain the Italian economy, which could not function in its current state without a migrant labour force. The dominant rhetoric originating from political parties is quick in defining migrants as a valuable labour force, but also in reproducing the old strategies of scapegoating that have been employed to victimize and criminalize Italian migrants all over the world. Literature and film uncover the complexity of migratory movements and appropriate a location in culture in which migrants are agents of change in the context they inhabit. Still, migrants' texts await validation as the most innovative representations of contemporary Italian culture to interpret the experience of migration, transmigration, and nomadism.

I offer a final introductory comment. This book would have never been written without the help of migrant writers who have encouraged my research from the very beginning. Their voices have followed me throughout the difficult process of writing, and they deserve all my gratitude and friendship. Tahar Lamri has been an amazing friend who has kept me informed about the latest publications and has supplied me with invaluable texts. Pap Khouma has allowed me to read his unpublished manuscript and Saidou Moussa Ba has discussed with me his work in film and literature. Thanks to Saidou, I had the privilege of meeting Shirin Ramzanali Fazel, who keeps in touch even after transmigrating to Kenya. I miss my conversations with Nassera Chohra, who was so open in discussing her life in France and in Italy. For reasons concerning her personal safety, contacts with her are not possible any longer. I am indebted to all the people who made it possible for me to participate in the literary award for migrant writers, Eks&Tra. Thanks to the annual award I was able to read unpublished material and meet writers including Martha Elvira Patiño, Jadelin Mabiala Gangbo, Gëzim Hajdari, and, last but not least, Christiana de Caldas Brito. Kossi Komla-Ebri, who has won a number of Eks&Tra prizes, is the person who has given me back the enthusiasm for politics that can really change the status quo. Special thanks go to Ron Kubati and Clementina Sandra Ammendola. I hope that this book will help them acquire a larger readership and allow them to be known as the writers of a history of cultural hybridization in contemporary Italy among scholars of global migrations.

CHAPTER ONE

Strategies of 'Talking Back'

It was not just that Italians did not look white to certain social arbiters, but that they did not act white.

Matthew Frye Jacobson[1]

Strategies of Sameness

In September 2000 a controversy captured the attention of Italians, highlighting the need for a redefinition of Italian culture. Cardinal Biffi, archbishop of Bologna, expressed the opinion that immigration to Italy should be limited to Catholics in order to preserve the identity of the Italian nation. He argued that even though Catholicism is no longer the official religion of the Italian state, it has traditionally been Italy's religion. Biffi's position was informed by the prescriptive obsessions of the pope, and by statements by Cardinal Ratzinger affirming the superiority of Catholicism over all other religions.[2] It was also supported by the immigration bill proposed in the same year by Silvio Berlusconi's party, Forza Italia, and the Northern League, which claimed the need for a Christian society standing against a multiracial society.[3] Cardinal Biffi's proposal of granting entry visas according to religious practices not only violated Article 43 of the current immigration law (which declares any discrimination based on ethnicity or religion illegal), but also took on the tone of an internal cultural crusade that privileged the rights of the majority at the expense of the minority.[4]

Endorsed by too many Italian politicians, Biffi's assertion represents a historical narrative about Italy based on continuity, homogeneity, and linearity. This narrative is often questioned, but still recurs as a fantasy useful in dominant politics.[5] In this specific case, religion is a structure within which Italians (or what Cardinal Biffi imagines Italians to be) see their past and present and wish to shape their future. This fascination with sameness aims to prove that migrants are 'breaking and entering' a culturally unified country that needs to defend the rights of the majority from cultural contamination.[6] While 'difference' is at the centre of international discussions of multiracial and multicultural countries, a conservative discourse is attempting to construct a homogeneous Italian culture and to rewrite history. It is also attempting to ignore loud dissident voices within Italy itself that problematize both sameness and difference.

Étienne Balibar's discussion on the 'imaginary singularity of national formations' is particularly relevant to my discussion on the imaginary unity of Italian culture at a particular juncture when the issues inherent in migration provoke a debate of what constitutes Italianness.[7] The operative word here is 'imaginary.' In fact, Balibar reminds us, '*Every social community reproduced by the functioning of institutions is imaginary*, that is to say it is based on the projection of individual existence into the weft of a collective narrative, on the recognition of a common name and a tradition lived as the trace of an immemorial past (even when they have been fabricated and inculcated in the recent past). But this comes down to accepting that, under certain conditions, *only* imaginary communities are real.'[8] These communities do not 'possess a given "ethnic" basis,' adds Balibar.[9] Therefore, 'the fundamental problem is to produce the people. More exactly, it is to make the people produce itself continually as a national community.'[10] Interpellated in Althusserian terms as subjects of an imaginary community, members of that community are surrounded by differences that are, however, relativized because 'it is the symbolic difference between "ourselves" and "foreigners" which wins out and which is lived as irreducible.'[11] Balibar argues that 'ourselves' is rooted in fictive ethnicity produced through language and race, which 'constitute two ways of rooting historical populations in the fact of "nature" (the diversity of languages and the diversity of races appearing predestined), but also two ways of giving a meaning to their continued existence, of transcending its contingency.'[12] While schooling reproduces the national language that has so dramatically changed the linguistic profile of Italy in the last fifty years, the hereditary nature of a fictive ethnicity has created a narrative of homogeneity that is threatened by migration.

Migration to Italy and the debates it has provoked have brought to the surface the fragility of the country's 'unity.' A construction of homogeneous *italianità* is necessary in order to create dichotomies such as 'us' and 'them,' 'Italians' and 'foreigners,' *comunitari* and *extracomunitari*, and also in order to forget deliberately that the rights of migrants do not replace, contrast, and negate the rights of natives.[13] These binarities ignore the multilingual and multicultural entity that Italy inherently is and was, even before the migratory waves to Italy of the 1980s and 1990s. Because of its late colonialism, a long history of migrations, and strong internal separations between North and South, Italian culture is the ideal location to reopen the discussion on the relationship between outside and inside, and examine the ongoing processes of integration in Europe. Against the background of Italian history, it is necessary to analyse certain aspects of contemporary Italian culture and processes of identity construction that are based on an ad hoc (that is, a contingent and pragmatic) manipulation of the concepts of sameness and difference by migrant and native authors alike.[14] This ad hockery allows an investigation of the cultural politics at work in specific historical moments and in the varied constructions of concepts of Italian identity, of *italianità*.

Abdelmalek Sayad has stated that through a geographical dislocation in migration, people inscribe themselves in a new culture that deprives them of equality. It does not accept their alterity, but still needs them as a work force.[15] In contemporary Italy, native Italians' fear of immigrations and of migrants has escalated in direct proportion with the increase in Italy's need for an immigrant labour force. In the 'host' countries, migrations bring to the surface nationalisms. Therefore migrants witness the strengthening of an obsession to regulate their lives and bodies through laws that sanction inequality and protect the rights of a dominant majority. Migrants experience a double absence: absent as they are from their country of origin and a familiar culture and pushed into a position of erasure and expendability at the margins of the country of immigration. In Italy, both the Left and the Right have been articulating discourses that reproduce the rhetorical strategies that have victimized migrants who are needed and marginalized at the same time. Influenced in part by Sayad's work, Alessandro Dal Lago has articulated the concept of being a non-person.[16] He describes the undocumented migrant as an individual who occupies a contradictory position. He/she is often a productive member of that fictive community that is a 'host country,' and can establish social relations with native Italians. However, the migrant can be expelled and the conditions of the expulsion originate from a decision that does not take into consideration the inalienable rights of an individual who is, according to Dal Lago, reduced to being a non-person. The majority that accepts laws and behaviours that give negative meaning to the position of being a migrant could understand what being a non-person means only if the members of that majority were placed in the position of a non-person. It is a difficult and problematic operation that different narratives about the internal otherness inherent in Italianness can only attempt to perform.

Narrating that double absence that is inscribed within Italian culture and Italian identities can challenge the inability to go beyond traditional discourses that reproduce structures of oppression. In his article '"Italy" in Italy: Old Metaphors and New Racisms in the 1990s,' David Ward brings the discussion on the identity of contemporary Italy back to Marcus Garvey and his provocative statement that under fascism Italians were attempting to pass for whites through an elaborate ideological construction.[17] Ward argues that Garvey's point was that the whiteness of Mussolini and of Italy itself was highly questionable. Ward's contextualization of Garvey's statement is accompanied, in the same article, by a cartoon that juxtaposes the attacks, from the end of the second millennium, on Italian migrants in Germany with those on African migrants in Italy, a parallel that supports Garvey's definition of Italian off-whiteness.[18] Absence therefore becomes one of the supporting structures of that sameness that connects native Italians and migrants. That double absence which characterized the lives of Italian migrants all over the world defines, in a different social/historical context, the experience of contemporary migrants for whom Italy is a destination. Italy is their America.

In his work on Italian Americans, Fred Gardaphé has sketched the changes in the perception of the Italian identity in the United States, a perception that has classified Italians as non-white, off-white, or white at different times in the twentieth century. In his book *Whiteness of a Different Color,* Matthew Jacobson documents the non-whiteness of Italian migrants in the United States through newspaper articles published in the late nineteenth and early twentieth centuries.[19] Italians were non-white 'dagoes' whose exotic and dangerous identities coloured a 'race colony' in New York.[20] Jacobson quotes a piece from *Harper's Magazine*, titled 'Italian Life in New York,' in which the 'exoticized accounts of the human landscape echoed then-current travel accounts from Africa or the Levant.'[21] In the south of the United States, adds Jacobson, 'immigrants who were white enough to enter the country as "free white persons" could also lose that status by their association with nonwhite groups. This was precisely the case with Italians in New Orleans.'[22] By living, working, and accepting 'economic niches marked as "black" by local customs,' 'dagoes' became 'white niggers.'[23] Jacobson adds that 'from being "like Negroes" to being "as bad as Negroes" was but a trifling step in dominant Southern thinking ...; and hence in states like Louisiana, Mississippi and West Virginia, Italians were known to have been lynched for alleged crimes, or even for violating racial codes by "fraternizing" with blacks.'[24] Therefore, a double absence is also marked by an imposition of essentialized definitions of racial identity that assimilate new migrants into prescriptive categories.

In their book *Are Italians White?* (2003), Jennifer Guglielmo and Salvatore Salerno explore the colour-coding of being Italian outside of Italy. Officially considered white, but having a darker complexion, throughout the twentieth century Italians in the United States have experienced on their own skin the slippery nature and ambiguity involved in assigning a colour to a cultural identity. Once deterritorialized, Italian identity became a malleable text that reflected the politics of colour inherent in the new cultural context in which a multiplicity of Italian identities were being inscribed. In his book *Malcolm X on Afro-American History* (1970), Malcolm X reminded Italians that '[n]o Italian will ever jump in my face and start putting bad mouth on me, because I know his history. I tell him when you talk to me, you are talking to your pappy, your father. He knows his history, he knows how he got that color.'[25] The dark complexion assigned by official forms to Italians in the United States narrates something different for Malcolm X. He recalls for Italian Americans that Hannibal was in Italy for many years and left his mark on the inhabitants of the peninsula. His irreverent revision of Italianness does not focus on the Arab presence in southern Italy, but rather on the impact of a northern African invasion in Northern Italy. In one fell swoop he reminds Italians of their otherness rooted in a mixed cultural heritage and challenges any rigid separation between North and South in the Italian peninsula.

The many arbitrary definitions of Italianness uncover the complexity of the construction of a multiplicity of Italian identities. Together Massimo Ciavolella and Luigi Ballerini have edited a new history of Italian literature for the University of Toronto Press. They place an Arab poet, with his verses in Arabic, as a key figure in their revisionary history of

Italian literature because, they argue, his poetry is a key element in the later constitution of a Sicilian school of poetry.[26] Revisions of the history of 'high' Italian culture complicate the definition of what is Italian, but they are in the privileged hands of academic alone. Italian popular culture has kept alive the unfamiliar within the familiar, that is, that otherness that the prescriptive definition of Italian culture could not completely erase. Italian pop music has evoked an African Italy with songs such as Almamegretta's *Figli di Annibale* (1993), Pino Daniele's Neapolitan-African sounds, and the remake of traditional Neapolitan songs as creations at the border between Italy and the South of the world.[27] Italian musicians stress that Italian cultural and genetic roots are in Africa and talk back to the traditional colonial project that repeatedly has taught Africans about the Western origins of all civilizations. In his book *Neyla* (2002), Kossi Komla-Ebri states: 'Among my memories, I still carry the weight of the anxiety I felt when they taught us that our ancestors were "Gauls with blond hair and blue eyes."'[28] Both academic discourses and popular culture work together in talking back to the fiction of Italian homogeneity and to the norms that dominant narratives create about origins. The goal is not to construct a privileged position for otherness, but to reveal an internal asymmetry and the artificiality of homogeneity. That asymmetry is the internal alterity that cannot be completely suppressed and that gives meaning to that difference which connects old Italian migrations and contemporary immigrations. Such disruptive statements disturb, but often fail to undermine, the monolithic construction of Italy as part of the European north.

The portrayal of a multicultural Italy is a fragmented construction that needs to be narrated by recovering and connecting the dispersed narratives scattered in diverse cultural practices. Since the beginning of a literature written or published in Italian by migrants at the beginning of the 1990s, even the publishing industry has paid attention to 'other' narratives that had been previously ignored. Italian American literature is being translated into Italian a century after it appeared in the United States, Italian colonialism is finally being narrated and talked about, and Italian migration to northern Europe is told in tales constructing the 'minor' identity of being Italian in Italy and elsewhere in the world. The result is a much more complex construction of Italy and Italian history than the one proposed by official political discourses. Once dominant and prescriptive definitions of Italianness are contested, identities and identifications multiply and fragment, creating a paradigm that is useful in talking about otherness and migration in contemporary Italy.

Resisting Homogeneity in Acts of *Talking Back*

Balibar's work is again very useful in stating that if ethnicity is a fiction, fictive ethnicity is produced through language and race.[29] 'They constitute,' adds Balibar, 'two ways of rooting historical populations in the fact of "nature" (the diversity of languages and the diversity of races appearing predestined), but also two ways of giving a meaning to their continued existence, of transcending its contingency.'[30] This linguistic community and ethnic community is validated and reinforced through schooling, the media, and a fictive 'hereditary substance of ethnicity' that assigns 'different "social destinies" to individuals.'[31]

The fragmented voices that question today the hegemonic construction of an imagined Italian community construct a non-homogeneous corpus of texts that resist the construction of the myth of a culturally unified Italy. They can only be weak acts of resistance that I call 'acts of talking back.' They are able to question hegemonic discourse, but often have a marginal impact on contemporary Italian culture. They uncover the process of turning people into non-persons, but they are unable to resist those legal, political, and rhetorical processes of oppression grounded in exclusion. The concept of resistance within an Italian context is identified with a specific historical narrative that, however fragmented in its different components, represents a strong myth validated by the political system and its rhetoric. In that historical context, resistance is defined as an organized movement and needs validation and recognition even though they are not contemporary to the act of resistance.

In his article 'Resistance at the Margins: Writers of Maghrebi Immigrant Origin in France,' Alec Hargreaves calls resistance 'a number' of oppositional acts and stances.[32] In the case of the rock-singer and novelist Mounsi, it is resistance to incorporation through writing. In fact, Mounsi wants to assert his identity as 'that of a child of the "Maghrebi periphery."'[33] Mounsi's individual construction of a counter-discourse constitutes the example of an act of talking back very different from the act of resistance performed by the march that took place on 17 October 1961 when, Hargreaves describes, thousands of Algerian migrants protested in Paris and openly disregarded the curfew. The police intervened and brutally repressed the protest. Censorship prevented the information about the subsequent killings from being disclosed and only recently have historians revealed them.[34] This combination of intellectual engagement and praxis is what I would call resistance. It also connects to a more recent episode in France when, in February 1997, fifty French intellectuals signed a self-accusation, declaring that they had welcomed undocumented migrants in their homes. It was their response to the Debré bill that allowed the legal prosecution of French natives who gave shelter to *sans papier,* whose presence had, by law, to be reported to the police. This collective and intellectual act of talking back through civil and civic disobedience was complemented by a campaign in the press that promoted transgression and created resistance to a frightening bill that echoed the 1941 French law requiring people to report the presence of Jews to the police. While the Debré bill was being discussed in France, Italy was struggling with the proposed creation of temporary holding facilities where undocumented immigrants would await the result of their appeal against expulsion. In light of the slowness of the Italian justice system, these 'camps' could become more than transitional and had frightening echoes in recent history.[35] Scattered articles expressing outrage to such a proposal appeared in the press, but failed to have the impact and the strength to create effective opposition to the bill. It was a failed attempt at resistance; the Italian bill was approved while the Debré bill was not. What is taking place in Italy is a less concerted effort that cannot yet be called resistance. Rather, it 'talks back' and embodies a marginal discourse that fortunately cannot be erased.

In order to define the difference between resistance and acts of talking back, it is useful to trace definitions of what resistance is. In his article 'Unsettling the Empire: Resistance Theory for the Second World,' Stephen Slemon eloquently summarizes different interpretations of the concept of resistance.[36] In fact, he distinguishes a resistance text as a complex text responding in an often-contradictory way to ideological interpellations that it attempts to resist. Starting from a concept of resistance literature as a fundamental contribution to the political opposition against colonizers, Slemon problematizes this notion by arguing the resistance text can end up being trapped in the system it has tried to oppose. Following Foucault, Slemon reminds us that power '*itself* inscribes its resistances and so, in the process, seeks to contain them.'[37] He adds that 'resistance itself is therefore never *purely* resistance, never *simply* there in the text or the interpretative community, but is always *necessarily* complicit in the apparatus it seeks to transgress.'[38] Inscribed within a migration context, the relationship between resistance and power involves analysing the political structure of the country that is creating discourses aimed at defending the 'home' from a potential *anabasis*.[39] In the case of Italy, the political armed resistance against fascism and the occupying German forces was an opposition against specific and negative embodiments of power. The Italian armed terrorist 'resistance' of the 1970s and 1980s still functioned by targeting symbols of institutional power: judges, policemen, journalists, and politicians. Hitting at the very heart of power was their slogan, ignoring the fact that such a 'heart' had been fragmented into multiple centres of power; their actions played into the hands of more conservative forces and brought about the demise of the terrorist movement. The fragmentation of power also involves the fragmentation of resistance into acts of talking back that migrants in Italy have embraced. Acts of talking back constitute the unassembled skeleton of resistance and the groundwork that points toward the possibility of constructing resistance. Talking back inevitably becomes a site of compromise, whether it is in collaborative writing projects or in catering to the demands of the publishing industry. Literary talking back can only be 'complicit in the apparatus it seeks to transgress,' as Slemon stated, because it is within such an apparatus that immigrants want to carve a niche without completely embracing identities that the dominant culture wants to impose on them.

Relegated to being published by minor companies, and appearing in critically acclaimed, but not well-distributed journals, the text that talks back is at times brought to the attention of the general public as a token, but it quickly disappears. This was the case with Pap Khouma's autobiographical text *Io, venditore di elefanti* (*I Am an Elephant Salesman*, 1990), which became a best-seller in the early 1990s, but rapidly disappeared from public attention. However, margins, imposed limitations, and legalized rules exist to be challenged and that is the goal of weaker acts of resistance, of talking back. The aim is to construct enough 'disturbance,' background noise, and talk to weaken dominant discourses, and to undermine their attempt to contain transgression completely. Texts that talk back claim a space for topics, themes, characters, locales, and identities that have been previously ignored or deliberately suppressed. In contemporary Italy, migrants write their lives talking back both to the alarmist press releases concerning mass invasions from poorer countries and to the opposite excess embodied in the construction of the immigrants as pitiful entities in constant need of assistance.

Jivis Tegno's experience with writing and the publishing world is particularly relevant to my discourse on weak resistance. After working in the tobacco fields of the Umbria region for a salary of five thousand lira an hour (about $2.50 U.S.) and after completing a degree in political science from the University of Perugia, Tegno wrote a book entitled *Ma come sono gli Italiani? Un viaggio alla scoperta della mentalità degli italiani. Dieci anni di studi meticolosi fatti da un immigrato con una visione distaccata sulla abitudini di un popolo* (2001; *But What Are Italians Like? A Journey of Discovery of Italians' Mentality. Ten Years of Careful Studies Performed by an Immigrant with a Detached Approach to a People's Mores*). He rejected the possibility of writing a narrative placing the experience of a migrant at its centre, and turned the tables by casting himself in a narrative as an observer of Italian society. His book highlights the contradictions inherent in a rich society whose problems do not originate from immigration, but are intrinsically connected to its internal structure. Poverty, drugs, criminality, and politicians' corruption are endemic problems that Tegno discusses in a book that no Italian publisher wanted. He financed the publication of the first one thousand copies, but heard the printer state: 'I have been doing this job for thirty years, and I had never seen an African publish a book.'[40] Tegno realized that marketing a book authored by a migrant who criticizes the same society that sees him as a problem was a difficult endeavour. His solution was to found his own publishing company and to begin by focusing on a micro-distribution of his work in the region where he lives. Named Jivis Editore Multimediale, Tegno's publishing company is certainly not a challenge to the major publishing companies, but has succeeded in achieving visibility and enough distribution to attract attention from the media. Minor publishing companies have, therefore, published texts that can only aspire to be marginally visible, but have also guaranteed the publication of texts that otherwise would have never been made public.

Talking back and looking back must go hand in hand in the constructions of (my own) narratives about contemporary Italian culture. Native-born and migrant writers look back at Italian histories and those uncomfortable stories about Italians that have been conveniently set aside and excluded by official educational programs in order to present a history in which migrant presences within Italy can be constructed on discourses of both sameness and difference. Italian colonialism is intrinsically connected with a discourse on migration, whether from or to Italy. Soon after the unification of Italy, a plan was formed to occupy areas of Africa that would constitute the Italian presence in that continent. This effort would help to obscure the internal economic problems within Italy, and place Italy on the map of colonial and international powers. Paradoxically, the colonial conquest took place at a time when a large number of Italians from the poorest northern and southern regions were migrating to richer countries. In the new lands of migration, Italians were often racially profiled as non-white. One could speculate that Italian colonialism was an attempt to 'whiten' the Italian identity. In fact, by becoming a colonial power, Italy could become a member of an elite of Western powers and acquire the right 'to belong.' Until 1860, Italy had been geographically and politically fragmented in small states directly and indirectly dominated by foreign powers. After being subjected to colonialism, Italy reproduced the same models, becoming an agent of colonial oppression. Whiteness and a first-world identity became the objects of desire that could be achieved by subjugating people whose skin colour was considered the embodiment of otherness and inferiority. Mussolini reframed Italian colonialism in the language of Roman imperial glory. He deliberately rewrote the narrative about Italian migration to richer countries into Italy's right to conquer territories in which Italian men could exercise their power. Mussolini's agenda was to dust off the past and cover it with the patina of propaganda in order to justify war and genocide. He also wanted to 'heal' national pride hurt in the defeat of Italian troops in Adwa, Ethiopia, in 1896.[41] As a consequence of its Ethiopian invasion of 1935, Italy was penalized by economic sanctions and mocked by black intellectuals who reminded Italy that it was the only 'colonial' power defeated in Africa by native troops. In 1935, during the Italian colonialist campaign in Ethiopia, Marcus Garvey articulated his verbal attack against Italy by criticizing the racial politics at play: 'In the South of Europe, Mussolini, who claims to be a white man, although the Italian race cannot be really called purely a white race, is preparing to devour a set of people in far off Ethiopia.'[42] Directly calling them off-white cannibals, Garvey placed Italians in the position of savages and brought them back to a position of inferiority that Italy's colonial endeavours had tried to negate. While the Italian colonies lost in 1941, were taken over by other colonial powers, Somalia became an Italian protectorate for about a decade until its independence in 1960.

Italian culture has traditionally reserved very little space for a discussion of Italian colonialism.[43] History has tried to ignore the Italian atrocities in Africa; native voices have been absent. Nuruddin Farah has written books in English that partially discuss the negative influence of Italian colonialism and its post–Second World War protectorate in Somalia.[44] Erminia Dell'Oro has recently narrated stories of women's exploitation in the history of the Italian presence in Eritrea.[45] Ennio Flaiano created an allegory of colonialism in his narrative of a soldier and intellectual during the African campaign.[46] Alfredo Antonaros and even the outrageously orientalist Enrico Emanuelli have supplied narratives of colonization filtered through the eyes of the transgressive colonizer.[47] These isolated works have influenced very little Italy's perception of its role in the history of colonialism. The February 1997 issue of *Nigrizia* announced that two historians, the English Ian L. Campbell and the Ethiopian Degife Kabré Sadik, were uncovering the facts concerning Rodolfo Graziani, the Italian governor of Ethiopia, who ordered the slaughter of 1600 people in retaliation for a murder attempt on his life. At the same time that this silenced history was coming to light, that same governor, known as the 'butcher' of Ethiopia, was being celebrated in his native town, which planned to use public funding to create a museum dedicated to its famous *Maresciallo*.

However, these blatantly rejected memories cannot be completely repressed, as they appear in fragments of native and non-native writers in order to place Italian colonialism beside other national imperialistic conquests. For instance, Saidou Moussa Ba has written both about his experience of migration from Senegal to Italy, and of growing up in a Francophone culture. In his short story 'Nel cuore di un clandestino' ('In the Heart of an Illegal Migrant,' 1995), Ba describes his father's experiences in the French army and death in the Vietnam War.[48] In a narrative in Italian for Italian speakers, Ba connects old and recent forms of colonialism. Employing Italian as the language in which to inscribe stories of oppression serves to indict the silenced Italian participation in colonialism. Ba decided to publish this text in a South African journal so that his Italian narrative about French colonialism could be inscribed in a post-apartheid context. Ba's text functions on different planes, talking back to colonialism and talking with other revisionist historical discourses. His short story is a valuable example of an act of talking back. The complex narrative is published and therefore made public, but remains a text read by a limited number of people. Because of its limited impact Ba's story contributes to, but in itself does not constitute, resistance. That can only come about if it can be brought together with other acts of talking back that together can contribute to public discourse.

Within post-colonial and post-independence theory, the discussion on resistance has placed a particular emphasis on the agency of the colonized/migrant and on the political role played by such resistance. In an Italian context in which revisionary narratives by migrant writers have often been co-authored by non-migrants or internal migrants, such dichotomies reveal their limitations.[49] A system of binary oppositions only works in a context in which one side resists and the dominant side imposes the authoritative representations of both dominant and dominated.[50] The often-controversial collaboration between native linguistic experts and migrants complicates oppositional relations and the practice of resistance. Even more so, the emergence of narratives of otherness and unequal relations within the Italian history of internal and external migrations fragment resistance into acts of talking back that need to be brought together. The exploration and discussion of unequal relations takes place therefore in both a revision of the master narrative on Italian history/identity and in the singular acts of talking back. Echoing Sara Suleri's observations on colonial cultural studies, I recognize that if migration cultural studies in Italian 'is to avoid a binarism that could cause it to atrophy in its own apprehension of difference, it needs to locate an idiom for alterity that can circumnavigate the more monolithic interpretations of cultural empowerment that tend to dominate current discourses.'[51]

Internal migrations and the articulation of degrees of difference in Italian culture have been at the centre of narratives, sociological studies, and films such as Luchino Visconti's internationally known *Rocco and His Brothers* (1960).[52] In the 1960s, at a time when Italy was struggling to become a major industrialized power, Italian external and internal migrations became a subject of texts and, at the same time, were subjected to institutionalized priorities that allowed a marginal role to representations of an internal otherness (i.e., weakness). In 1973, one of Italy's biggest publishers, Mondadori, distributed *Le scapole dell'angelo* (The Shoulder Blades of an Angel) by Giovanna Righini Ricci, a novel for young adults. The text was adopted by schoolteachers who wanted to expose their students to 'other' identities in the Italy of the economic boom and to provoke discussions on how Italians were and are ethnically located in and outside of Italy. The book's ostensible purpose was to generate tolerance, but it is all about reinforcing stereotypes and social hierarchies of power. The cover of the book presented the stereotypical picture of two southern Italian migrants to northern Italy with their possessions in suitcases held together by ropes. The book told the story of a young immigrant boy, of the same age as the target reader, living on the outskirts of Milan. He suffered discrimination and stereotyping, and emerged as a hero when, in an attempt to distance himself from the criminalized portrayal of all southern Italian migrants, he reported the criminal activities of other immigrants to the police. In his exceptionality, the protagonist declared his loyalty to the nation/state that guarantees his status as hero in the narrative. This book wanted to have an impact on young people's perception of migrant identities at a time when northern Italy fed itself on discourses against the 'invasions' of internal others coming from southern Italy. It also placed at the centre of a narrative those sons and daughters of migrants who had, following the national educational program, fed their imaginations with literature that privileged a more traditional identity, language, and subject matter. However, norming is the clear agenda of the book that stresses loyalty to the nation rather than to the community and becomes an instruction manual for the process of 'whitening' and belonging. Despite the influence of linguistic experts, the first books by migrants written in Italian are not as prescriptive as Ricci's educational tool. They focus on strategies of differentiation in order to fragment the perception of a monolithic mass of interchangeable and expendable foreign identities. In *Le scapole dell'angelo* the protagonist wants to earn the right to equality and to be just like northern Italians; contemporary migrants' literature focuses instead on the right to enjoy equal rights and the right to be different.

In the 1960s and 1970s, newspaper headlines announcing, 'Calabrese uccide la moglie' ('Calabrian kills his wife') or 'Siciliano coinvolto in una rissa' ('Sicilian involved in a brawl') captured readers' attention. Those headlines were replaced in the 1980s and 1990s by others: 'Albanese coinvolto nel traffico della prostituzione' ('Albanian involved in the business of prostitution') or 'Marocchini arrestati per spaccio' ('Moroccans arrested for selling drugs'). Even the categories employed in describing migration have recycled labels: the *questione del mezzogiorno* has now become *la questione immigrati* that identifies people as problems and, very often, migrating people as potential criminals. In July 2000 an article titled 'Tre Italiani su quattro con l'incubo immigrati: "Colpa loro se aumenta la criminalità"' ('Three Italians out of four see immigration as a nightmare: "It is because of immigrants that crime increases"'), published in *la Repubblica*, eloquently described the disconnection between the impact that immigration has in Italy and the perception that native Italians have of migration.[53] The Censis (the Centre for Socioeconomic Research, established in 1964) issued an official report stating that since 1997 the number of victims of 'reati' ('crimes') has decreased 2.6 per cent and Italy only occupies eleventh place among European countries in the number of crimes reported. When, on 20 July 2000, the president of the Camera Luciano Violante, the vice-chief of police Antonio Manganelli, the commander of Carabinieri General Sergio Siracusa, and the director of Censis met to discuss the results of the report, they devoted their attention also to the data that demonstrated Italians are more worried about a perceived increase in crime brought about by immigration than by unemployment, even though Italy has one of the highest unemployment rates in Europe. The 'knife wielding' Sicilian ('Dago' comes from the word 'dagger') that once attracted the attention of newspaper readers in the United States seems to have become the protagonist of a different narrative, while the old racist framework has been recycled with foreign-sounding names in the old motherland.[54]

It is right at this crossroads of narratives that analysing past and present discourses of discrimination constructs new meanings, and allows the articulations of 'other' identities that cannot be considered completely other. The imagined Italian community that Cardinal Biffi wants to defend contains characteristics that connect rather than separate same and other in contemporary Italy. Narrating the Italian identity at this juncture builds on Julia Kristeva's theoretical articulation of 'ourselves' as being strangers to ourselves and creates the possibility of interpreting difference in a non-separatist framework.[55] Theories of *métissage* (Françoise Lionnet), of in-betweenness (Homi Bhabha), of nomadism (Rosi Braidotti), and of inevitable hybridity resulting from the encounters of cultures, even in hierarchical structures, find in the turn-of-the-millennium Italy a unique interpretation.[56] Past and present narratives on internal and external otherness propose Italy as a crossroads where difference and the recognition of sameness meet and invade cultural and linguistic territories.[57]

Charles Taylor's definition of the politics of recognition in multiculturalism is particularly useful in my discussion of the role of migration culture in contemporary Italy.[58] In fact, my emphasis on the multicultural identity of the Italian culture in which recent migrants inscribe their identities belongs to a cultural practice of recognition. Such a practice is grounded, in Taylor's words, on the realization that 'my discovering my own identity doesn't mean that I work it out in isolation, but that I negotiate it through dialogue, partly overt, partly internal, with others,' that is, 'my own identity crucially depends on my dialogical relations to others.'[59] Granting recognition to those others who dialogue with processes of identity formation that concern both the individual and the national context challenges universalisms, even legal universalisms, that declare equality in rights. Taylor argues that with the politics of difference, what we are asked to recognize is the unique identity of this individual or group, their distinctness from everyone else. The idea is that it is precisely this distinctness that has been ignored, glossed over, assimilated to a dominant or majority identity.[60] The recognition of the distinctness within the majority is a necessary uncovering that acts of talking back can perform within an Italian context.

In talking about contemporary Italian multiculturalism, one must stress that the encounter between native and migrant cultures takes place in the plural, as both are constituted by a distinctive multiplicity of identities and by a plurality of cultural influences. There is not one Italian culture or a single monolithic culture denoted by the name of the country of origin of the migrant; there is not one culture that is threatened by the monolithic embodiment of another way of life. As Jürgen Habermas has eloquently stated the matter:

> Even a majority culture that does not consider itself threatened preserves its vitality only through an unrestrained revisionism, by sketching out alternatives to the status quo or by integrating alien impulses – even to the point of breaking with its own traditions. This is especially true of immigrant cultures, which initially define themselves stubbornly in ethnic terms and revive traditional elements under the assimilationist pressure of the new environment, but then quickly develop modes of life equally distant from both assimilation and tradition.[61]

The protection of a style of life that motivates a rigid defensiveness against outsiders has led to an artificial construction of cultural homogeneity in Italian culture that is also influencing the protectionist stance that immigration laws currently serve. In such a homogenizing context, even the politics of recognition, which respects the differences among native Italians (and that is supposed to be a pillar of contemporary democracies), is secondary to patriarchal, Western, and artificial universalisms that do not even serve the recognition of opportunistically whitened members. As Étienne Balibar states, the only threats to

Western civilization are the consequences that follow the exclusion and marginalization of migrants.[62]

Anthony Appiah has criticized current discourses on multiculturalism and on the politics of recognition for containing 'conceptions of collective identity that are remarkably unsubtle in their understanding of the process by which identities, both individual and collective, develop.'[63] In fact, those scripts that create collective identities become normative and exclude the fact that 'the personal dimensions of identity work differently from the collective ones.'[64] This is an issue that all students of multiculturalism have to confront, because 'the last thing one wants at this stage from Eurocentered intellectuals is positive judgments of the worth of cultures that they have not intensively studied,' as Taylor asserts.[65] Therefore, any project on the processes of cultural hybridization taking place in Italy can only aim for a narrow understanding of a limited set of critical negotiations. Such negotiations must inevitably confront the circumscribed knowledge of the critic and open a dialogue with different discourses and approaches to the construction of a field of Italian multicultural studies.

Internal and External Otherness

It is possible to talk about Italian contemporary multiculturalism only if we connect it to a long pluricultural history and analyse the different embodiments of otherness that have been constructed. In this exploration, literature is a privileged medium that has allowed articulations of selves, which in turn have created a vernacular of difference contained in the narrative process of telling a story. Carmine Abate's work on the Albanian minority in Italy is particularly relevant in this context. He traces the construction of difference within national borders and then projects it outside the Italian cultural context. The catalyst of such movement is, of course, migration. The imbrications and interplay of sameness and difference in Italy is highlighted in Abate's four books *Il ballo tondo* (*The Round Dance*, 1991), *Il muro dei muri* (*The Wall of Walls*, 1993), *La moto di Scanderbeg* (*Scanderbeg's Motorcycle*, 1999), and *Tra due mari* (*Between Two Seas*, 2002). Abate grew up in an *Arbëresh* community in Calabria, and in his books he tells of the acquisition of Italian as a second language in public schools. Albanian communities in Italy preserved traditions and oral narratives for centuries, and have participated in the recent migrations to northern Europe and to Germany. There Abate himself has lived and published his work in German, then retranslated it into Italian (*I Germanesi*, 1986).[66] Abate eloquently describes the layers of foreignness that follow his characters, who inhabit the borders of a marginalized culture within Italy, but become stereotypical 'Italian' immigrants outside of the country's borders. However, the identity construction of Abate's characters is further complicated by their illegibility in the panorama of migrating people within Europe, where they become opaque texts to be interpreted. In their native Calabria they are scolded by an authority figure, the schoolteacher: 'But what's this Arbëria! We live in Italy. But what's this with an eagle! You are just asses. You don't even know how to speak Italian. Get it through your thick heads that, according to the law, you are not to speak Albanian, at least in school. Asses, that's what you are!'[67] This teacher who belongs to the *Arbëresh* community imposes on them what Tullio De Mauro has called the 'acceptance of a preferred linguistic norm as a shibboleth, as a pass that gives access to the ruling classes,' or at least to geographical mobility.[68] Coming from outside the local community, another teacher in the same story by Abate validates his students' linguistic diversity by collecting their narratives and putting himself in the position of a student who has to learn from the local people. His project articulates itself outside of the limitations of the educational programs established from above by the minister in Rome. In his article 'Linguistic Variety and Linguistic Minorities,' Tullio De Mauro tells of a report to the Italian minister of the interior written by a *carabiniere* (policeman) reporting a teacher who had published texts in Greek in order to value and preserve the language of the community in which he was living. The policeman also supplied some mitigating circumstances for the teacher's transgressive approach to teaching Italian: he stressed that the teacher could still be qualified as a good citizen and a good Catholic. De Mauro adds:

> There could only have been [on the part of the *carabiniere*] the deep, instinctive conviction that those who speak differently from others can be suspected of not being good citizens, good Catholics etc. Linguistic diversity is a strangeness, and it legitimizes any other suspicion, even though the honest writer of the report wished to forestall any possible suspicion. The fact remains that an implicit, deep unassailable conviction exists that, in the end, speaking in a different and particular way compared to others is a very strange thing.[69]

The strangeness of speaking differently seems to undermine even

Cardinal Biffi's concept of homogeneity based in religious practices. In Abate's work, that unerasable strangeness marks the separation between belonging to and being excluded from a larger community in which speaking differently carries connotations of inferiority. One of Abate's characters eloquently voices his exasperation with the demands and cultural paradigms of a host country: 'I must have told Ingrid [his German partner] a thousand times that it is not right that it is always the stranger who must adapt. Why don't you adapt to us for once. I have had it with this adapting. These people want your soul not just your body. But my soul is not for sale, dear ladies and gentlemen, it is already booked, it has always been spoken for.'[70] Additional complications arise in daily practices of dominant recognition of otherness. In Germany Abate's Italian/*Arbëresh* character runs into problems:

> 'Police, come with us.'
> 'They checked my passport. Then doubtful they asked me: You are Italian?'
> 'And while walking away they said: "We are sorry, we took you [*scambiata*] for a Tunisian."'[71]

A mistaken identity becomes in Italian *scambiata*, exchanged, and inscribed in an economic discourse that assigns meaning and value to the identity of the migrant. In their new country, migrants represent the workforce necessary to guarantee and validate a comfortable lifestyle for a majority. In exchange, they are 'tolerated' as long as migrants' problems remain marginal and can be publicly ignored. In the country left behind, migrants represent an economical resource on which the survival of the family is often based. Back in Italy, Abate's returning migrant is renamed the *Merikano*, even though his migration was to Germany. Nationalities become mistaken in a discourse that conflates the countries of migration into a generic *Merika*, not really a cultural identity but a location of potential economic and social mobility.[72] *Die Germanesi* are the self-named Italian migrants to Germany who feed the myth of their exchanged identity in order to construct the idea of a successful migration. This mobility in self-definition changes according to the linguistic and cultural context in which the migrant traveller inscribes himself (and in Abate's narratives the focus is on male migrations).

In Abate's texts in Italian, a German experience is marked by a mixed text intertwining many languages that construct the multilinguism of memory: 'When a kind German woman brought me *shtridhëlat*, I was very surprised. But this is an *Arbëresh* dish, I told my friend. The woman looked at me slightly upset: No, this, Italian pasta. Cook comes from the Calabria.'[73] The ungrammatical Italian of the kind German woman names the food of memory as a culturally translated entity. The food is Italian, and all differences become erased in this economic enterprise of selling the 'gourmeted' identity of a country. The *Arbëresh* component is exchanged for a Calabrian one that, in turn, is exchanged for a generic Italian label: 'In the end, I asked to be taken to the kitchen. The cook from Arbëria was directing, ladle in one hand, a small group of four women: two were German, two Italian. I just said: "Une jam nga Karfici, I am from Carfizzi." He answered: "Nice to meet you, Franco Moccia, nga Spexana."'[74] The process of uncovering mistaken identities is indeed a matter of words. In his attempt to see and see again and to revisit one's identity, Abate talks back to Cardinal Biffi's ideological position, which demands homogeneity and a clear definition of identity boundaries and obscures economic discourses behind religious screens. Abate's narratives trace identities at the intersection of languages, such as standard and non-standard Italian, German, and *Arbëresh*, and of changing economic conditions. The economy of language acquisition and that of social mobility ground themselves in parallel hierarchical structures that Abate connects using different languages and cultural contexts. His books describe the changes between several generations of people who can only choose migration to a richer North, even at a time when Italy is attracting immigrants willing to accept jobs that native young people reject.

In this regard, Maria Pace Ottieri, novelist and essayist, author of books on the lives of migrants in contemporary Italy, has stressed the particularity of Italy's position in the panorama of current global migrations. In her article 'Ancora pane e cioccolata' ('Still Bread and Chocolate'), she brings to the reader's attention the fact that Italy at the beginning of the new millennium is a country that is experiencing migration to and from itself. It is still 'bread and chocolate' because the Italian identity narrated in Franco Brusati's film *Pane e cioccolata* (1973) portrays the phenomenon of Italian emigration, that although smaller in scale, still characterizes contemporary Italy. Brusati focuses on the experience of an Italian migrant to Switzerland, where, even now, people of Italian origin constitute a large community. Brusati's protagonist focuses on the disorientation of displacement, on being different because being a migrant makes a person 'other' even vis-à-vis other richer Italians who travel as tourists. Class therefore plays a big role in his film and still plays a role in today's emigrations from Italy. Ottieri illustrates such a phenomenon by gathering oral narratives from a group of migrants leaving Palma di Montechiaro, Sicily, to migrate to Germany. On the bus that takes them to northern Europe there is also one African man, Yaya Konte, a migrant from Mauritania. 'I don't understand,' he states, 'why young Italians go to Germany rather than to northern Italy where there is so much work.'[75] Rosario, one of the young Sicilians on the bus, can supply an answer: 'Because in the north of Italy I don't know anybody and I would be more afraid of being exploited. *La vie c'est difficile.*'[76] External and internal migrations, as well as otherness, stand side by side in the microcosm of a bus, like many others travelling the intersecting roads of migration and nomadism. At the crossroads of migration trajectories, Italy is a North with economic connotations that still connect it to a South that has little to do with a geographical location. The emphasis is still on separation and internal differences that trace migratory paths parallel to, but different from, those of the recent migrants to Italy.

In order to define the specificity of contemporary Italian migration culture, it is crucial to stress that Italy has been experiencing e-migration and, *at the same time*, im-migration.[77] In the decade of the 1990s, while immigration increased, thousands of Italians elected to emigrate. Data about the migration of Italians is now difficult to collect, as migrations within Europe do not require the documentation that was needed before the unification of Europe. Tangential data could, however, give an idea of the size of the phenomenon. Tracing the number of people that transferred their residence abroad in the 1990s does not supply the exact number of migrants (as their act of migration probably took place much earlier), but contains information regarding the mobility of Italians. In 1990, 48,916 Italians officially transferred their permanent residence abroad. The number peaked in 1994 at 59,402, and decreased at the end of the decade, with 38,984 residency transfers in 1997.[78] In March 2004, the financial newspaper *Il Sole 24 Ore* reported that every year between 30,000 to 40,000 native Italians leave the country to work mostly in other European countries, and a smaller number in the Americas.[79] These are not small numbers for a country that has fewer than 60 million citizens. The article also specified that not all Italian migrants have a standard level of education. In 1998, only 6.4 per cent of the e-migrants had a university degree; 14% had a high school degree, 32.7% had only an elementary school degree, and 9% did not even have an elementary school degree.

The spectrum of migratory movements concerning Italy becomes even more complex if we also consider the phenomenon of 'return migration.' Motivated by her own experience, Clementina Sandra Ammendola insists on the necessity of discussing the cultural impact of people with Italian ancestry, and often an Italian passport, who migrate back to Italy.[80] Ammendola migrated from Argentina, a country that has experienced a serious financial crisis that fuels a migration of return. Carrying Italian passports and Italian names, but having a different mother tongue, they return to bring a different Italian cultural 'accent' back into the heterogeneity of Italian culture. People left the northern and southern regions of Italy for countries such as Argentina, and their descendants return at a time when roles are totally reversed. Regions such as Friuli Venezia Giulia or Veneto have developed plans to facilitate their return.[81] However, the professions that are open for the protagonists of a migration of return are often inadequate to their level of education. Therefore, their return to the paternal or maternal motherland is fraught with difficulties. Often, they migrate to another region that is different from the one where their relatives' migration started. In a migration of return, people perform a double act: that of participating in internal and in external migrations as foreigners and as Italian citizens.[82] In order to recognize the artificiality of dichotomies and geographical separations, intellectuals such as Abate or Ammendola challenge limiting discourses on southern chronic economic depression and do not perpetuate the stereotypical separation between North and South. They reject a dominant normative ideology about the superiority of the North vis-à-vis the South, and contribute to that cluster of narratives uncovering Italy's complex role in world migration.

Raul Rossetti's *Schiena di vetro* (*A Glass-Like Back*, 1989) tells of his migration from the north-west of Italy to the mines in Belgium. The recently translated book *Gente con me* (*People with Me*, 1998) written in Spanish by Syria Poletti, who migrated to Argentina from the north-east of Italy, proposes the representation of an Italian North whose economic conditions are very close to the ones of the South. Both Rossetti's and Poletti's works establish a counter-discourse to the one created by political forces (such as the separatist Northern League) that focus on a generic northern Italian economic superiority based on the suppression of historical narratives negating such a fact.[83] Being a migrant is now plagued with a connotation of inferiority in Europe, but Jürgen Habermas has reminded us that

> [i]n the period between 1800 and 1960 Europeans were disproportionately represented in intercontinental migratory movements, making up 80 percent of those involved, and they profited from this ... The exodus of the nineteenth and early twentieth centuries improved the economic situations in the countries from which they fled, just as decisively as did, conversely, the immigration to Europe during the reconstruction period following the Second World War. Either way, Europe was the beneficiary of these streams of migration.[84]

That separation between North and South is therefore grounded in an economic superiority of a European North that has also been achieved through processes of migration that are constitutive of the European identity. This is particularly relevant to the case of Italy, whose political, economic, and historical identity is intrinsically connected to present and past migrations.

In his autobiographical novel *Io, venditore di elefanti*, the Senegalese writer Pap Khouma narrates the experience of undocumented immigrants who became street vendors and were often arrested. In one of these episodes, Pap, the protagonist of Khouma's autobiographical text, experienced the homogenizing potential of racial stereotyping when policemen told him to start break dancing as all black people can.[85] While Khouma's text, written from the perspective of an outsider to Italy, cannot use irony as a weapon against Italian racism, Raul Rossetti, in an eerily parallel episode that he told thirty years after he experienced it, uncovers the absurdity of stereotypes: 'I wonder why outside of Italy they picture us all [all Italian men] with a guitar and a razor blade in hand. And what's more, all singers. I am naturally allergic to songs, in particular, to Neapolitan songs, but everybody invites me to sing. Bitte zigen ... No, no. Su zigen. Well, if you really want me to. And I went "O sole mio." I delighted everybody with my frog-like voice. What was in my favour was the fact that I was singing in Italian.'[85] Rossetti, a northern Italian who migrated to work in the mines of northern Europe, takes on the cultural identity of a southern Italian singing a Neapolitan song. Differences collapse in the structuring of stereotypes to which migrants have to comply. It is in the act of complicity, of mimicry of stereotypes, when migrants narrate and mock, that literary talking back becomes culturally 'corrosive' humour.

Outside of Italy, Italians have been called 'macaruni,' 'macaroni,' and 'macaronì,' whether their origins were southern or northern Italian. In September 1994 the monthly journal *Il calendario del popolo* (*The People's Calendar*) focused on the parallelism between 'macaroni' and 'vu cumprà,' placing recent and past migrations side by side while at the same time highlighting differences between the emigration of Italians from and contemporary immigrations to Italy.[87] About Italian migrants to America, Fred Gardaphé states: 'If the Italian was not seen as a gangster or a knife-wielding, mustachioed foreigner who had taken away American jobs from the earlier immigrants, then he was depicted as a "restless, roving creature who disliked the confinement and restraint of mill and factory," as "very slow to take to American ways," and as "volatile, and incapable of effective team work."'[88] Even more interesting in the contemporary context, the word 'guinea' has been used in the United States as a disparaging and offensive term to define a person of Italian birth or descent, creating a precise identification of Italians as originating from the African continent, and as black. At this crossroads where sameness and difference meet, literature takes the role of exposing the cultural anxieties that have so efficiently motivated the repressions of the narratives of Italian migration. The space of sameness between the Italian 'macaroni,' who worked the most humble jobs outside of Italy, and the immigrant 'vu cumprà,' who sells (often without a permit) lighters and imitation designer goods on Italian sidewalks, is further complicated by the origin of the term 'vu cumprà.' In the glossary of their co-authored novel *La promessa di Hamadi* (*Hamadi's Promise*, 1991), Saidou Moussa Ba and Alessandro Micheletti trace the origin of this expression. The term, they state, appears for the first time in a 1925 poem by Raffaele Viviano entitled 'O' tripolino,' which tells of an Italian street vendor in Libya. In Ba and Micheletti's book the term 'vu cumprà' is considered a linguistic hybridization between the French *vous* and the Italian verb *comprare* (to buy). Their interpretations create connections between migrations and even reverse traditional movements from South to North by introducing an Italian migration to Africa as a land of opportunity, however connected to Italian colonialism.[89]

If the infiltration of French into a discourse on migration points to the francophone migration to the former motherland, it also implies the often forgotten migration of many northern Italians (and not only southern Italian people), in particular Piedmontese people, who in the nineteenth and twentieth centuries were both permanent migrants and seasonal migrants to southern France. Popular literature such as the best-selling mystery novel *Macaronì: romanzo di santi e delinquenti* (*Macaronì: A Novel about Saints and Criminals*, 1997), written by the singer/university professor Francesco Guccini and Loriano Machiavelli, places at the centre of the narrative such a discourse of intersecting sameness. The protagonists migrate in the late 1880s to France from the Emilia Romagna region without proper papers. In France, *macaronis* became *briseurs*, strike-breakers, although the term meant nothing to them.[90] The initial migration of Italians to the United States consisted of a large group of political exiles who, because of their ideals and demonstrations against the economic policies of the recently politically unified Italy, had to leave in order to avoid prison time. The political role that Italians played in the working-class struggles in the United States at the beginning of the twentieth century, which has been explored by historians, culminated in the Sacco and Vanzetti executions of 1927. Raul Rossetti remembers that '[w]hen the weather changes I still feel the pain where they struck me. In Cracebarleur, a town located ten miles from Liege, during a strike, the police charged against us as if we were Indians.'[91] Stereotypes function only when they are not closely examined: Italians as violent, but musically talented people, as strike-breakers, as revolutionaries, as migrants from a poorer country creating unemployment among the natives. The banality of stereotypes guarantees the possibility of recycling them into different social contexts and paradigms of scapegoating.[92]

What is implicit in this discussion is that texts have contributed across genres to the construction of a new frame in which Italianness is inscribed. Such a frame constructs itself as a fragmented structure that renders fluid the boundaries of the categories of sameness and difference. The narratives that describe the links between categories that cannot be kept separate successfully negate the possibility of a singular imagined Italian community. They also run counter to the deliberate political effort from above to construct such a community. The construction of a national literature that followed the unification of Italy in the nineteenth century and aimed to create such an imagined community cannot be sustained any longer.

At the beginning of a third millennium even concepts of residency, citizenship, and language cannot be solely connected to one national context whose lines of demarcation are rigid. Italian migration has created a new brand of Italian citizenship whose alliances are split into multiple citizenships. The plurilinguism that the new Italian Nation had marked with connotations of inferiority and tried to suppress by creating 'the' standard Italian remained the language of a migration from the motherland. That fictive ethnicity produced by language and discourses on race could not shape Italianness in the deterritorialization inherent in migration. Other fictive creations of ethnicity played a role in constructing Italianness abroad, as many migrant writers have testified in their writings. In contemporary Italy, the demand placed on migrants is to become fluent with that standard Italian that in turn signifies Italian unity and assimilation. The texts published by migrant writers in Italian ostensibly embrace the standard language. However, they employ Italian to define their differences from the fictive unified ethnicity that 'standard' Italian represents. These highlighted differences connect their constructed identities to the different embodiments of Italianness produced by Italian migrations within and outside the peninsula. Therefore, the narrative of Italianness that emerges negates homogeneity and grounds itself on disjointed and overlapping cultures that find continuity in the discontinuity of cultures and languages brought by contemporary migrants to Italy.

Recolouring Italian Culture(s)

Armando Gnisci has highlighted the complexity of geographic coordinates of North and South in movements of migration to Italy.[93] Judging from early texts by Ba, Khouma, and Salah Methnani, migrating to Italy from the South has involved migrating to Italy's south and the south of Italian culture. Employed in the tomato-picking fields, confronted by similarities rather than differences between past and present cultures, these authors explore the North of their diasporic journey by encountering that South which in the local culture has been coloured by connotations of inferiority. This movement toward a North that is seen by many as a South appears in the narratives of Italian migration to France. Approaching French culture, or Italian culture, from the South opens the possibility of questioning the construction of a North and the impossibility of doing so without uncovering the South already inherent in its septentrional geographical and cultural location. Not without humour one must conclude that one person's North is someone else's South until one moves geographically so far north that the roles are reversed, as in Scotland vis-à-vis England, or Finland vis-à-vis Sweden. The contingency and relativity of definitions of geographically challenged economic/social/political identifications of dominant and subordinate sections of the world highlight the inherent ad-hockery of cardinal points.[94]

Giulio Angioni's *Una ignota compagnia* (*An Unknown Friendship*, 1992) places two characters experiencing migration at the centre of the narrative. One is a Sardinian who moved to Italy's North in the early 1990s because his school degree had not guaranteed employment in his native region; the other is an African who tries to pass for American in order to become a more acceptable embodiment of difference. The protagonist of Ricci's *Le scapole dell'angelo* returns in a different shape and form in Angioni's book, and this time he is exploring the shared spaces of sameness with a fellow migrant. However, in this construction of complementary experiences of migration, the reader witnesses the contingency of the construction of skin colour. Similarly, the Ethiopian Italian writer Maria Viarengo underlines the fact that when she came to Italy in the 1960s her skin colour was considered lighter than that of immigrants from southern Italy. While southern Italians were openly discriminated against in rental policies, she, the woman recently arrived from Africa, was welcomed by landlords and considered exotic, but 'whiter' than immigrants from the Italian *meridione*, because her identity held no negative connotations. In the new economic landscape of contemporary Italy, the non-white Italian from the 1970s, the internal migrant, becomes whiter as the black immigrants from Africa now occupy the location of absolute otherness. Now, after thirty years in Italy, Maria Viarengo, who looks like other more recent immigrants, is confronted by the prejudice she had not previously experienced. These parallel reversals eloquently demonstrate the anxieties inherent in the construction of race and space according to a racialized geography based on ad-hockery in patterns of discrimination.

Aware of this arbitrary process of colour and racial identification, Saidou Moussa Ba focuses his co-authored text *La memoria di A.* (*A.'s Memory*, 1995) on a teenager's discovery of his own 'coloured' identity outside the familiar paradigms of racial identification in Italy. Antonio, the protagonist, fights alongside his parents to keep black immigrants out of their neighbourhood so as to maintain the value of their property. This otherness to be kept at bay is reframed in Antonio's trip to Germany, where he joins relatives who had migrated there. Rather than discovering, in a Kristevian move, the other within himself, Antonio is confronted with himself as other as constructed by the natives whose country he temporarily inhabits. Discovering otherness within oneself in order to remove the distance between sameness and otherness is an act of privilege that can be performed only from a particular position. Antonio is forced into an identity that other people have constructed for him. This slippage from being same to being other invites the Italian readers of Ba's text to confront the arbitrary processes in the construction of meaning employed in discourses on racial identities.

I would name the strategic process employed by these authors the *recolouring of a culture*. To recolour the Italian national identity in this context means to respond, by talking back, to an ideologically motivated attempt to whiten, 'catholicize,' and celebrate a first-world Italian identity in order to defend the rights of a majority. I offer an alternative model – that of the crossroads, which defines Italian culture as a context into which the past flows and encounters the present in order to create a plurality of hybrid future representations of national, international, and transnational identities. The cultural politics employed in the process of recolouring a culture expose, once more, the arbitrary construction of colour as a signifier whose content is supplied by contingency. Both migrant writers and native Italian writers emphasize in their narratives that the others are agents who talk back to and disrupt the negative stereotypes of alterity through a game of musical chairs in which marginality is disseminated. The strategy of recolouring is grounded on a two-way movement; the issue at stake is not only an Italianization through cultural contamination of incoming cultures, but also a xenophilic infiltration by other cultures that modify the pre-existing paradigms for the construction of meaning in Italian culture. The emphasis is on agency on the part of both native and migrant people in the construction of a collective counter-narrative about the past and the present of *italianità*. Such emphasis is at the centre of the process of recolouring a culture that goes far beyond the superficial multicultural aspects of contemporary Italy, such as ethnic restaurants, stores, and music, which reduces 'otherness' to a market product.

Recolouring is inevitably an inadequate term, but it is useful in identifying Italian culture and locating Italian identity as the crossroads of the Mediterranean. It is a term that allows talking about the location of a culture and the multiple subject positions within such a culture. It describes the uncovering of the fabrication of fictive ethnicity. Talking about recolouring Italian culture is also a provocation that brings to the surface anxieties in describing local cultures, Italian culture(s) in particular. It is by bringing destabilizing definitions of Italianness into a discussion on fictive ethnicities that we can generate questions and answers that interpret the present multicultural profile of Italy, grounded in continuity with a Mediterranean, already multicultural, past.

Literature plays a considerable role in my discussion of Italian multiculturalism, for it tells stories that run counter to any homogenizing project and allows the individuation of experiences that are excluded from public political discourse. In his essay 'Post-Colonial Transformations and Global Culture,' Bill Ashcroft argues that 'writing is one of the most interesting and strategic ways in which diaspora might disrupt ... problematic national formulations of identity.'[95] Ashcroft adds: 'If, as Stuart Hall suggests, the crucial concern of diasporic identity is not subjectivity but subject *position*, then the diasporic writer provides the prospect of a fluidity of identity, a constantly changing subject position both geographically and ontologically.'[96] In writing, diasporic writers in Italy have experimented with changing the subject position of the native. Both native and migrant writers have contributed to this literature that talks back. In particular, Martha Elvira Patiño has programmatically attempted to propose a revision, a recolouring, of one of the best-known myths in Italian culture. Her 'Naufragio' ('Shipwreck,' 1999) is a short story that rewrites the migration of Aeneas to the Italian coast and thus talks back to the myth of Italy's noble beginnings.[97] Patiño rewrites Virgil's didactic and celebratory construction of noble Trojan roots for the Roman Empire into another journey through similar adversities. Patiño's characters leave from the same coast whence Aeneas escaped after the destruction of his city, but they also represent that side of the Adriatic Sea where not only war but also the collapse of economies and political structures have forced people to migrate. Like Aeneas, the protagonist of 'Naufragio' leaves hoping to find a new place to settle: 'We escaped wounded and in pain. There were my son, some friends, my father, and myself. If others have managed to survive, they will be among the many refugees wandering the globe.'[98] Landing in Italy brings them into contact with the local people. Patiño reminds us that Aeneas conquered the new location with force and rape and that Virgil sang the glory of a culture constructed on violence. The migrant Aeneas at the end of the second millennium does not present himself as an invader, but as somebody who wants to gain access to a new country:

> I waited in vain for a reply to my letter. The news that reached me said that the most powerful man around here had agreed to welcome us in

> peace, but he had been pushed aside and silenced by a majority that questioned my origin. A strong, arrogant young man led that majority. He considered himself the direct heir to power, and the reply we got was a forceful invitation to leave. He explicitly threatened us, unwelcome people, with every kind of hostility. There was nothing we could do. We were forced to engage in that sorry battle in which men of these lands often fought. It seemed predetermined that peace could only be obtained through violence.[99]

The representation of a modern Aeneas as other turns 'high' into 'low' culture and myth into the daily construction of new representations of changing Italy. Pessimism pervades 'Naufragio,' and colours the new epic journey. Quoting Virgil, Patiño reminds us that 'it is easy to descend into hell,' a hell that can be the condition of the migrant, of the new hero without glory. Violence in fact marks the experience of a migrant: it is the violence caused by an obsession about constructing a fortress Italy in a fortress Europe, about the forced expulsion and preventive carceration of undocumented migrants, about defending the rights of a majority. Patiño's protagonist becomes a hero or heroine who, as Jadranka Hodzic tells in her 'L'altra parte dell'Adriatico' ('On the Other Side of the Adriatic Sea,' 1996), crosses the sea leaving war behind in order to tell a story in a new language and then obliterates himself or herself in suicide. Originating from a country in conflict, Hodzic's protagonist still finds violence and isolation in Italy. What is left are texts of a minor literature, revisionary acts that talk back to the structural myths of a culture, and disrupt through recolouring Italy's construction of its whiteness.

Conclusion

In his *Cinque scritti morali* (*Five Moral Writings*, 1997), Umberto Eco argues that 'there is only "immigration" when immigrants (those who are granted documentation according to political decisions) accept most of the customs of the country to which they migrate. There is 'migration' when migrants (whom nobody can stop from crossing borders) radically transform the culture of the land into which they migrate.'[100] His assertion constructs categories that, however attractive in their specificity, bring back the discussion on Italian multiculturalism to binary structures and collective identities that are marginalized into passivity. Immigration and migration and their impact on a culture cannot be kept separate and defined according to degrees of influence. Any individual embodiment of a culture impacts the new contexts in which he/she reinscribes himself or herself. The unpredictability of such impact is connected to various planes of interpretation that the local culture has of the migrant/immigrant and vice versa. Italian culture has developed protectionist discourses based on strategies of belonging and unbelonging. However, such monolithic strategies contain overdetermined definitions that disparate discourses have challenged in acts of talking back. Even if fragmented, that weak form of resistance has exposed the intrinsic multicultural entity that Italy is and responded to a dominant ideology on Italian whiteness.

The articulation of the concept of 'talking back' supplies a tool for understanding how the subaltern, the migrant, achieves agency under the pressure of the normative structures of a destination culture, which in turn is at the centre of a subsequent process of recolouring. Recolouring Italian culture is a provocative articulation of that process that interrupts discourses on cultural homogeneity and demands a revision of any simplistic definition of what constitutes Italian identities, histories, and cultures, stressing their plural forms. Recolouring Italian culture involves moving away from the defensive constructions that characterize relations between natives and non-natives. It allows not only the redrawing of boundaries, but also a questioning of the concepts of cultural boundaries and of binary oppositions in order to explore the locations of sameness and difference.

Both native and migrant practitioners of culture collaborate in reading Italy as a crossroads and a border whose geographic and cultural locations demand hybrid strategies, contaminated by different disciplines, in order to be investigated. The creation of a new language for migration is necessary for talking not only about migration, but also about its protagonists. Following Appiah's and Taylor's criticism about Western approaches to otherness, my goal is to create a script that can allow talking about migration issues without forgetting the dialogical process that constitutes identity construction and the necessity to redefine the terminology that critics employ to talk about the subjects of 'otherness.'[101]

CHAPTER TWO

Minor Literature, Minor Italy

L'eredità, figlio Sohn bir,
è questo tesoro di more mir e mir
che ho sulla punta della lingua,
këto fjalë parole Wörter,
queste autostrade del sole:
prendile tu che puoi,
mein Sohn bir figlio mio,
e attraversale come vuoi:
il pedaggio l'ho pagato io

Carmine Abate[1]

Durante gli antipasti e il primo si parlò di me, della traccia Est-Ovest, Sud-Nord della mia rotta, della laurea in lettere che non serve a nulla, di editori e di lavoro ...

Ron Kubati[2]

Issues of Language

In some of my earlier articles on migrants' literature, I employed the term 'Italophone literature' in order to define texts written by migrant authors in Italy and in Italian. My use of the term was motivated by affinities between examples of migrants' writing in Italian and the francophone tradition. However, the Italophone context that I traced starting from the early 1990s must be analysed in its specificity and the use of such a term must be questioned.

The term Italophone places the emphasis on language and on the difference between native speakers and non-native speakers, who acquire a new language through the process of migration. Although useful in describing the beginning of a migrants' literature in Italian, such a binary separation places migrants' literature outside a tradition and a linguistic 'genealogy.' In Derridian terms such a separation differentiates between those who own a language and those who do not.[3] However, Derrida asks, 'Who exactly possesses [a language]?'[4]

In his *Monolingualism of the Other; or, the Prosthesis of Origin* (1998), Derrida contests any possibility of ownership of a language and analyses the extraneous position of an individual to his or her native tongue. This is particularly useful in talking about Italian and its character as a national language. I need to reiterate what I already, in part, stated in chapter 1. Following the unification of Italy there was a concerted effort from political and social institutions to establish a national language. In fact, Derrida states, 'Every culture institutes itself through the unilateral imposition of some "politics" of language.'[5] For Italy such an imposition translated into an attempt to erase other native languages, which were downgraded to the status of dialects. Étienne Balibar has argued: 'There is no contradiction between the institution of one national language and the daily discrepancy between – and clash of – "class languages" which precisely are not different languages. In fact, the two things are complementary.'[6] However, the variants between 'dialects' and the Italian language are not, or at least not always, marked by class but by a whole set of characteristics that also involve the existence of a corpus of literature. In the 1960s, both television and a longer mandatory education achieved the goal, articulated a century earlier, of linguistically unifying the nation. Nonetheless, micro-politics of language mark standard Italian and allow dialects and regionalisms to permeate today's national language.

This infiltration of dialectal variants within the language reveals that a native speaker of Italian 'owns' the language and is, at the same time, a stranger to it. Consequently, the national language is not one language, and the native speaker cannot really own it, but rather negotiates his or her own linguistic difference vis-à-vis the language that is the standard tongue. Even migrants in Italy have learned to perform at different linguistic levels in daily practice, establishing market strategies grounded in linguistic localism. Street vendors have mastered the skill of acquiring enough knowledge of the dialect of the place where they are selling their goods. This linguistic appropriation establishes familiarity between two different embodiments of distance from a national language (that of the native Italian and that of the migrant). Simultaneously, the migrants' linguistic appropriation undermines the resurgence of the use of dialect on the part of natives who linguistically perform their belonging, at the expense of the 'others,' in favour of the local, 'original,' linguistic 'nature' of a place. This conservative micro-nationalism that parties such as the Northern League have embraced has also had the effect of demonstrating how weak the connection is between Italians and their national language.

Tracing the 'genealogical force,' in Derrida's words, intrinsic to being a stranger to one's own language – which is not a 'natural possession' – leads to a 'disorder of identity' and uncovers that otherness already present in the relationship between speaker and mother tongue.[7] Therefore, the native speaker is that individual who embodies extraneousness to a language that others attempt to master in order to occupy a special position of belonging to a culture. It is in the shared space of otherness vis-à-vis a national language that both native speakers of Italian and the migrants who acculturate themselves in Italian meet. Consequently, the linguistic modifications brought about by migrants, and their languages, in their use of Italian directly connect to a local tradition of linguistic transgressions and modifications that a linguistic 'homo-hegemony' cannot erase.[8]

The 'impossible property of a language' in Derridian terms uncovers the unfamiliarity of the familiar language that contains a multiplicity of languages that are the languages of the others, the native speakers.[9] The impossibility of owning a language also reveals the impossibility of using a term such as Italophone in talking about migrants' writings. What remains is the possibility of inscribing language 'in proximity' to a standard national idiom and, according to Derrida, 'not simply in it, like a complaint lodged next to it, a grievance and, already, an appellant procedure.'[10]

The Relevance of Minor Texts

Quoted at the beginning of this chapter, Abate's *'këto fjalë parole Wörter'* words find a home in Ron Kubati's literature and an heir in Kubati himself. Abate is an *Arbëresh* author who migrated from Italy to Germany and transmigrated back to Italy. Kubati belongs to a more recent migration from Albania to Italy. The tradition established in the writings of an 'other' Italian outside of Italy stands next to another generation's experience with migration. The words that express such migrations become tangled in plurilinguisms that mirror the intertwined lines and directions of migrations and languages. The geographical movements of people from and to Italy reflect themselves in literature's fragmented mirrors that are the words expressing the personal memories, the history, and the collective and singular experiences marked by migration. Literature becomes therefore the signifier of cultural hybridizations contained in weaker texts that reject policies and politics of exclusion. Speaking from a marginal location, migrants' writing narrates the role of the migrant as agent of change in the new culture he/she inhabits and the strategies of exclusion employed by the dominant culture. My critical approach to these texts fulfils the function of highlighting the relevance that migrants' literature has in shaping the future of Italian culture in a new multiculturalist direction that inscribes itself in the already multicultural Italian profile. Literature contains a crossroads of cultural lines that, even with a weaker voice, interpellate readers and demand validation. In this chapter, I want to analyse and validate the innovative appropriation of literary traditions on the part of migrants who create narratives in Italian. I also want to enact the relevance of literature in an interdisciplinary discussion on migration and contemporary Italy.

Interpreted in a Deleuzian sense, the minor literature being written in contemporary Italy is 'that which a minority constructs within a major language.'[11] The issue of language in contemporary Italian minor literature is a complex interplay of translations from other major languages. At a time when writing in local dialects has become a characteristic of Italian postmodern narratives and speaking in dialects has, in daily life, lost its connotations of inferiority, hyphenated Italian texts (that is, works authored by Italian migrants all over the world) are translated from major languages into Italian. At the same time, migrants to Italy learn a new idiom, abandoning other major colonial languages in order to write their lives in Italian, which is a third or fourth language for most. In this interplay of languages Italian fulfils a mediating role, as it is from an international perspective a minor language. Nassera Chohra, a second-generation Algerian migrant in France wrote the autobiography *Volevo diventare bianca* (*I Wanted to Become White*, 1993) in Italian. Chohra devotes most of the book to the narrative of her life in France as a *beur* or, more accurately, a second-generation Algerian in France, with only a final chapter on her experience in Italy. She chooses to write her minor narrative in a language that has a minor status in relation to the language in which her experiences as a member of a minority took place. After acquiring Italian by using a French-Italian grammar book, Pap Khouma wrote his autobiography, inspired by a book written by Günter Wallraff, a German native who posed as a Turkish man and lived as a member of the German Turkish community.[12] Khouma read this narrative either in French or in Italian (even he cannot remember which) and used the book written in German by a German pretending to be a member of a minority as a model for writing his own life in Senegal, France, and Italy in Italian. Languages, whether national or local, become deterritorialized in the context of minor literature in Italian and used as tools to move the concept of minor literature, written in one language, beyond the borders, whether political or geographic, that delimit the location of such languages.

Language is a tool for writers such as Ba, educated in French and in French culture in Senegal, to talk back to the colonial environment in which he became an adult. His refusal to migrate to the ex-motherland imbues the choice of writing in Italian with ideological connotations. In a short story in Italian entitled 'Nel cuore di un clandestino' ('In the Heart of an Illegal Migrant'), Ba discusses the role that France and French have played in shaping his life. In particular, he dwells on his father's death while serving in the French army and fighting in another French ex-colony. Pap Khouma stresses that his attempted migration to France was a failure because both the French and the older Senegalese communities he encountered made him feel unwelcome. The choice of another language and another culture opens the possibility of interrupting the colonial and post-independence connections with France. However, French – not African languages – is the mediating idiom in the acquisition of Italian. While it took generations for Italian migrants to become visible in the literary arena outside of Italy, recent migrants to Italy started telling their stories in Italian while in the actual process of learning the language. As in Italian American literature, the role of the linguistic expert or native speaker functioned as the necessary mediating entity that would 'correct' the language and develop the connections with the publishing world.[13] On the one hand, this strategy sets a number of limitations on the way the story is narrated; on the other, it allows migrant narratives to be published and migrants' voices to be heard. This transitional phase is a powerful tool to create a distance from the colonial language and talk back to the colonial paradigms by pointing at other processes of cultural hybridization.

In his book *Decolonising the Mind*, Ngugi Wa Thiong'o asserts that adopting a new language involves a separation from the past 'toward other worlds.'[14] He refers to the colonizers' languages imposed over the African native languages, such that acquiring an education has meant abandoning an African past to embrace the superiority of Western knowledge. As language is intended as both a 'means of communication and a carrier of culture,' such a separation becomes a mutilation, an exile from a community.[15] 'Language as culture[s],' adds Ngugi 'is the collective memory bank of a people's experience in history.'[16] This evident separation from the 'original' languages appears in the Italian texts written by Africans in Italy. However, the context is somewhat different from the one described by Ngugi, as the centre of the discussion is migration, and the inevitable coming together of different languages and cultural contexts in a process of geographical and cultural translations. Bill Ashcroft eloquently connects post-colonial and migrants' writing by stating that 'diasporic writing is ... a pre-eminent demonstration of the post-colonial tendency to problematize imperial and global boundaries.'[17]

The multiplication of other worlds in migrants' writing also involves a rewriting of that imagined community that could be called home, land, and culture of origin. In *The Post-Colonial Critic*, Gayatri Spivak states that 'the diasporic cultures are quite different from the culture that they came from originally.'[18] Most migrant writers in Italy, in particular African Italian writers, come from already diasporic cultures and their background is already multicultural. Since many of these writers come from former French colonies, they know French, not to mention a multiplicity of local languages and dialects. Embracing Italian means creating another collective memory bank that aims to construct other 'people's experience in history.' The emphasis is not so much on one history, but on plural interpretations of many histories and, in this case, on a specific community and a specific history of migrants and immigrations to Italy. Italian has become the language shared by many groups of migrants from Africa, Asia, and eastern Europe, groups that do not share any other common language. The narratives created in Italian by migrants themselves define their present history and the history of migrations, and address a large reading public. The need to respond to the alarmist discussions of invading foreign identities makes it impossible for migrant writers to write in any other language than Italian. On the one hand, this necessity creates, 'the feeling of irreducible distance' from their mother tongues and cultural context; on the other, migrants' narratives in Italian become a means to talk to the other migrants originating from different parts of the world, because by creating a minor literature in Italian these writers also write a literature that can unify rather than separate the degrees of otherness represented by the migrant groups in Italy.[19]

This minor literature addresses native Italians by revising the stereotypes presented in the press, addresses other others by representing their experiences that are parallel to the ones described, and approaches language as a malleable entity permeable to other languages. The dispersion of untranslatable terms originating from other languages is present in Italian minor literature: *gorbha*, nostalgia, or *saudade*, and rhythms and inflections foreign to traditional Italian narratives contribute to the deterritorialization of language. This specific minor literature creates spaces of proximity to a national language that, borrowing Derrida's words, 'make something happen to it.'[20] For instance, the linguistic game played by Christiana De Caldas Brito in her 'Ana de Jesus' (1995), the monologue of a Brazilian maid in Italy, is based on the ungrammatical grammar of language acquisition and of migration. According to Deleuze and Guattari, 'a major, or established, literature follows a vector that goes from content to expression'; 'a minor, or revolutionary, literature,' instead, 'begins by expressing itself and doesn't conceptualize until afterward ("I do not see the word at all, I invent it").'[21] This transgressive approach to literature can be interpreted in disparate ways: the ungrammatical expression of Ana can become for an Italian audience the reassuring comic ramblings of an illiterate woman. Salah Methnani states in his novel *Immigrato* that although he had a university degree and became rapidly fluent in Italian, he soon discovered that it was much safer for him in Italy to disguise his linguistic ability and hide in the ungrammatical articulations of the mass of immigrants to which natives expected him to belong. The sense of alarm that his fluency provoked in native speakers made him retreat into the stereotypes and broken Italian that people found more reassuring. His autobiographical text in Italian is therefore an attempt to talk back to the expectations imposed on him. Writing also allows Methnani to make himself visible in his singularity, to appropriate Italian and demonstrate his mastery of it, and to establish on/in his own terms a discourse in sameness and difference.

The construction of a vernacular of a migrant literature in Italian places the migrant writer as agent of linguistic change and hybridizations. Kossi Komla-Ebri deliberately eliminates the use of subjunctives in his novel *Neyla*, and inserts words from his native country, Togo. He adopts, therefore, a more oral Italian as his literary language, employing the simplifications that characterize daily exchanges between people. He wants to bring Italian closer to the signifiers of those oral African languages that appear in his narrative. He assigns dignity to both by inscribing them in a novel that validates the innovative approach of migrants to a newly acquired language. Even more complex is Tahar Lamri's approach to linguistic experimentation. In his short story 'Il pellegrinaggio della voce' ('The Pilgrimage of the Voice'), the emphasis is again on the language of orality and its translation into a written text, but with a twist. He involves a theatre group from Mantua that translates sections of his short story into Mantovano dialect, borrows from texts in Romagnolo dialect by Luigi Dadina, and in Veneto dialect by the poet Ennio Sartori. His protagonists speak in both Italian and Arabic, and are called Abdessalam, Orsolina, and Antavleva; this third character is an unwanted child whose parents called her by the revealing first name 'Didntwantyou.' Lamri's characters are the witnesses of poverty and ignorance in different cultures. His linguistic discourse is structured around issues of class, as his exploration of languages reveals that sameness which connects the poor and the oppressed, whose lives are told in minor languages and inscribed in a narrative in standard and literary Italian.

Inventing identities by experimenting with language, by manipulating stereotypes and a literary tradition, has given unexpected results. In 1997, the Albanian poet Gëzim Hajdari, who had been writing in Italian since leaving his native country for political reasons in 1992, won the most prestigious poetry award in Italy: the Montale Prize. Hajdari's style, which conflates both Albanian and Italian poetic traditions, became the model for poetic expression at a time when Italy was alarmed by the nightly invasion of Albanian boat people. Migration and marginalization are at the centre of Hajdari's poetry:

Piove sempre	Bie shi vazhdimisht	It is always raining
in questo	në këtë	in this
paese	vend	country
forse perché sono	ndoshta ngaqë	maybe because I am
straniero.[22]	i huaj.	a stranger.

An emphasis on strangeness and foreignness dominates Hajdari's poetic work. He places otherness at the centre of a body of work that is officially recognized and represents 'the best' poetic production in Italian of 1997. Hajdari portrays history outside of any traditional narrative, emphasizing the exotic attractions for the tourist and the utopian-American dream for migrants. Italy becomes for Hajdari a country of an unfriendly rain that envelops the life of the stranger whose unbelonging becomes a physical sensation. His appropriation of literary Italian and his infiltration of the Olympus of Montale prize-winners makes Hajdari's work a manifesto of migrants' literature as minor literature within Italy's cultural production. However, Hajdari's poetic work is also sustained by the other narratives published by migrants in Italy. As poetry is the least commercial genre in the publishing market, Hajdari has been canonized as a voice in Italian high literature and, at the same time, been marginalized in that same privileged group that he has succeeded in accessing.[23]

At the end of many of my oral presentations on migrants' literature in Italian, I have been asked if what migrants are writing is considered literature or something that comes close to literature, and whether these writings will graduate to the status of literature, or perhaps are merely at an experimental stage that would locate migrants' texts outside the realm of literariness. From the standpoint of a more traditional idealistic approach to literature, I have been asked if migrants' texts are good literature. Literature is a special form of discourse that has multiple partial definitions, but cannot be limited by normative and prescriptive methodological approaches. In his *Guida allo studio della letteratura* (*Guide to the Study of Literature*), Remo Ceserani reminds us that when Dario Fo won the Nobel prize for literature, the literary Italian establishment reacted with indignation because Fo's work did not really belong to literature, but to a sub-category to which connotations of inferiority were attached.[24] Published in the winter of 2003/4, the anthology of Italian poetry *Poesia Italiana*, edited by Cesare Segre and Carlo Ossola, contains only two women poets in its two volumes devoted to the twentieth century: Antonia Pozzi and Amelia Rosselli.[25] The volume devoted to the nineteenth century contains no texts authored by women. By virtue of this exclusion, what women wrote in that century stands outside the canonical definition of what poetry is. The historical relativity of literary experience and values is evident in the process of selecting what belongs and does not belong to 'literature'. Migrants have written texts that have been 'canonized' into the Italian literary roster, as in the case of Gëzim Hajdari, in addition to novels and short stories that dialogue with the canonical texts of Italian literature. Positioning themselves at the crossroads of disparate literary traditions, migrants have performed a literary synthesis that borrows and selects, filtering intellectual heritages through the process of migration. They create narratives that in their linguistic proximity to a national language revise the literary languages of many traditions. It is a minor literature that aims to create a minor tradition whose complexity also demands a complex critical approach that can include issues of literary quality, provided that one takes into consideration the arbitrariness of such values.

In confronting literature from the point of view of cultural studies, I am interested in what Maurizio Viano has called the 'use value' of a text in literature, of migrants' literature in this case.[26] Viano argues for privileging 'the valorization of texts that, beyond the categories of beautiful and ugly, strongly solicit our attention because of their capacity of *forcing* us to deal with questions of incomparable urgency.'[27] The questions of incomparable urgency that are relevant to this book concern the future of literatures in Italian, the future of Italian cultures, and the relationship between local and global cultures seen under the light of migrations from and to Italy. Often interpreted as a process that amplifies inequalities among people and between peoples, globalism can also be interpreted from below, from the individual act of writing that documents the location of the individual within the global. Therefore, migrants' literature talks back to the homogenizing process of globalization, by appropriating local languages in order to create literary texts as use texts. These use texts are agents of change that can create a minor literature in which change is *imagined* and made public in a narrative structure.

Migrants' literature as a minor literature exists at the beginning of the second millennium as an entity that has acquired visibility thanks to a gradual acquisition of space – in the literal sense, on the shelves of bookstores and in the catalogues of publishers. Deleuze and Guattari assert that a 'characteristic of minor literature is that in it everything takes on a collective value. Indeed, precisely because talent isn't abundant in a minor literature, there are no possibilities for an individual enunciation that would belong to this or that "master" and that could be separated from a collective enunciation.'[28] Unfortunately, such an enunciation can lead once more to an approach to migrants' texts in the negative, as non-literature, as cultural manifestations in the domain of social studies. Even the commercial success of Pap Khouma's *Io, venditore di elefanti* has been considered as just a temporary surfacing of an exotic narrative and as an isolated phenomenon that cannot be considered a contribution to literature. Even Oreste Pivetta, who edited Khouma's work, wondered:

> Will a literature of the immigrant 'other' be born in Italy? I have doubts for at least two reasons: because of the language, as French and English are for a Moroccan or an Indian languages that they have heard since childhood. We cannot say the same about Italian for a Senegalese or a Moroccan. Second: because immigration to Italy is too recent and too limited (the so-called 'wave' never took place). That's a pity. Our fight against 'the fear of difference' would have been encouraged.[29]

Yet, Pivetta has been proved wrong, as a large number of texts have been published in which writing in another language has not been an obstacle but a way to talk back to the colonial languages in which migrants have been educated.

The large number of writings marked by very different levels of complexity and sophistication have created a non-homogeneous corpus of texts. This may be, suggest Deleuze and Guattari, the paradoxical strength of a minor literature, in which the 'scarcity of talent is in fact beneficial and allows the conception of something other than a literature of masters.'[30] The collective narrative of migration that is at the centre of my discourse is eloquently described by Deleuze and Guattari's articulations, but at the same time points beyond their definitions. The fact that migrants' literature can occupy both the centre of high literature with a poet such as Gëzim Hajdari, the Olympus of the publishing market with a best-seller by Pap Khouma, and the margins of literary production with the texts of many other migrant writers demands a redefinition of the concept of talent and scarcity of talent inherent in minor literature. Understood in its traditional sense, talent has been recognized in Hajdari and commercial talent in Khouma, but such talents still stand outside the canon of Italian literature. Even Hajdari's success has not guaranteed his inclusion in canonical anthologies. However, the position of marginality imposed on migrant writers has been modified by native Italians' texts on contemporary migrations.

A minor literature in Italian constructs itself on non-separatist strategies that allow native voices to participate in its definitions. Writers such as Giulio Angioni, Marco Lodoli, Antonio Saponaro, and Emilio Tadini participate in the construction of a migrants' literature by connecting past and present migrations.[31] They articulate discourses in which sameness and difference share flexible boundaries, as well as malleable geographical and historical borders in strategies of identity construction. In *Una ignota compagnia,* Giulio Angioni tells of the affinities between internal and external migrations embodied in his two characters, who originate in Kenya and Sardinia. In *I fannulloni,* Marco Lodoli focuses on the relationship between people at the margins of Italian society: an elderly man and an African immigrant. Giorgio Saponaro describes, in *Il ragazzo di Tirana,* the agony of escaping Albania locked in a container in which the dreams of a better life turn into tragedy. At times melodramatic, Saponaro's novel, seeking to destroy the myth of a 'better' life in migration, describes the desperation of those who decide to return to their point of origin. Emilio Tadini's play *La tempesta,* inspired by the Shakespearean classic, describes the relationship between a Prospero-like Italian and an African immigrant who together confront the establishment. In the performance on stage, Saidou Moussa Ba played Tadini's African character, which exemplifies the fact that Ba has privileged collaborations with a linguistic expert (Alessandro Micheletti) and native intellectuals. Ba's active participation in collaborative projects makes him an intellectual engaged in bridging the separations between native and migrant productions of meaning, between Western and non-Western representations of identities and margins.

In her *Lontano da Mogadiscio* (*Far Away from Mogadishu,* 1994), Shirin Ramzanali Fazel tells of her hybrid identity and cultural background when she writes about her Asian father and Somalian mother, her Italian education in Somalia, and her escape from the dictatorship there with her Somalian Italian husband in 1970. Writing her autobiographical text more than twenty years after her migration, Fazel blurs the boundaries between native and non-native Italians by constructing a narrative in Italian in which she witnesses the war in her native Somalia through the Western eyes of Italian television. She feels part of a privileged group whose cultural whiteness has contaminated the interpretation of her own past:

> Sadness overcomes me, and in my mind I again see the innumerable images of so many reports that every newspaper has published. Snapshots of children, women, and old people, skeletal from hunger, with wrinkled faces and enormous eyes. Exactly like those the television is showing at this moment. The camera freezes the images, and a momentary wave of indignation and compassion overcomes us when we watch them.

> We are beautiful, white, and our skin is smooth. Our bodies are muscular and our faces smiling, like the mineral water commercial shows us. Those people, however, have no name, no story. They are only images, images of ghosts who are not ours.[32]

Starting from a description of her familial community at the dinner table, identified as an initial 'us,' Fazel changes the representation of community, of the 'us,' beyond the domestic sphere into a public 'us' that is not defined along colour lines. That 'us' made of people watching the same images on Italian television involves an elaboration of the concept of sameness that includes those who participate in and validate narratives on otherness that seem so distant on television. In her minor text, Fazel plays with strategies of hybridization in a very effective way: she begins her book with the nostalgic narration of Somalia as a mythical location; defines her Western education as a shared space with her Italian readers; tells of her migration and of the construction of her own different identity within a country that at the time, the 1970s, did not have a large immigrant population; connects her present identity with that of more recent, less privileged migrants; and finally places herself among the natives who read their white difference in the distance between the starving, warring, Third World people and the well-fed Italians, citizens of a First World. Same and different become, in Fazel's work, permeable entities that collaborate in defining the large community she is addressing. Fazel expresses the need for a redefinition of community and for a collective act of witnessing the construction of multicultural Italian identities.

'Literature,' state Deleuze and Guattari, 'finds itself positively charged with the role and function of collective, and even revolutionary, enunciation.'[33] Still, individual authors claim the right to write against the grain of the strategies of migrant identity construction that dominate public discourses in Italy. The mass of immigrants (actually, a small number compared to those in other European countries) appears in the press as a homogeneous entity from which native people have to protect themselves. Individual writers respond with autobiographical acts that talk back to such racist discourses and contain the narrative of one identity, one experience, different from all the other experiences of the group. 'I am an other like many other immigrants, but I am also an other like no other' is the statement at the centre of each migrant's text. This individuality is evident in the first novels published at the beginning of the 1990s. Pap Khouma told of his life in a community of Senegalese migrants that shared language and origin and talked of their collective experience as street vendors, as undocumented immigrants harassed by the police, as a community functioning as separate from the rest of the Italian communities. At the same time, this is an autobiographical narrative with a very specific identity at its centre. The protagonist's success is based on separation from such a community in order to emerge as a writer who emphasizes his uniqueness within a discourse on the similarities that connect him to a community.

This minor literature within the narrative of contemporary Italy places migration issues at the centre of the discussion. What is at stake here is the possibility of constructing non-separatist paradigms and, in part, the articulation of processes of sameness in identity construction. In such processes and in immigrants' minor narratives, the boundaries between sameness and difference demand a redefinition that takes into consideration disparate cultural narratives whose agenda is the recolouring of the Italian identity. In this regard, it is important to analyse the construction of difference within migrant literature. It is a difference identified in disparate relational contexts: between migrants and their communities, between immigrants and natives, and between men and women.

The role that women's literature plays in the debate on migration parallels the traditional role that women writers have played in Western society and, at the same time, challenges it. One of the best-known texts in Italian American literature is Mary Hall Ets's *Rosa: The Life of an Italian Immigrant*, which narrates the life of an Italian woman who migrated to America at the beginning of the twentieth century. This testimony recorded by Ets, a social worker, is a text created from an oral narrative by Rosa Cavalleri. The storyteller had no control over the final product; the book is Ets's rendition of Cavalleri's hybrid linguistic ability. This problematic first attempt to publish an Italian immigrant woman's life proves once more how much harder it is for women's voices to surface. In contemporary Italy, men have migrated and become visible by selling in the streets. They have supported each other, living and travelling in communities. Women, who were among the first immigrants to Italy, responded to the need for domestic workers and caretakers and experienced migration dispersed in native familial spheres. Because of the complexity of migrating as a woman, migrant women's narratives have appeared later than men's and have been authored by privileged subjects of migration. Nassera Chohra moved to Italy after spending her childhood and adolescence in France, where she was born in an Algerian family. Her autobiographical narrative, *Volevo diventare bianca*, is not in Deleuzian terms a 'collective enunciation.' On the contrary, Chohra focuses on her unique experience and life as a *beur* in France, describes her condition as a second-generation immigrant, and once in Italy is careful to separate herself from the trials of recent immigrants to Italy. She even employs stereotypes that were used against her: while in France she pursued a career as an actress and was rejected for the part of an Arab woman because her skin was too dark. She did not embody the stereotype because her sub-Saharan origin made her into a non-Arab. Once in Italy, she looks at the street vendors from a distance. Nassera, the protagonist of *Volevo diventare bianca*, has come to Italy as a tourist and stays because she meets her future husband. In her description of the changing multicultural landscape of Rome, she is careful in locating her identity in a cultural frame that validates her claim of being already French Algerian: 'I would not know why, but I instinctively compared my skin with the poor and unfortunate salesman's skin. He stood there with downcast eyes and a resigned expression. He must be Senegalese, I thought. They have this trade in their blood.'[34] The genetically determined profession of the Senegalese immigrant is negated by Khouma's story, which explains that, although he is Senegalese and for a time a street vendor, he failed in the trade. Chohra finds the employment of stereotypes reassuring and a validation of the cultural separation between first- and second-generation immigrants and of her belonging, through complicity, to the dominant discourse on otherness she had tried to undermine in her narrative of growing up *beur* in France. When she narrates her return to the Sahara as a teenager, Nassera decides that the people who are her relatives have more in common with Native Americans than with her. Her rejection of them is drastic: they are savages, she is French.[35]

The 'collective enunciation' of Deleuzian tone is not to be found in the attempt to describe a familial community along ethnic lines, but needs to be constructed by the readers through an intertextual reading of, for instance, the disseminated women's narratives, and is grounded in the plot of isolation and invisibility. In her autobiographical narrative *Con il vento nei capelli: vita di una donna palestinese* (*With Wind in My Hair: The Life of a Palestinian Woman*, 1993), Salwa Salem looks back at her life through the experience of a terminal disease that prevents her from finishing her book. The editor Laura Maritano completed and published the book after Salem's death in 1993. In her nomadic existence, Salem experiences forced migration as her family has to give up its property in the occupied territories. She describes her active resistance against the Israeli occupation and voluntary migration in order to begin her working career. Her arranged marriage forces her to abandon her position as a teacher in Kuwait in order to follow her husband, a student of architecture, to Vienna. Her critical position vis-à-vis the patriarchal culture that she sees embodied even in the community of her husband's Palestinian friends in Vienna, the unwelcoming Austrian cultural context, and her ambivalence toward her identity as a wife and mother are the defining characteristics of her isolation and loneliness. It is in her double isolation as migrant and as a mother whose work takes place inside the home that Salem's story speaks of the experience of other women migrants. In fact, while her husband pursues his studies and inscribes himself in a university community, she remains isolated in a private sphere.

Salem's final migration to Italy relies on a construction of the new culture as a border culture: the geographical location of Italy in the middle of the Mediterranean coincides for her with the construction of a locale able to function as a connection between the South and North of the world. Italy becomes for her a place where her loneliness is mitigated by encounters with southern Italian women who, like her, know what it means to migrate: 'I began going to the public garden with Rosalba.' Even though they struggle to communicate in English because Salwa cannot speak Italian, 'I later discovered that she came from the South and understood what it means to be alone, far from one's land, from one's family.'[36] Rosalba's South is different from Salwa's, since Rosalba's ability to function within Italian culture is facilitated by being a native speaker of Italian. Still, Salem wants to construct a sense of community, of a female nomadic community. She thinks that Italians perceive her as a 'normal foreigner,' somebody who originates from outside the culture, but is 'acceptable' within the landscape of a country that is a crossroads in the Mediterranean.[37] Salem's construction of a subjective map of Italy and its culture plays, on the one hand, with Italy's internal history and, on the other, with the Palestinian struggle. On a trip back to visit her family, Salem realizes how absurd it is that she needs an official visa to visit her own people. Taking a walk with her father, she listens to his description of neighbours and locations that had long disappeared: 'Lui aveva l'antica mappa stampata nella sua mente' ('He had the old map printed in his mind').[38] Maps, whether geographical or cultural, are for Salem subjective constructions that can deprive people of their home/land, as in the violent Palestinian/Israeli history of relations, or can talk back to the official invention of borders and cultural identities within migration. In her provocative construction of herself as a migrant within the paradigm of 'normality' in a subjective mapping of history and traditions, Salem establishes a counter-narrative that both talks back and stresses the role of agency in the construction of a destination culture.[39]

The Destination of Italian Culture

Traditionally a destination culture is a culture toward which migrants move. In my discussion of Italian multiculturalisms, I would like to articulate the possibility of theorizing a destination culture that can be such for both native and non-native people. A destination culture is a site of cultural intertextuality and a location in which the validation of processes of cultural hybridization takes place. The Italian multicultural past intersects a multicultural present that projects a local culture into a European context of hybrid cultures. In my usage, a destination culture is therefore not only the culture toward which migration moves, but is a new hybrid culture that is the result of both the changes brought to a local culture by incoming people and the influence of that Western culture (with its internal hybridizations and pluralism) on incoming cultures. In a present cultural context in which the Western culture(s) occupy a privileged position, it is clear that the difficulty in constructing a shared destination culture is 'to honor and do justice,' according to Radhakrishnan, 'to the specificity of the subject position such as black ... immigrant, ethnic, ... and at the same time, to enable structurally homologous and isomorphic readings of one situation in terms of the other.'[40] A destination culture is, therefore, a projection and development into the future of present cultural turmoils and tensions. A destination culture in Italy is structurally grounded in processes of recolouring, that is, in the fluid boundaries between sameness and difference, between past and present cultural paradigms. The possibility of an Italian destination culture relies on the strategy of talking back and recreating a context, marked even by changes to a specific national language, that revisits both the culture of the 'origin' and of the diaspora. Isolated acts of talking back build on strategies undermining traditional cultural practices in order to debunk them from their privileged position. A destination culture is also a site of hybridization in which the construction of the meanings of otherness is based on 'talking with' the local cultures and the cultures geographically inscribed in the country from which the journey of migration started. In Italy, a destination culture is grounded on the right of migrants to access and appropriate a location of culture in which they bring to the surface the inner tensions of the already multilayered local culture. A destination culture grounds itself on cultural turmoil as a site of production of meaning and of identity.

It is in the context of a politics of contamination that one can question the position and the definition of what is marginal and what is dominant. The Italian language is a privileged site into which otherness translates itself. However, such a context creates counter-narratives that are only relatively empowered and can be easily marginalized as they are not granted entrance into a tradition. A destination culture requires a re-drawing of lines of identification beyond migration and ethnicity into less-confining post-migration and post-ethnic realms that make the use of the term 'migrants' literature' start to lose its validity. In fact, writers such as Jadelin Mabiala Gangbo, whose native language is Italian, or Nassera Chohra, whose cultural and geographical migrations trace generations and disparate locations, problematize terms such as 'migrants' writing' vis-à-vis their texts and 'ethnic identity' vis-à-vis their multiple cultural identifications.

It must be reiterated that the concept of Italophone literature is a term too limiting to describe the phenomenon of the construction of an Italian destination culture. In fact, a destination culture is situated, but not geographically restricted. Tahar Lamri's plurilinguistic experimentation and Christiana De Caldas Brito's grammatical transgressions go beyond an interest in constructing identities in one language. In addition, what constitutes the creation of a destination culture is also the retranslation into Italian of narratives of Italian migration that were articulated originally in other languages but are constitutive elements thanks to how an Italian destination culture articulates itself.

Italian destination culture is the site in which the construction of one homogeneous imagined community connected to a traditional concept of national identity within the bounds of national lines cannot be sustained. A destination presupposes a journey that metaphorically, and in practice, translates, that is moves across borders and betrays them.[41] It involves a process of remapping geographical and cultural terrains that overflow the bounds of national lines. In fact, a destination culture is also 'imbricated in wider processes of globalization.'[42] We cannot discuss a destination culture that originates from the hybridization of an Italian context without connecting it to other processes of cultural transformation in which migrants are the protagonists. We cannot talk about the specific case of an Italian destination culture without connecting it to other destination cultures across subjective border limitations.

Although the translation into practice of my articulations of destination cultures is projected into the future, it is possible to trace its roots in present developments. In December 1998 Maria Corti spoke to the Collège de France on 'L'Europa come "luogo mentale" e i "mondi possibili" della letteratura' ('Europe as an "imaginary location" and the "possible worlds" of literature).[43] She placed literature at the centre of her discourse on post-unification Europe by stating that the future of the European culture could already be 'imagined' within literature itself. Migration literature in Italy fulfils the same function of 'imagining' a destination culture that is a future intercultural context. Gëzim Hajdari's Albanian Italian texts have made him the winner of the most prestigious poetry award in Italy. Mohsen Melliti's work in Arabic, published only in Italian, contains a linguistic contamination between Italian and Arabic that imagines a hybridized Italian language. The Algerian Italian writer Amara Lakhous continues to write in Arabic even after living in Italy for a long time. He has stated that his linguistic choice is based on the assumption that Arabic is a language that has returned to Italy; it is part of Italy's past and can be considered a dialect of Italy.[44] Nassera Chohra allows us to imagine the possible cultural contaminations not only between migrants and Italians, but also between the cultural elaborations of second- or third-generation migrants in European cultures and Italian culture. Pap Khouma and Saidou Moussa Ba have stressed the connections between the processes of identity construction in their narratives in Italian and the post-colonial French context in which they were acculturated.

The privileged position of literature as an indicator of future developments is the site from which my theoretical articulations originate. In migration literature a writer can construct 'identity in difference' and 'difference in identity' that constitute the framework of cultural intertextuality that, in turn, has to negotiate between the demands of assimilation and the 'rights' of an alleged majority. Created at the intersection of local traditions and incoming cultural practices, literature within a destination culture projects its hybrid components into a fluid present and an unpredictable future grounded on the crises of the articulations of sameness and difference. Literature, therefore, constitutes the location in which it is possible to construct an imagined destination culture.

The Crisis of the Same Difference

Italian destination culture constructs itself on old and new migrations and colonial cultures that dialogue with Italian culture(s) in order to deterritorialize contemporary migrants' cultures and traditions. In the context of Italian American culture, Fred Gardaphé, William Boelhower, and Werner Sollors describe the progression from narratives centred around strictly autobiographical themes to autobiographical fiction.[45] To quote Sollors, 'ethnic writing' moves from 'folk and popular forms to high forms,' 'from lower to higher degrees of complexity.'[46] In a truly postmodern move, a first generation of migrants to Italy has created a corpus of texts that simultaneously contains testimonies, autobiographies, autobiographical fiction, and poems in Italian. The difference between Italian American and contemporary migrants' narratives in Italy lies in the historical and economic contexts in which these two literatures have developed. The emergence of texts, written in Italian by non-native speakers, is a process that has taken only a few years, while the process of the acquisition of a new language and of literary skills spans a couple of Italian American generations. However, it is a methodological imperative to return to Italian identities layered in difference when discussing the construction of contemporary Italian multiculturalism. Helen Barolini's *Umbertina* (first published 1979), for instance, describes the painful process of becoming fluent in the cultural discourse whose margins Italian Americans inhabited for generations. In describing second-generation autobiographical narratives in France, Alec Hargreaves argues that 'where the Beurs [a term that Hargreaves himself finds now problematic] are concerned, the split is effectively between two different parts of the self: one which identifies with the secular values of contemporary France, and one which, through the family home, remains engaged with the Islamic traditions of North Africa.'[47] In this context, Italy becomes the third possibility for a writer such as Nassera Chohra, born in Marseilles in an Algerian family. Chohra writes in Italian of the generational split she experienced in France, translating experiences of migration across generations in a language in which it did not take place. These chronological and geographical shifts and conflations constitute the core of Italian destination culture. Autobiographies, autobiographical texts, biographies, ventriloquized first-person migration narratives, and pulp fictions of migration form the varied landscape of a first-generation migrants' literature in Italian, which already contains varying degrees of complexity.

In the 1990s, migrants' texts in Italian such as Chohra's articulate the elements that characterize second-generation narratives in francophone culture.[48] 'The Beurs,' Hargreaves writes, 'carry within themselves conflicting cultural imperatives which make it impossible for them to feel unequivocally rooted in a single territorial base.'[49] Tahar Lamri, born in Algeria, educated in Libya, migrated first to France and only later moved to Italy. His work in theatre and literature focuses on the intertwining cultural lines that constitute his intellectual identity and the impossibility of identifying with one clear national and cultural identity. Lamri's 'Solo allora, sono certo, potrò capire' ('Only Then, I Am Certain, I'll Be Able to Understand,' 1995) is a short story devoted to the impossibility of a return to a first generation cultural identity.[50] The effort to understand the familial roots originating from a specific cultural context proves the impossibility of re-appropriating an identity that the family has worked hard to suppress. Lamri writes in Italian and constructs a protagonist who represents the voice of a *Beur* generation displacing it into an Italian context in order to discuss the cultural dilemmas that are already present in Italian immigration experiences. In his work on francophone culture, Alec Hargreaves stresses the struggle between cultures in *Beur* literature and, in particular, describes the second generation's distance from a first generation's Algerian past. Lamri's short story eloquently describes the second-generation impossibility to return to a paternal land because it is characterized by a double unbelonging. Torn between a loyalty to the culturally hybrid familial environment and the assimilationist imperatives of the host country, second generations translate into narratives the tensions that a first generation could not voice. Lamri creates a synthesis that bridges first- and second-generation cultural turmoil and opens the doors for other intergenerational narratives of both absence and acculturation.

Lamri's short story contains a plot of double unbelonging that cannot be resolved. The protagonist's identity is filtered through the cultural space his Algerian parents claimed for their son in France, where he became an adult without learning his parents' language. Named Jean-Marie by his father, the protagonist embodies a linguistically disguised identity that is revealed in a brief encounter with an Algerian man. He asks Jean-Marie whether his mother is French: 'No, no, both my parents are Algerian ... You mean because of my real name? My father wanted it, because for him, it was part of integration into French culture: ours and above all mine. You know, one of the many illusions of the immigrants.'[51] The concept of double unbelonging is inscribed within Jean-Marie's full name: Jean-Marie Ben Arjoun. His first name makes him French; his last name reveals the patrilinear connection to a country and a culture that the father himself had tried to efface by calling him Jean-Marie and identifying him with a Catholic culture. Frances Bartowski argues that 'the demands placed upon the subject in situations of unfamiliarity and dislocation produce a scene in which the struggle for identity comes more clearly into view as both necessary and also mistaken.'[52] She adds that 'identities are always mistaken,' which in the case of Jean-Marie Ben Arjoun translates into a mistaken identity of double unbelonging that motivates Jean-Marie's decision: to return to France after burying his father in Algeria, settle his affairs in Paris, and move back to his father's territorial and cultural point of departure. He chooses to re-migrate to the father country where he is a stranger, intent on looking at the place as a tourist enchanted by the exotic beauty of Algeria. Determined to live and learn what his father tried to erase, he attempts to create a familial memory of which he is the sole author. His attempt to 'understand,' which motivated his reverse migration from North to South, seems destined to fail as Jean-Marie stares at a television screen, unable to understand the language he hears. In the end, he can only associate with those Algerians who are closer to his own Western upbringing. The effacement of the stranger in himself cannot take place, and Jean-Marie is bound for a journey in which he will discover 'the moment when the headiness of motion turns to anxiety, disavowal, the abyss in the ground.'[53] Unable to 'claim a space, culturally speaking,' Jean-Marie becomes the epitome of the nomad, as Bartowski defines it, whose 'representations of selves [are] shaped in relation to an elsewhere,' or a repetition of elsewheres.[54]

Lamri's narrative of migration to Italy does not talk about Italy at all. His non-autobiographical narrative wants to trace the impossibility of discussing one's experience through cultures without ventriloquizing other migrations. It is a narrative about elsewheres that problematizes the concept of movements from and to a place and creates a manifesto for the literature of migration in Italian. In fact, in his involuntary manifesto, Lamri proclaims the impossibility of writing an Italian migration experience without reflecting on a more global and historically charged movement connecting colonial, post-colonial, and post-independence relations between countries. The silencing of his experience as other in Italy declares the possibility of looking at the Italian case as only a chapter in a narrative that relates the complex relations between countries and people.

Post-Migration and Post-Ethnic Identities in Italian Destination Culture

In *Verso la notte Bakonga* (*Toward the Bakonga Night*, 1999), Jadelin Mabiala Gangbo portrays the recolouring of Italian culture through a construction of identity in difference and of difference in identity. The title already presents a convergence of cultural influences. A quotation from Conrad's *Heart of Darkness* opens the novel and creates the Bakonga 'night' in Gangbo's title. It also points to the unknown entity that Africa is even for Mika, the protagonist of Gangbo's narrative, who paradoxically embodies for everyone else the identity of the black African man. In this novel with autobiographical undertones, Gangbo narrates the story of a young man of Bakongo origin, born in Brazzaville but raised in Italy. He tells of his family's privileged migration to Italy in the 1970s, of their wealth and their loss of it, and of the disintegration of the family unit. Mika is raised in a religious institution until he finds a home with an Italian family, from whom he feels an insurmountable distance. With no news from most of his biological relatives, Mika becomes the embodiment of unbelonging. At the same time, his only connections can be established in one country and one language, the only one he knows. Yet, his foreign name embodies his estrangement. His connection with Italian society can only exist at the margins shared with Gianmma, his best friend, whose original Italian first name and identity are changed into a foreign sequence of consonants. Like Lodoli, Giulio Angioni, and other Italian writers, Gangbo portrays unbelonging in a non-separatist pattern. Gianmma, the local boy, and Mika the racial other, become a transgressive 'unit' that dissolves only when Gianmma's behaviour turns tragically self-destructive and Mika begins to write his identity in Italian. With Mika, Gianmma experiences violence, drunkenness, and drug-induced stupor, and wanders in the urban landscape of an Italian city. Bologna plays an important part in Mika's story. It is the place where he has lived most of his life, and it represents the heart of Italian culture, from food to high culture, as it is the seat of the oldest university in the Western world. High culture is not part of Mika's life; in fact, school has failed to attract his interest. His omnivorous search for knowledge turns into random readings and a process of cultural appropriation based on geographical and cultural wanderings all over Europe. In his life as a *flaneur*, Mika moves from identity to identity, becoming for a short time a cook of Italian specialties.

Food as a cultural marker often appears in migrants' texts. It is a reductive but effective trope that allows a migrant writer to manipulate stereotypes about Italianness. As in Carmine Abate's 'Il cuoco d'Arbëria,' food becomes the cultural element that connotes the paradox inherent in identity construction. While Abate tells of the mistaken naming of *Arbëresh* food as Italian food in Germany, Gangbo narrates Mika's ability to construct representations of Italian food culture. On the one hand, the smells and tastes of Africa are for Mika part of a myth of Brazzaville that lies at the centre of his memory. These smells and tastes both fill his retrospective narrative and tell the lies inherent in reconstructing one's life: 'Running, running, among the noise, the smell of manioc and chickens, among the papaws and the India rubber merchants, among banana, avocado, and mango trees. Running, running among the drums, the fights, and the good luck charms. Running, running, barefoot like snakes, sticky like bark, without doubts and without limits. Never thinking of my brothers in Italy. Africa was here ...'[55] On the other hand, his Italian family pushes him to attend the culinary institute in Bologna. Even his foster mother tells him that he has learned how to prepare first courses just like they do in a local restaurant.[56] The new tastes and smells transform him into a creator of one of the most popular symbols and fetishes of Italian culture, and turn him into an Italian other who manipulates Italian stereotypes.

His translational adoption of what is defined as Italian is marked by transgression. Mika eventually rejects this role as a cook of cultural products as he wants to pour his creativity into writing. However, his ambition is lost in the maze of his life, torn between his need to explore his difference and the influence of his Italian family. Pressure from the adoptive family is combined with the desires of his African sister, who pushes him toward conformity and assimilation, which he sees embodied in his nephew, whose colour tends to be 'più bianco che nero' (more white than black).[57] Mika is a black man who has only known life in Italy, but who still gets complimented for being fluent in Italian. He is both trapped in the only language he speaks and labelled a stranger in the only culture he knows. The result is his desire to transgress, on the one hand, with petty crimes and drugs and, on the other, with a journey through Europe where other identities are assigned to him. He attempts to go against contemporary market rules that promote the free circulation of goods and restrict the circulation of people, unless people can be treated as a temporary work force with very few rights.

In Paris, Mika experiments with processes of cultural proximity in a culture that offers him a plurality of migrant communities. He is trapped, however, in his monolinguism. In an Arab restaurant, the waiter has to translate his 'desolante francese' (poor French) and has to tell him that Arabic food is the only food he can have in an Arabic restaurant.[58] The Italian African reveals his foreignness to multiculturalism:

> The waiter had brought me a quarter-litre of wine. I poured out a glass to speed up the process of integration. Then the couscous with vegetable and beef came. In the meantime, a young black man asked the band if he could sing. Somebody complained about the interruption. They started with a rap-beat and the black man could perform ...
>
> It was a party. I would have liked to join in, but I had a different character from theirs. My personality is more that of an Italian black man than that of an uninhibited man ...
>
> Somebody slapped me on the back, opening his eyes wide and offering his hand in a friendly gesture. Another one shouted at me: 'Allez! Allez! Mon ami!' ...
>
> I had been accepted. I had made it. I had made that flavour of skin my own, those breaths and those lively eyes. Very little was needed to play, in the end.[59]

Mika defines himself as an Italian black man outside his country of residence and cultural formation.[60] Far from the isolation experienced in Italy, and in a new location where his difference is permeable to other differences, Mika wants to participate in a game of differences that finally has many players. In his search to deterritorialize his difference, Mika realizes he is the embodiment of a new kind of Italian culture, that of a black man whose affinities with other black men in other post-colonial contexts are not defined by skin colour. His foreignness in Italy translates into a different kind of foreignness along colour lines as defined in French culture, but affinities can develop and a temporary sense of community can envelop him. Mika, the catalyst in a redefinition of Italy, points the discourse on Italian multiculturalism toward the exploration of a European racial and cultural periphery constructed on the imbrication of cultural experiences through generations of migrant lives and local cultures. Yet language betrays him. The 'nero' who wants to perform becomes a 'negro,' which in Italian can also mean 'nigger.' This slippage betrays the stakes in a game that is not changing, as the sense of community and isolation are only temporary and are permeable to the predetermined connotation inherent in the language in which he is fluent.

Jadelin Mabiala Gangbo creates a post-migration narrative in which the act of travelling becomes nomadism and uprootedness. Even in the Italian context, his characters' identities were constructed along post-ethnic lines, that is, according to chosen alliances beyond ethnic identity.[61] Outside of Italy his transmigration leads Mika to travel along the path of migrants, and his post-ethnic identity comes in close contact with the tensions that inform being ethnic. After Paris, Mika moves again and explores Spain before returning to Italy and focusing his attention on writing his identity within a changing country:

> That spring the soccer team of Bologna was in eighth place. While pretending to be members of Bologna's Ku Klux Klan, the customs officers had beaten three students from Cameroon. The Hale-Bopp comet strolled across the atmosphere. At the Fiumicino airport smuggling of an underage prostitute ring was discovered. Eighty-five Albanians had forgotten their life jackets. The Spice Girls sold more records than the Beatles. Sandokan became a mama's boy. I received the results of the literary competition. I won the first prize.[62]

This concise summary of events at a specific time locates Mika's success within an apparently random list of Italian, European, racist, universal, and personal experiences and occurrences. In its paratactical structure, such a list represents the multiplicity of cultural tensions in Mika's construction of a text about himself. His portrayal of Italian destination culture highlights difference as the paradigm, and the changes in Italian culture is a subtext with which he is very familiar. He embodies contrasting elements that contribute to the creation of what he calls an 'Italian black man.' His position lies in-between old and new migrations, old and new discourses of racial identities, and his work in Italian functions as a translation into practice of the issues that concern generations of migrants. Gangbo as cultural translator and interpreter points outside the national delimitation of a culture toward a more global analysis of influences, and connects his experience as an Italian black man to the narratives by recent migrants such as Khouma, Ba, or Chohra.

The role that autobiography plays in Gangbo's text highlights the role that autobiography plays in migration literature. Seen as a less sophisticated, first-generation expression of a first-person experience in a foreign culture, autobiography becomes a genre from which to begin that is later rejected in order to embrace multivoiced forms of expression. However, autobiography as a genre that borrows from many other genres is already quite a sophisticated form of expression, as proven in *Verso la notte Bakonga*. Like his character Mika, Gangbo is the winner of a literary award for migrant writers, and has been raised in Italy after being abandoned there by his biological parents. Gangbo's novel translates his life into a retrospective narrative of an Italian man with a complex history of mixed identities. His rereading of himself as an other allows for a distance by proximity, turning autobiography into a fictional representation of the self as same and different. The relationship between narrator and protagonist, between sameness and difference in a life story, parallels the relationship between self and culture described by Gangbo. His cultural identity is marked by Italy and its traditions, and is grounded in sameness. His biological identity signifies a difference that both sets him apart and highlights a multiculturalism that is an inherent component of Italian culture. In fact, his belonging to the local culture makes him 'different' from the difference of the more recent immigrants.

The changes brought by the new immigration create new cultural spaces in which Gangbo's autobiography can acquire a collective voice:

> In the Fall of 1998 I was 23 years old.
>
> After a year of Albanians' illegal entries into Italy, Italy had guaranteed a visa to thousands of undocumented people coming from outside Europe. The news spread and the immigrants arrived in large numbers from other countries in Europe.
>
> Colours were finally changing. People talked of marginalization, of solidarity and of reforms that would guarantee a framework for the new kind of Italians. I felt good.[63]

The disparate planes in which difference and sameness converge allow a theorization of Gangbo's role in the birth of a new kind of Italians, finally at the centre of discourses on tolerance, marginalization, and legal rights. This newly acquired sense of community creates the possibility of investigating a transition and a change in Gangbo's autobiographical text. From an isolated act of self-identification through difference, Gangbo moves to documenting how the new migration inscribes itself in his own definition of sameness and otherness within Italian culture. He can document a transition in the construction of meaning in an Italian context in which he is both protagonist and witness.

In her article 'Resisting Autobiography: Out-Law Genres and Transnational Feminist Subjects,' Caren Kaplan argues that resistance literature is marked by geopolitical situations that translate a global phenomenon into political conflicts originally provoked by colonialism. Resistance literature, adds Kaplan, 'is comparative but not always linked to a national language; it is overtly political, sometimes anonymous, always pressuring the boundaries of established genres.'[64] Following Kaplan's statement, autobiography appears to be a privileged location of resistance or, in the context of Italian migration culture, a privileged location from which one can talk back to a whole set of paradigms. Gangbo's autobiographical act revolves around practices of transgression: Mika's relationship with Italian culture is based on confrontations. He is in many ways the other who breaks the rules through crime and becomes protagonist in a text that rejects the construction of the 'good immigrant' that other autobiographies had presented. Talking back to Italian institutions, Gangbo also talks back to a simplistic construction of otherness in Italian society. His character, Mika, describes his brother's violent life and death in prison; Mika himself is a rapist, for he forces himself on the girlfriend who represents his past (he met her as a child in Africa) and present. Mika is a character who can separate himself from any stereotype by recontextualizing generalizations in a complex narrative about destination cultures. His strategy is to move between opposites and provoke his readers by creating mediations that are always filled with unexpected tensions.

Published by Feltrinelli, a major publishing company in Italy, Gangbo's second novel *Rometta and Giulieo* (2001) places the author *in fabula* and offers a new model for post-migration and post-ethnic narratives. Through the use of irreverence, breaking linguistic codes, and entering into the realm of Italian literature, *Rometta and Giulieo* conclusively challenges the limitations inherent in defining migration literature in Italian as Italophone literature and is a provocative text for the development of Italian destination culture(s).[65] It also plays the role of enacting the relevance of literature at a juncture in time when describing what Italian culture is involves a construction of new paradigms, challenges prescriptive theoretical practices, and defies normative structures.

Gangbo's text grounds itself on irreverence and defiance vis-à-vis canonical cultural productions, as is evident in the linguistic manipulations he performs. Inspired by Shakespeare's *Romeo and Juliet*, Gangbo uses different linguistic registers for the two narrative plots and sets of characters in his book. This novel is structured around theatrical frames and scenes; Rometta and Giulieo speak an archaic Italian borrowed from the Italian translations of Shakespeare's plays, a language that is a re-elaboration of nineteenth-century Italian. Jadelin, the narrator in the story, employs contemporary colloquial Italian in telling how the novel came about and describing the process of writing it. His modern, native ability to speak the slang of young Italians who are the same age as his characters becomes a problem, however, when Jadelin also becomes a character in Rometta and Giulieo's love story. They do not understand him and accept his justification that his is an archaic form of the language they speak. Gangbo's linguistic manipulation defines the author, that is himself, and Jadelin, the alter-ego, narrator, character, and Italian black man, as the internal and, at the same time, external others that challenge any preconceived idea on literature as a multicultural artefact.

Rometta is white and a native Italian. She is a twenty-year-old wealthy student writing a paper on Peter Greeneway. Giulieo is a Chinese pizza-delivery boy who was abandoned as an infant by his mother and raised by nuns in a religious institution: 'Giulieo was nothing but an object forgotten somewhere. He was like the slime of a slug, like the fart of a snake. Giulieo was the result of the unfortunate act between two migrants, who, in search of fortune, had met by chance in Verogna. They made love there. Then they disappeared. One went north. The other gave birth to a boy, threw him into the garbage, and then went east.'[66] In the undefined time warp of the novel, the characters live in the city of 'Verogna,' a name that suggests *vergogna* (shame), and also sounds like 'Verona,' the setting for the Shakespearean play. Today's Verona is marked by northern Italian politics that claim the superiority of the rich North where the other is appreciated for his/her market value and is acceptable because of the need for unskilled workers. However, there is no room for the pathetic or the directly vindicatory in this novel. Disadvantage turns into anger, isolation into a tragedy that takes place in a degraded urban environment.

Jadelin, the narrator, describes his topic choice for this novel along commercial lines and in provocative terms. He tells the reader that his first novel *La seconda volta di Clemente* (*Clemente's Second Time*) did not achieve much success. This time he wants a love story that can surpass and replace the Shakespearean model and, after checking the list of available literary competitions, decides to create an ethnically defined character. First, he thinks of his main character as Colombian, but he would be 'too flimsy, when have you ever recognized a Colombian in the street? You would not even be able to tell the face of a Colombian apart from all the others. Let's make him a Chinese instead. Shit, write the Chinese their story. They are scattered everywhere, disgusting as they are ...'[67] When he chooses his male protagonist, Rometta has already been introduced, as is the privileged Western reader to whom the story is told, addressed as 'Sire.' The vernacular, a street Italian with which his main protagonist is introduced, accompanies the description of his literary agent, a wheelchair-bound middle-aged man with whom he discusses women as 'cunts' and whose sexual organs become the necessary topic around which he narrates his story. Political incorrectness and provocation are at the centre of Gangbo's creation of a narrative on sensitive issues of race: 'The bearer of the pizzas arrived before the world, Sire. Yellow face and black shiny hair, slicked back as if it had been run over by something. Carrying an unpleasant odor that smelled like plague, he handed over three hot white boxes and the ice beer.'[68] Collecting all the most derogatory stereotypes about racial identity, Gangbo makes his Chinese man into an unlikable character. Once Jadelin himself becomes a character in Rometta and Giulieo's love story, Jadelin the narrator deliberately attempts to make Giulieo expendable. Giulieo becomes a petty criminal and Jadelin falls in love with Rometta, the character he has created.

Distancing himself from all the rules in talking about racial issues, Gangbo jumps into the 'messiness' of dealing with migration, ethnicity, and individual and national relations with otherness. Jadelin, the narrator, meditates on his narrative plots sitting on an external window sill of his apartment building, from which at the end he decides to jump and end his life. Jadelin has tried to erase the manuscript he has written, but the computer icon of *Rometta and Giulieo* has a life of its own and cannot be eliminated. At the same time, it cannot be made public because it leads back to the author's own identity, who has turned into a character. Jadelin thus concludes his narrative and his life:

> I was still a bastard, a son of a bitch on a windowsill. I am still looking up and I see things in the sky, and I then look down and see the sea slap the coast where there could be only asphalt.
>
> It was up to me, Sire, I had to decide what to see: the sky or the asphalt. I would decide in my flight down and understood on impact ...[69]

Deciding what to see, and putting one's identity at risk is a game that Gangbo plays in his novel. The result is a desire to destroy and for self-annihilation. Breaking the rules and entering into a literary domain creates isolation, but also provides a powerful model for talking about Italy and the location of race and migration in its destination culture. In fact, Gangbo's linguistic irreverence talks back to disparate literary traditions. In *Rometta e Giulieo* he appropriates a cultural icon and giant such a Shakespeare, bringing his work into a literary context that revises separations between high and low culture and reappropriates Italian sources and locations that Shakespeare had appropriated centuries before.

Gangbo's vernacular creates a model shaped on acts of breaking and entering into a language, and a literary tradition that proves inadequate as a host of disparate identity constructions. This language talks back to any attempt to enclose Gangbo's work in normative categories and rejects the limitations that a label such as 'migrant' literature subsumes. His literary language ranges from street lingo to an original construction of obsolete Italian. It is a mixed vernacular that frames the situatedness of Gangbo as an intellectual who positions his work in a post-migrant, post-ethnic context. His approach to Italian turns into a practice of transgression that turns the tables on the linear process of the development of migrants' writing. Migrants' literature was initially marked by collaborations with linguistic experts: Pap Khouma wrote with Oreste Pivetta, Saidou Moussa Ba with Alessandro Micheletti, Nassera Chohra with Alessandra Atti Di Sarro, to name a few. In these collaborations the native speaker was the problematic collector of stories and testimonies, and the facilitator between the migrant writer and the publishing market. In 2002 Jadelin Mabiala Gangbo co-edited a collection of short stories, *L'Africa secondo noi* (*Africa According to Us*), written by well-known contemporary Italian writers such as Aldo Nove, Laura Pariani, Simona Vinci, and Dario Voltolini. These stories are not actually a collection of narratives about Africa, but rather about Africans in Italy seen through the eyes of native Italians, a concerted effort supervised by Gangbo and Piersandro Pallavicini. In this project. Gangbo positions himself as editor of native Italians' writings, outside of any traditionally hierarchical structure of belonging and unbelonging, and adds another layer to such an innovative approach. *L'Africa secondo noi* was published by the Edizioni dell'Arco, also known as 'Gruppo Solidarietà Come,' which prints a street paper sold by immigrants themselves. Migrants have an invested interest in selling the paper, as a considerable amount of money from the sales remains with the vendor. Even the books published by Edizioni dell'Arco are sold in the street. In the particular case of *L'Africa secondo noi*, immigrant vendors sell a collection of stories about migrants authored by native Italians who have published before with commercially successful publishing companies. Gangbo himself has published with Feltrinelli. Inverting hierarchies at the level of distribution, and constructing a new vernacular to express post-migrant and post-ethnic identities, is Gangbo's successful agenda. It allows him to position himself as an Italian intellectual engaged in the construction of both theory and practice. In fact, he places in the hands of migrants the stories that portray them, changing the market logic by allowing migrants to benefit economically from selling stories about them. Last but not least, Gangbo also manages to intervene in a critical approach to his work by demanding that any critic interested in his work approach a street vendor to purchase his edited volume. He demands a repositioning of the intellectual and the critic of migration who must directly establish contact with a subject of study and, even in minimal terms, turn theory into practice, as Gangbo did in the creation of his vernacular.

Gangbo's transgressive approach to writing turns problematic if read with a feminist approach. The female body in his work is often a site of tensions and of physical violence. In *Verso la notte Bakonga*, the protagonist rapes his girlfriend. In *Rometta e Giulieo*, the female protagonist is the object of desire for both the protagonist and Jadelin, the author in the story, but other women are reductively defined as 'cunts.' The female body as the embodiment of a Western culture is abused, and as an object of contention between men is filled with meaning that leaves little room for the individuation of an independent female identity in the narrative.

In the context of Italian post-migration and post-ethnic identity construction women's issues emerge in a number of narratives that talk back to Gangbo's *reductio ad unum* of female identities. Viola Chandra's *Media chiara e noccioline* (*Medium Light with Nuts*, 2001) creates a powerful model for discussing migration, race, and gender issues in a destination culture that drags both migrants' culture and local culture into future developments that make dichotomies impossible. Her novel opens with a description of overwhelming rage that turns self-destructive as Valentina, the protagonist, becomes anorexic and bulimic. The female body is at the centre of the narrative and becomes the location in which Valentina performs her private and public conflicts. Her narrative connects to a long tradition of women's narratives that explore the relationship between femininity and the female body (which Chandra reinscribes within a post-migration context). In *Lontano da Mogadiscio*, the Somalian Italian writer Shirin Ramzanali Fazel described the female body as both the site of conflict in Western society and a sign of oppression through starvation in poor countries. Valentina's process of identity construction revolves around issues of control of her body and therefore femininity that connect her to many other Western women. At the same time, her body is the site 'coloured' by connotations of otherness that she has difficulty reconciling with her Italian, that is Western, education. Valentina is the daughter of an Indian man who came to Italy to attend the university. He married and later divorced an Italian woman, Valentina's mother, and became a successful lawyer in Italy.

Valentina finds herself located at an uncomfortable crossroads of identities in which *essere e apparire*, to be and to appear or look like, contain the ambiguity of her self-definition. She knows she looks different, even if her hair is straight and she uses a solar protection cream to keep the colour of her skin as light as possible. She wants to displace attention from her appearance as a signifier of otherness. Thanks to the heterogeneity inherent in the Italian genetic pool, she could pass for Italian; however, she also wants to explore that cultural and ethnic patrimony that cannot be invisible to her. Her very absent father refuses to help in her exploration of her 'Indianness' and reminds her: 'They shat on your head, what the fuck do you have to do with India?'[70] Searching for a paternal figure, Valentina encounters eating disorders and paradoxically discovers the Italianness in her father's difference. Her friends think it is exotic and interesting to have an Indian father who can supply spiritual 'pearls of knowledge.'[71] Her father exposes the

Italian stereotype about Indians, and only voices ideas and wisdom that originate from the Western context in which he identifies himself. Valentina forcefully states: 'Well, I'll tell the next person who has seen Gandhi four times and has read Siddharta at least twice and then talks about Indian spirituality to go down there, in the material world of the Varese area, where he can find my father.'[72]

Valentina inhabits a destination culture in which second-generation issues combine with processes of identity construction that are grounded in conflict inherent in her family and in being a woman in a society that is rapidly changing. At the same time, that society contains patriarchal rules and privileges that her father treasures. She is the daughter who is not so important after the birth of a son, born to a woman who is not her mother (she is her father's second wife). The second wife is a local woman who could help her father become 'naturalized' in Lombardy. While her father loves to tell how through hard work he has become a powerful lawyer, he despises the new immigrants, pushing Valentina to choose a new alliance with others whose experiences are, however, radically different from hers: 'I was Western, too white and too different for Indian children who, even then, looked at me and laughed. I was too black for some Italians I met on the bus or in the street. I was too black for them just like the Africans, who in the street, at the corner of the street, wash his car windows, are too black, and poor, and smelly, and annoying for my father. They don't study and don't work but live off other people's money.'[73] The search for her father leads her to discover his racism, and consequently she resists her desire to discover her otherness through him. If originally Valentina decided to privileg the non-whiteness of her identity through an exploration of her Indianness, she later discovers that the hybridization of her identity can only take place in putting herself in relation to other constructions of difference that reveal both her privileged position and her deterritorialized cultural location. In search of a home, Valentina affirms: 'Every time I see an Indian or an African in Italy, I hope that he will recognize me as a member of his family, as a daughter. I don't belong to my father's family any more, as I am no longer my father's daughter.'[74]

Hybridizing her identity by deterritorializing difference and refusing biologically determined genealogies of race and colour is Valentina's agenda. Instead of travelling to India, she decides to 'immerse' herself in 'smells, tastes, lights, flies, landscapes and other dark skinned people' in Morocco, Mexico, and Guatemala.[75] She can only return to India in her thirties to discover once more that in that male-dominated country she cannot find acceptance for her hybridity, but remains one among many tourists whose money is welcome, but whose difference is insurmountable. The destination culture in which Valentina locates herself challenges the national boundaries in which she lives. She situates her identity in relation to external and internal otherness; her position is grounded on choosing difference as a connection rather than an agent of marginalization.

The fluidity of the boundaries of Valentina's identity echoes other women's selective alliances in their narratives about migration and post-migration. Nassera Chohra grounds her identity in experiences in two cultures: the familial Arab traditions and the Western traditions she encountered throughout her life in France. Once in Italy, Chohra presents herself not as a culturally hybrid Arab woman, but as a culturally hybrid European. Her French post-ethnic, post-migrant identity translates into the Italian context, where Chohra lives and marries an Italian man, by creating her self as different from the new migrants who are living the life her parents experienced. Even Shirin Ramzanali Fazel portrays the Africans as unable to look back: they are boxed in the square picture on the television screen and distanced from the viewer. Fazel witnesses war, famine, and the starvation of her fellow Somalians by feeling like a white observer separated from this tragedy. Her empathy makes her reject a forced alliance to First World observers and complicates definitions of ethnic, post-ethnic, migrant, and post-migrant identities. After more than thirty years in Italy, Fazel has moved back to Africa, but not to her native land. She is currently living in Kenya, where her identity mirrors important aspects of a destination culture. Inscribed outside the boundaries of both her birth country and the country of her migration, Fazel has opened an Italian restaurant in Kenya that caters to nostalgic tourists and markets the Italian culinary tradition. In Kenya, a geographic location that the West considers exotic, what is Italian becomes the exotic 'cooked up' by a Somalian-Italian woman who in Italy embodied the exotic and who continues to write in Italian.

As Fazel's narratives of life eloquently show, migrants' writings constitute the groundwork on which a destination culture can develop. The relevance of literature lies in fact in its role as a corpus of unerasable texts that enable unpredictable articulations of cultural hybridizations that rigid boundaries cannot contain. Literature can imagine changes in power relations that cannot be translated into practice.

Thus, it is a blueprint of future developments envisioned by migrant writers who engage in a dialogue with the local culture. Literature is therefore the location in which volition is enacted; that is, agency on the part of a migrant becomes a unique story that only the migrant can tell. It is a story about himself/herself and it is the story of the encounters of different cultures that come together and hybridize. Literature is, therefore, a possible agent of social change, able to articulate what is absent from dominant narratives. It is through a validation of literature as an agent of social change that a destination culture can be theorized.

It is also possible to articulate the concept of a destination culture that soars over national borders and linguistic separations. In fact, a destination culture that grounds itself on narratives that are acts of cultural hybridization is always situated, but cannot be restricted. Elvira Dones's work describes the dissemination of what is Italian, hyphenated, and migrant as well as the relational context in which such definitions are created. An Albanian writer living in the Canton Ticino, Switzerland, where the official language is Italian, Dones writes in Albanian and narrates the experience of Albanian migrants to Italy. Translated into Italian, her novel *Sole bruciato* (*Burnt Sun*, 2001) is revised by Dones, whose migrant identity in Switzerland places the author within the Italian language context and at the same time outside of Italy. The plot of her novel focuses on a group of Albanian women who embody several degrees of otherness as women, migrants, undocumented immigrants in Italy, and prostitutes. Their experience in migration is that of entrapment and exploitation in a market economy in which female bodies can be used, bought, and, in the context of this novel, mutilated, because nobody in Italy will bother to look for an immigrant prostitute's killer. Expendable like all undocumented migrants and street prostitutes, Dones's protagonist, Leila, dreams of 'one day walking toward her own return.'[76] Locked in the coffin that finally will take her back 'down there,' as Albania is called throughout the novel, Leila is allowed to speak and tell of her past, her decision to leave for Italy, and her life with other women. Gender issues are at the centre of Dones's work: she describes the ease of movement across borders when the goods are women's bodies to be sold for prostitution, in contrast with the rejection of other immigrants and forms of immigration. Located outside any acceptable category of migration, their encounters with the new country are based on debasement and exploitation. Prostitutes cannot create alliances, acquire mobility, or have a voice. Dones writes sections of her novel as a diary so that the 'first person' can emerge and allow the female protagonist to speak. *Sole bruciato* defines the new directions in which Italian destination culture is moving. In the case of Dones's narrative, the act of talking back modifies borders to include other languages that eloquently present migration as a global phenomenon that modifies local cultures. Stressing the importance of one language, Italian, to define migration literature in Italy would exclude texts such as *Sole bruciato* that narrate contemporary Italian stories of migration in a language that is not Italian.

At the beginning of the third millennium, the cultural emphasis is on transmigrations, that is, non-linear paths of migration marked by 'impermanence,' by repetition of the processes of leaving and arriving. The convoluted trajectories contained in transmigration complicate the concept of a migrants' literature that finds the adoption of only one language too limiting. Dones's text represent an example of a literature of transmigration able to disregard irreverently the borders between countries, languages, and local literatures in order to conceptualize articulation of what is global from below, that is, in the story of a prostitute whose body returns to the country where she was born. *Sole bruciato* further complicates the definition of what a destination culture is because it recasts the term 'culture' as always intrinsically plural. Consequently, Dones's text helps to articulate a concept of migration literature that rejects final definitions by talking back at any attempt to create a limiting terminology to describe narratives of (trans)migration. The 'impermanence' of terms turns theorizing about contemporary migration literature into a double challenge, that of connecting the local and the international linguistic and cultural contexts in which a migration text locates itself. In the case of *Sole bruciato*, the invitation is to focus on contemporary migrations to Europe through the shared experiences of migrants who create the common denominator of a destination culture across national boundaries.

Yet other texts reiterate the importance of the specificity of cultural location in which a migrant creates the narrative of his or her hybrid identity. In this context, a destination culture articulates itself at the intersection of many different cultures, but in one specific language. For Albanians, Italian culture and language were a daily presence even before migration thanks to Italian television programs. In his novel *Va e non torna* (*Leaving Without Coming Back*, 2000) Ron Kubati assigns the role of translator to his protagonist, Elton, who is an Albanian student in Puglia. Located in the part of Italy that has witnessed the arrival of ships often filled to capacity with Albanians, Kubati's protagonist mediates between local institutions and the many Albanians who are at times as foreign to him as native Italians are supposed to be to a migrant. Appropriately, Kubati's translator is also a doctoral student of philosophy at an Italian university located in Puglia, which is also that in-between space where Albanian communities have been established since the fifteenth century. The specificity of Puglia as a geographical location in Kubati's work privileges a destination culture that reveals its multilayered planes of difference: that of being in the south of Italy, of having a tradition of e-migration and of im-migration, and of being an important crossroads of migrations from Albania.

Carmine Abate has narrated the cultural predicament of southern Italian/*Arbëresh* people, who acquire Italian in school and then migrate and inscribe themselves in other languages. Abate grounds his narratives on a re-appropriation and historical revision of an Albanian culture that inscribed itself within Italy centuries before the recent migrations from Albania. Kubati, the recent migrant from Albania, focuses again on the Italian South and on working in between languages outside of any established *Arbëresh* community. Abate's and Kubati's work collaborate in describing what a destination culture is across centuries. Cultural repression from above filled the *Arbëresh* language with connotations of inferiority, as described by Abate. Kubati instead creates the character of the translator from Albanian into Italian as the key figure for the future of a culture. In *Va e non torna*, the protagonist/translator mediates between Albanian migrants and the representatives of the Italian state, constructing a cultural dialogue that revolves around language.

In his second novel, entitled *M* (2002), Kubati creates another cultural intersection in which language is not a major concern. He delineates a protagonist who is not situated in a narrow geographical location. *M* is a generic Italian urban space in which a migrant from eastern Europe tries to find work and publish his first novel. In *M* there is a deliberate lack of specificity in the description of the cultural and geographical points of departure and arrival in the unnamed protagonist's migration. The book focuses on a migrant's difficulties in finding work and negotiating relationships with native Italians. The context in which the protagonist's story takes place is unnamed, but is nevertheless defined by political and cultural characteristics that make it generically Italian. The other characters are teachers and *badanti*, who take care of old people and share that work with the protagonists. They are also people engaged in political protests that reveal their leftist ideological stance. Yet, because of their lifestyle they are all inhabitants of margins of Italian society and welcome the protagonist, a migrant, to share that space with them. Professor Andrea, for instance, is an idealist left-wing intellectual who shares his home with whoever needs a shelter, including the protagonist. Andrea chooses to look like and dress like a homeless man. He is, Kubati's protagonist states, 'the eternal antagonist of an eternal system and stank of sweat worse than I did.'[77]

The complexity of the different locations of otherness that Kubati inscribes in the role of the migrant as translator, and as mediator between internal and external marginalization, is grounded once again on an exploration of sameness and difference within migration. Dones's deliberate dismantling of cultural and linguistic borders through the experience of migration becomes in Kubati an exploration of differences in disparate embodiments of otherness. The protagonist in *M* becomes in the end a privileged observer of the society in which Kubati as a writer scripts himself. As an observer, the protagonist witnesses the hierarchical structure of otherness. Tensions in the hierarchy of difference are performed through the female body of Betti, another character in Kubati's *M*. Betti is a prostitute, an undocumented migrant who hopes to find respite from oppression among the group of friends to which the protagonist belongs. She in fact becomes 'Betti' among them and sheds her identity as a prostitute ('Donna B') that she embodies on the streets. Yet Fabio, a member of that marginal group, rapes her, thus revealing the presence of a hierarchy of power even at the margin. That sameness inherent in their marginality is a temporary link between Betti and Fabio, who then turns around and reproduces traditional strategies of oppression.

Kubati's text is particularly useful in my discussion on the relevance of minor texts written by migrants, because it signals potential developments in migrants' literature and continues the narrative strategies developed by Jadelin Mabiala Gangbo. The dialogue that migrant writers nurture between narratives about migrants authored by native speakers and their own writing weakens the separation between linguistic experts and migrants. In editing the volume *L'Africa secondo noi* (2002), Gangbo proposed a new collaborative paradigm that changes the hierarchies of power. In the same year Gangbo's anthology was published, four other collections offered models of collaboration that attempted to change the separation between migrant writers and Italian writers, canonical literature and marginal texts. Originating from a sociological/literary experiment on integration, the anthology *Matriciana/Cuscus: storie di integrazione* (2002), edited by Giulio Mozzi and Marina Bastianello, returns to the metaphor of food as culture to collect short stories by migrants and native Italians. Thanks to public funding from the Veneto region and the city of Padua, the editors created the contexts in which separations could be challenged and lines of difference redrawn. In this anthology the Algerian-Italian writer Amor Dekhis writes about his attempt to stop helping other Algerian migrants and the internal conflict that derives from such a decision: 'I was aware that, behind my back, people thought that I had to be a real selfish son of a bitch. In other moments in my life, if I'd heard that I would've thrown myself off a bridge to escape some moral judgement that found me guilty of lack of solidarity toward my people. Those were different times!'[78] He exposes the artificiality of solidarity along genetic lines and steps outside any traditional definition of migrant communities. This collaborative project similarly redraws the lines of a community of writers and creates a shared space for different definitions of the roles and the identities of writers. *Matriciana/Cuscus* was published in the Veneto region, a wealthy region that has required a large number of immigrant workers and is a Northern League stronghold, a party known for its racist agenda. Publishing such an anthology was therefore a political act.

Literature as a means of talking back to master political narratives about identities is particularly successful in another anthology, *Parole di sabbia* (Words of Sand, 2002) published by the southern Italian publisher 'Il Grappolo.' Edizioni il Grappolo had previously published translation of books authored by Italian Americans. Thanks to this publishing company early texts of Italian American literature became available to Italians for the first time. In the volume *Parole di sabbia*, edited by Francesco Argento, Alberto Melandri, and Paolo Trabucco, the heterogeneity of voices is remarkable. Seven migrant writers' texts cohabit the anthology with work by Alberto Masala, an artist in Bologna and an internal migrant from Sardinia; Carmine Abate's linguistically multilayered texts; and Serge Pey's writings in Occitan, still a minority language in Italy. Geographically situated in a specific south, Il Grappolo's anthology elaborates a literary representation of Italian culture and adds layers of complexity to previous experimentations with anthologizing a culture.

Diaspore europee & lettere migranti (*European Diasporas & Migrant Texts*, 2002), edited by Armando Gnisci and Nora Moll, braids still other strands of difference. The anthology is divided in two sections: one devoted to fiction and the other to critical essays. The Brazilian Italian writer Christiana De Caldas Brito contributes to both sections, theorizing on what a migrant writer is and on her own contribution to migrants' literature. The creative texts included in the anthology are published with parallel texts: the original language in which the poem or short story were written and the Italian translation. These are texts authored by migrants who originate from countries both outside and inside the European community. This combination re-proposes a discussion on internal and external otherness: Italian/non-Italian, European/non-European, Western/non-Western. *Diaspore europee & lettere migranti* collects the proceedings of the 'Primo Festival Europeo degli scrittori migranti' organized by Armando Gnisci. Thanks to a monetary contribution from the Department of Italian Literature and the Performing Arts at the University 'La Sapienza' in Rome, the anthology came to light in a book series edited by Armando Gnisci and published by Edizioni Interculturali in Rome.

Probably the most original experiment in writing published in 2002 is *Piovono storie: romanzo collettivo* (*It's Raining Stories: A Collective Novel*), edited by the Laboratorio paroleMOLEste.[79] This experiment in co-writing took place in Turin. The intention of the Association Laboratorio was to create a collective narrative about the lives of people on the outskirts of the city. Eighty non-professional writers, divided in small groups, wrote the novel. Each group would follow the previous one in developing the plot. Native and non-native people together wrote this border narrative that is a novel that borrows from other genres including poetry, prose, and autobiography.

What stands out among these texts is a shift in focus. Not only do they analyse what non-Western, migrant identities are, they also explore what that entity called the West is. This is true also for Kubati's 'M,' an imaginary location in which his characters act and perform their marginal lives and embody the tension inherent in trying to expand margins into a mainstream. 'M' is above all a Western urban space that represents any unwelcoming city for a migrant. It is 'the West' for the protagonist who is aware of its local and essentialized Western characteristics. It is a 'here,' with which the migrant has to come to terms because of its specificity, but it is also an 'elsewhere' disconnected from the local cultural characteristics. 'M' is an attempt to go beyond the particularities of a space of migration connected to a local culture, and describe a universal Western space that any migrant inhabits. Kubati questions the constraint of the particular, that is, of the singular description of one experience of migration. This tension, which is also a tension to break away from the constraints of marginality, points toward a need to overcome the limitations imposed by writing a literature that does not have a wide audience.

Kubati's 'West' finds its visual representation in a remarkable film by the Italian director Corso Salani. *Occidente* (*The West*, 2000) explores the same space, both local and universal, that Kubati has articulated in his novel. Malvina, the protagonist of the film is a Romanian woman who actively participated in overthrowing Ceausescu's dictatorship.[80] Following the collapse of the regime, changes in the Romanian economy created the conditions for her forced migration to the north-east of Italy, to Aviano (Friuli), a city of multilayered cultures. Aviano is an American city in Italy, full of soldiers of the local American military base, and caters to the soldiers' cultural and linguistic needs. Malvina works as a waitress in a country-western bar and wears the stereotypical cowboy dress that enforces the 'authenticity' of that location. The bar wants to embody what is familiar for an American abroad or what the locals in Aviano have interpreted as a representation of what is 'home' for an American soldier. The lingua franca in the bar is English, but some of the local women who work as waitresses speak the local dialect. This adds to the complexity of Aviano as a crossroads of languages and of cultures located within Italian borders. Malvina survives in this multiplicity of cultural identities by attending a local nursing school that could, in the future, place her outside that border culture of Aviano.[81] The privileged position of everything American becomes evident in the curriculum at the school, which focuses on combat nursing, catering again to the needs of the military base. Aviano is the 'West' for the protagonist of *Occidente*. In the film's construction of the 'West,' it is neither Italy, nor Europe, nor America, but a negative destination culture in which cultures cannot be mediated because they are trapped in a rigid hierarchical structure. Malvina's Romanian identity is irrelevant here because difference is irrelevant, and everything is reduced to essentializing categories.

Making sense of that 'West' in Aviano is impossible for Malvina because it leads to a destination culture grounded on illegibility and on inequality. What is 'Italian' in Aviano is itself marginal, minor: dialects, conversations with teachers who do not live in that area but travel to teach at the local school, and silence. The pessimism that pervades the film is mitigated by encounters at the margins. In fact, in the bar where she works, Malvina meets Alberto, who is an Italian teacher working at a school in Aviano.[82] Alberto and a few other colleagues spend time at the bar 'Occidente,' but look like strangers and speak like foreigners in that environment dominated by American stereotypes. The connection between the Romanian migrant and the Italian 'other' lies in difference vis-à-vis the dominant American presence in Aviano. Alberto's loneliness and isolation in Aviano makes him an outsider and a foreigner in an Italian city. American culture is 'the' Western paradigm that in Aviano marks any other Western cultures and embodiments of culture with connotations of inferiority. The connection between Malvina and Alberto created through the recolouring of the native, who is 'other' in Aviano, talks back to the privileging of American culture, weakens hierarchies, and hints at the possible future development of a destination culture beyond marginality. Cultural contamination is the supporting paradigm in a destination culture. Contamination develops into processes of cultural hybridization grounded in practices of relation between what is native in its multicultural identity and what is non-native and embodies the otherness of the migrant. Aviano in *Occidente* represents the impossibility of translating into practice my articulation of a destination culture in a location marked by absence and the unquestioned signifiers of a Western culture. Aviano is a degeneration of Kubati's urban space in *M*.

Alberto's localized migration, Malvina's loss of direction at a crossroads of Western identities, Kubati's community at the margins, Dones's dislocation of narrative content and language, Gangbo's manipulation of genres and languages, and Chandra's complex identity constructions testify to the complexity of narrative strategies that characterize texts about migration issues in contemporary Italy. These are sites of conflict between traditional articulations of migrant identities and post-migration and post-ethnic elaborations of a destination culture. Grounded in the refusal of traditional separations and categories, these texts still inhabit the margins of Italian culture, and therefore embody the temporary failure of that destination culture that they help to theorize.

Market Strategies: Literary Awards, Anthologies, and Publishing Companies[83]

In 1995 Roberta Sangiorgi, a journalist in Rimini, founded the association Eks&Tra, which organized the first literary award for migrant writers. Financed in part by public funding from the city of Rimini, the association's organizers also raised money from the local community and, in particular, from local shop owners. A local publisher, Alessandro Ramberti, supplied the means to collect some of the poems and short stories submitted, in a volume published by his company Fara Editore. The result was *Le voci dell'arcobaleno* (*The Voices of the Rainbow*, 1995), edited by Roberta Sangiorgi, which was to be the first in a series of volumes. The jury of the literary award included Armando Gnisci, who teaches Comparative Literature at the University of Rome, Saidou Moussa Ba, who at the time had published his first book and was involved in acting, Shirin Ramzanali Fazel, author of *Lontano da Mogadiscio*, and myself.[84] I was responsible for assembling the jury, which went through changes throughout the years. I left the jury in 2001. My analysis of this literary award and its publications cannot be performed at a distance, as I remember the tentative nature of its first edition and the later discussions on the purpose of a literary award for migrant writers. At the beginning, it was intended as a space for migrants to make their voices public and for migrant writers to begin publishing short stories and individual poems. However, other members of the jury would disagree with my interpretation of the goals of the award. In 1995 Gëzim Hajdari submitted his poetry and won the award. He went on a few years later to win the most prestigious poetry award in Italy, the Montale Prize. Tahar Lamri participated with a short story and later became a member of the Eks&Tra award jury. Christiana De Caldas Brito, who won a prize and later turned her short story into a play, went on to write children's books.[85] Other submissions were very disparate: autobiographical and semi-autobiographical narratives, and ventriloquized narratives of migrations in which a migrant writer filtered his or her own migration experience through the stories of other migrants originating in different countries. Many of the short stories revolved around the issue of documentation, of the *sanatorie* (amnesties for undocumented migrants), and of migrants' renaming themselves or being renamed in order to forcefully fit within Italian culture.

When Tahar Lamri became a member of the Eks&Tra award jury, he articulated the goal of a literary award for migrant writers. If other literary awards are deemed successful when they achieve continuity, the success of a literary award for migrant writers is proved by the demise of the award. What Lamri highlighted was, on the one hand, the need to create a space in which a literature written by migrants can develop and, on the other, the danger of establishing a creative ghetto that can only marginally contribute to the literature written in one language. Not needing a separate context for migrant writers would then become the real success for the Eks&Tra literary award. In the meantime, the award association has successfully collected migrants' narratives from 1995 until today, publishing an anthology of poems and short stories every year. The volumes trace the changes in stylistic sophistication, levels of narrative complexity, and topics that have characterized migrants' writing since the mid-nineties.[86]

If the Eks&Tra award appears to function as a launching pad for writers, the limited distribution of the yearly anthology volumes also highlights a market dominated by the major publishing houses. Distribution becomes a key issue to the financial survival of small publishers, such as Alessandro Ramberti (Fara Editore), who are willing to lend their expertise to ethically motivated experiments. The 1998 anthology *Destini sospesi di volti in cammino* (*The Suspended Destinies of Transient Faces*), edited by Sangiorgi and Ramberti, and the 1999 volume *Parole oltre i confini* (*Words Beyond Borders*), under the same editors, were published by Fara Editore. In 2000 the publisher could no longer sustain the financial loss of publishing the literary-award anthologies and had to withdraw his support. Later anthologies were published by ADNKronos, a publisher and press agency. In 2003 ADNKronos withdrew its support and the anthology, entitled *Impronte* (*Footprints*), was published by Besa Editore, a publisher located in the region of Puglia, which had published Ron Kubati's work. Currently the anthologies are published independently by the Eks&Tra association. In 2000 the city of Rimini withdrew its support for the award, which then moved to the city of Mantua, whose left-wing administration welcomed it.[87] Supported by local and regional public funding, the Eks&Tra award became a segment of the yearly Literature Festival that takes place in Mantua. One of the award's major achievements in recent years is its support of the initial writings of Jadelin Mabiala Gangbo, who later published two novels, of the poetry of Gëzim Hajdari, who later won the prestigious Montale prize, and of the work of Christiana De Caldas Brito, who subsequently turned her 'Ana de Jesus' into a play and travelled throughout Italy performing it. Because Italy is a country of too many literary awards and a dwindling number of readers nationwide, it is probably still too early to quantify accurately the impact that the Eks&Tra literary award has had in that process of cultural hybridization to which migrant writers contribute.[88]

In 1999 the Cultural Association 'Leoncavallo' financed an anthology titled *La lingua strappata: testimonianze e letteratura migranti* (*The Torn Tongue: Migrant Witnessing and Literature*). Located in Milan, the Leoncavallo Centre is a left-wing organization whose 'Gruppo Migrantes Leoncavallo' is engaged in politics that defend documented and undocumented migrants and their rights. Alberto Ibba and Raffaele Taddeo are the editors of the anthology. The former is a publishing consultant and author of a book on the history of the Leoncavallo Centre, the latter is the president of the multicultural association 'La tenda,' and has promoted meetings and lectures on the subject of migration. Their anthology is divided in two sections: one devoted to literature, the other to witnessing. In the first part are short stories authored by Kossi Komla-Ebri, Abdel Malek Smari, Saidou Moussa Ba, and Hossein Hosseinzadek.[89] The second section, entitled 'Testimonianze migranti,' includes first-hand narratives by migrants like Marcelo Vega, whose narrative has the quality of an oral narrative, including ungrammatical and misspelled Italian, thus revealing that the editors decided not to intervene in the text. In this second section of the anthology, authors such as Kossi Komla-Ebri and Abdel Malek Smari also engage in testimonial narratives.[90] These testimony-like texts are first-person narratives of an experience of migration transcribed by an editor, in this case Komla-Ebri or Smari. The linguistic experts here are not native speakers, but rather published migrant authors who function as facilitators. The power position of the migrant linguistic expert is radically different from that of the native Italian, whose mediating role is expendable here, even though the volume in which the testimonies are published has native Italian editors. In fact, native speakers have more chances to access the publishing market, however marginal the publishing company is.

Major publishing houses have given space to token texts by migrant writers, but have not attempted to create a reading audience for migrants' texts. Garzanti successfully published Pap Khouma's best seller *Io, venditore di elefanti* in 1990, but did not capitalize on that success by creating a series in which migrants could publish their texts. DeAgostini published Alessandro Micheletti and Saidou Moussa Ba's co-authored novels *La promessa di Hamadi* (*Hamadi's Promise*, 1991) and *La memoria di A.* (*A.'s Memory*, 1995), marketing them as educational texts that catered to pedagogical programs devoted to multiculturalism in Italian schools. Other major publishing houses that have supported one-time token texts include Giunti, which published Salwa Salem's

Con il vento nei capelli (*With Wind in Her Hair*, 1993), and Bompiani, which published *La straniera* (*The Foreign Woman*, 1999) by Younis Tawfik. Jadelin Mabiala Gangbo's *Rometta e Giulieo* (2001) was published by Feltrinelli and Smari Abdel Malek's *Fiamme in paradiso* (*Flames in Paradise*, 2000) by il Saggiatore. All told, this is a very small number of texts compared to the number of books authored by migrants available on the market. One could also state that minor publishing companies allow far more experimentation than do the major publishing houses. Visibility could be a double-edged sword. Higher visibility could sensitize readers to important issues about migration, but one could also speculate that a series devoted to migrant writers might set the authors apart in a reductive category marked by isolation.

Exploring the universe of small publishing companies and the ideological stance that motivated their choice to publish migrant authors is a challenge. It is particularly relevant to pay attention to the ideological stance of individual publishing houses in order to analyse the connections between migrant texts and the ideological meaning assigned to the texts by publishers. For instance, Edizioni Lavoro published Mohsen Melliti's two novels and a number of texts such as Ugo Melchionda's *L'immigrazione straniera in Italia: repertorio bibliografico* (*Foreign Immigration to Italy: Bibliographical Selection*, 1993). Located in Rome, Edizioni Lavoro is the publishing company of a trade union, CISL (Confederazione Italiana Sindacati Lavoratori), historically linked to the centrist parties. Their publishing roster covers a large variety of texts, from translations of Paul Ricoeur, Emmanuel Levinas, or Michel de Certeau to a series on Islam and its impact on contemporary Italy, to texts on Italian migration. If class struggles foreground Edizioni Lavoro's publications, Fara Editore's work is grounded on Christian humanist values and Alessandro Ramberti's academic interest in linguistics. His Catholic beliefs motivated Ramberti's commitment to publishing texts by migrants and in particular the yearly anthology for the literary award Eks&Tra. Fara had to stop publishing the literary award anthologies because its pioneering work in the area was becoming a financial burden that the company could not sustain.[91]

Two publishing co-operatives founded in a Roman prison deserve a particular mention because of their commitment to multicultural publications. In 1990 at the Rebibbia prison, a number of prisoners and external volunteers founded the publishing company Sinnos, which in Sardinian means 'signs.'[92] One of their series, titled 'I Mappamondi' ('The Globes'), targets young adults with bilingual texts written by migrants in Italy who narrate their lives before and after migration. One such text, by Maria de Lourdes Jesus, entitled *Racordai: vengo da un'isola di Capo Verde. Sou de uma ilha de Cabo Verde* (*Racordai: I Come from Cape Verde*, 1996), is published with parallel texts in Italian and Portuguese. Introduced by the world-famous Italian linguist Tullio De Mauro, who teaches at Rome's University 'La Sapienza,' this book embodies the pioneering role of the publishing company Sinnos, which also supplied its printing services to other publishers such as Editori Riuniti and Newton Compton and to institutions such as the University 'La Sapienza' and the Catholic associations Caritas and *Azione cattolica*. The strategy of assuming the dual role of publisher and supplier of publishing services allows Sinnos to confront the financial challenges a small company/co-operative inevitably encounters.[93]

The publishing house Sensibili alle Foglie was founded by Renato Curcio, Stefano Petrelli, and Nicola Valentino, who were imprisoned for their involvement in left-wing terrorism in the 1970s. The best known among the founders is Curcio because of his position of leadership in the Red Brigades. Besides publishing a number of books that focused on life in prison and strategies for survival, texts on the history of Italian terrorism, and books authored by Curcio himself, Sensibili alle foglie published the most controversial books that deal with migration issues. For instance, the themes of transsexuality, prostitution, and crime are at the centre of Fernanda Farias de Albuquerque's *Princesa* (1994). Another book, Hassan Itab's *La tana della iena* (*The Hyena's Den*, 1991) gives a first-person account of a Palestinian's terrorist mission to Italy and his integration into Italian society through his encounters in prison. Deliberately created to give space to migrant writers in prison, Sensibili alle Foglie challenges any easy definition of the migrant as a 'criminal' within Italian culture. By publishing writings from prison, Sensibili alle Foglie dismantled that separation between spaces that makes the lives of prisoners invisible and irrelevant for a majority of people. They also collaborated with the late Luigi Di Liegro, director of the Catholic association Caritas, to publish one of his books on migrations.[94] Determined to challenge ideological and methodological preconceptions, the publishing company encountered numerous financial and social difficulties.

I need to reiterate that distribution and therefore visibility are the core problems for minor companies responding to the challenge of publishing migrant texts. Such problems place them in an unavoidably fragile position on the market, and are aggravated in some cases by deliberately provocative choices of texts to publish that require a reading public acculturated in migration issues. Some of the publishers have decided to focus on educational material that is useful in schools in order to bring the discussion on multiculturalism to younger readers who can, in turn, be educated to pay attention to marginal literary productions. Minor publishing companies have been fundamental in creating a corpus of literary texts that have documented the development of migrant literature in Italy and the history of migrations to Italy narrated in the first person. Therefore, the future of migrant published texts is strictly linked to the financial future of small publishing companies that the market crisis at the beginning of the third millennium seriously threatens.

Conclusion

Enacting the relevance of migrants' voices lies at the centre of an analysis of texts authored at the crossroads of disparate traditions. A minor literature originating in and from migration highlights the cultural strategies inherent in describing that movement from a multiplicity of 'heres' to a multiplicity of 'theres.' The validity of such literature is eloquently expressed by Gabriella Turnaturi in her book *Immaginazione sociologica e immaginazione letteraria*: 'In a word, literature compels us to take a stand. That's because what we know from other sources, in the shape of facts, numbers, statistical data, political and economic analysis, translates itself into life experiences, connected to human beings, although imaginary human beings.'[95] It is, in fact, in the ability of literature to imagine change that migrants' texts create new meanings in contemporary Italian culture. Often described only as texts with sociological value, migrants' literature is instead the most innovative contribution to contemporary Italian literature.

In imagining themselves within Italian culture, migrants have also interpreted literature as an agent of social change. Attempting to influence changes in the social context in which they live by imagining such change has involved grounding processes of self-representation in a multiplicity of cultural traditions. The narrative strategies involved have moved away from canonical representations of ethnicity to explore identities that are post-ethnic and post-migrant in order to complicate the concept of otherness. In fact, migrants' literature articulates possible developments in a destination culture that ground them in a hybridization of the past, and in irreverence toward a dominant rhetoric about an imagined Italian identity. The processes involved in writing oneself into a changing literary tradition question at the same time any narrow understanding of what literature is and the possibility of creating simplistic narratives on Italian culture.

The marginality of literature in reaching readers embodies the difficulty in making first-hand narratives of migration count in the process of interpretation of the changes taking place in Italian culture(s). However, strategies that mark the processes of cultural hybridization in an Italian context find a clear, albeit very complex, map in migrants' texts. These texts defuse the sense of emergency and fear created by 'others' entering the familiar borders of Italy, and reveal how little known those arbitrary borders are to the natives. In fact, the value of a minor literature authored by migrants lies in its ability to tell the story of a destination culture that connects local and global cultural changes.

What is at stake is the role of literature (and of film and art in general) as an agent of social change because of its ability to *imagine* change. In their articulation of post-migrant and post-ethnic identities, migrant writers have successfully theorized the complexity of the future of Italian culture. This destination culture that uncovers the hybridity of the Italian past and redefines the paradigms of future cultural developments through migrations and transmigrations formulates hypotheses of cultural change that are far reaching. These writers are grounded in Italian culture and language, but present alternatives in their vision of global migration and local cultural connections that address the anxieties of normative dominant discourses.

Unfortunately, very few Italian literature departments in Italy are paying attention to the ground-breaking work written by migrants. Literary critics in Italy have only marginally studied migration and post-migration and post-ethnic literature because it often is considered a phenomenon that belongs to social studies and is outside the aesthetic concerns of practitioners of literary criticism. It is necessary to contaminate such fields with contingent issues concerning today's Italian culture, because practices of exclusion (i.e., practices that define what is and what is not literature) limit research to discreet margins that cannot affect dominant discourses. Enacting the relevance of a minor literature involves, therefore, an arbitrary widening of discursive boundaries into interdisciplinarity.

CHAPTER THREE

Cinema and Migration: 'What' and 'Who' Is a Migrant?

'I write in the language of here.'

Tobias, in *Brucio nel vento* (dir. Silvio Soldini, 2001)

Film in Black and White

In his 1951 film *Miracolo a Milano* (*Miracle in Milan*), Vittorio De Sica depicts a magical side of poverty in an abandoned area of Milano where a marginalized community has constructed a city within a city. Two minor characters, an African American man and a white woman, are at the centre of a sub-plot that supplies a separatist paradigm of interracial relations still in place in today's media representation of otherness. The story unfolds between the black man and the white Italian woman as follows: They are attracted to each other, but they are of a different skin colour, and this is the muted and unspoken reason for their courtship performed only at a distance. When Totò, the protagonist, gains the ability to fulfil anybody's dream thanks to a magical dove, the white woman and the black man wish to acquire the other's skin colour. The white woman whispers her wish in Totò's ear, and the black man states his desire in two languages: 'I want to become white, voglio diventare bianco.' The dove works its magic, and the audience is confronted with the image on screen of a white woman with a blackened face, in the 'best' Hollywood tradition, and a black man whose skin we can only guess has become white because we see him from the back, and at a distance. The change in his skin colour is only hinted at and he quickly disappears from the screen and from the story. The couple can never be united, for the white woman who wanted to be black performs a mockery of blackness and the black man who wanted to be white cannot perform whiteness in full view of the audience. We are left with irreconcilable representations of otherness and attraction for the other, which remain fragments without closure in the plot of *Miracolo a Milano*.

The problematic model of racial representations scripted in *Miracolo a Milano* has not been thoroughly contested in contemporary Italy. Separation between differences and attraction for the Orientalist representation of the other proliferate in contemporary Italian culture, but such performances of racial identity for Western audiences have been challenged by self-referential writing and texts in different media authored by migrants in Italy. While literary narratives have created a space in which migrants inscribed their otherness, cinema is gradually becoming a medium that migrants can access, allowing them to reach larger audiences.

Relational Selves: Privileging the 'Who'

In a discussion on the construction of 'other' identities in film, I would like to focus on a theoretical framework that could facilitate the approach to film on migration issues and connect it to the Italian context in which it is produced and validated. However, it is still a difficult task to find a consistent body of theoretical work in the Italian context that would help interpret the relationships between migrant and native cultures. Fortunately, Italian feminism, which for a long time excluded racial issues from its discussion of difference, is becoming instrumental in addressing migrant identity construction in Italian.[1] Distancing Italian feminism from its traditional connections to French feminist thought, Adriana Cavarero articulated a feminist concept of 'relational identity' that is grounded in Christine Battersby's concept of feminist metaphysics. In her book *Le filosofie femministe* (*Feminist Philosophies*, 1999), co-authored with Franco Restaino, Cavarero summarizes Battersby's theories on identity, intended as individuality and constructed in a constitutive relationship between the self and the other. This relationship involves both dependency and reciprocity: 'It is a self that cannot exist without the other.'[2] Feminist metaphysics 'distances itself from both the metaphysics of the subject and its postmodern dissolution.'[3] The identity thus created is fluid and dynamic, is never fixed or permanent, and is not the fragmented self defined by social or sexual categories: 'The abstractness and universality of the subject in fact make room here for the incarnate and sexed existence of the self. Repeatable subjectivity makes room for unrepeatable oneness. A claimed autonomy makes room for intrinsic relations; becoming replaces being.'[4] Cavarero stresses that although there is a structure at the centre of feminist metaphysics, that structure is not identified with language: 'Removing the self, the way Christine Battersby does, from contemporary theory, a move that renders the self a result of the performative power of discourse, is decisive.'[5]

Cavarero considers Battersby's feminist metaphysics to be a theoretical framework that allows the rejection of both the 'metaphysical subject and postmodern fragmentation.'[6] Feminist metaphysics moves away from the traditional inquiries grounded in a search for universal entities such as Man, being, or subjectivity in order to privilege the single identity and the question 'Who are you?' instead of 'What are you?' Translated into Italian feminism, and Cavarero's work in particular, individuality and its *irrepetibilità* lead back to the moment of birth both as the moment at which one's uniqueness is recognized and as the stage at which the relational self is established in its connection to the mother. In *Tu che mi guardi, tu che mi racconti* (*You Who Are Looking at Me, You Who Are Telling My Story*, 1997),[7] Cavarero privileges the concept of the unique self, excluded from philosophical discourse, a self that she traces from the relational self established at birth with the mother to the consciousness-raising practices of early feminism. 'It is a self that always needs the other,' writes Cavarero, 'not an *other* as general category, but rather another man or woman who is always someone, other *selves*, unique and unrepeatable, flesh and blood, present here and now.'[8] Cavarero stresses that this relational self is an identity that lends itself to being narrated. Expelled from the realm of philosophy, the relational self finds its location within narratives: 'The uniqueness of a self that here shows itself demands a meaning that a general category cannot seize and lead back into the hierarchical order of a system.'[9] Cavarero distances herself from Levinas's construction of an absolute position of supremacy of the other. This allows Cavarero not to construct another hierarchy even if that order would displace the supremacy of the Western identity in favour of difference. In the end, Cavarero distances herself even from that theoretical framework grounded in feminist metaphysics that she initially borrowed from Battersby. Cavarero, in fact, focuses on the narratability of the self and on reciprocal relations between beings 'in carne e ossa' (flesh and blood) and the stories that mediate such relationships.

Cavarero's work articulates itself in feminist philosophy and focuses on responding to a theorization of identity that places an emphasis on fragmentation. Her articulation of 'whoness' and 'whatness' criticizes the postmodern fragmentation of identity in order to present a narratability of the self particularly useful in talking about otherness. I arbitrarily translate Cavarero's feminist discourse into the context of a discussion on otherness in immigration, taking the liberty of using her paradigms in my approach to film and to male and female embodiments of otherness in contemporary filmmaking. In a discourse on migration, whatness often presents itself as a *reductio ad unum*, a monolithic representation of multiple, stereotyped characteristics that prescriptively define the identity of immigrants. However, this *reductio* contains in itself a paradox: it flattens by essentializing and, at the same time, it contains an exasperated fragmentation made of prescriptive elements that define identity in otherness.

Alessandro Dal Lago's text on migration entitled *Non-persone: l'esclusione dei migranti in una società globale* (*Non-People: The Exclusion of Migrants from a Global Society,* 1999) is in direct dialogue with Cavarero's process of constructing the concept of relational identity. Dal Lago's interest in social, legal, and political constructions of other identities helps to describe the process through which migrants are deprived of their individual identities. Contemporary global economic developments rely on a redefinition of commercial boundaries between nations in order to promote a global circulation of goods. The rhetoric of a free circulation of 'things' is accompanied by a heightened control over the movement of people, for whom borders become harder to cross. Having crossed, their identity in the country of migration is weighed down by over-codification in political, cultural, and legal terms. In the Italian social-economic-political arena migrants become a 'what' and not a 'who,' as described by Cavarero. Dal Lago, on the one hand, and Cavarero, on the other, trace the framework of the discourses on migration and migrants and document the tension inherent in discussing the identity of migrating selves. Some representations of the experience of migration have, since 1990, extensively documented cases of migration to Italy. In doing so, these narratives validate the sociological and philosophical investigations carried out in Dal Lago's *Non-persone.* Literary work by migrants is increasingly challenging the dichotomy between natives and migrants by investigating the multilayered differences among the many identities and making impossible the notion of a universal concept of the migrant.

Recent cinema by both native and non-native Italians has constructed the paradigms of that relational self that in its plural form becomes the protagonist in film and documentaries.

Films in the 1990s have portrayed innovative representations of whoness and embodiments of otherness. Native and migrant filmmakers have used this medium to articulate complex revisions of stereotypes. They have used film as an iconographic mediator that portrays contemporary Italy, placing migrants at the centre of the narrative. For instance, Rachid Benhadj's *L'albero dei destini sospesi* (*The Tree of Pending Destinies*, 1997) focuses on the experience of a young Moroccan migrant in Italy.[10] Samir, the protagonist, works as a cook for a community of Moroccan men who earn their living in Italy as construction workers. He hates being enclosed in a domestic sphere that limits his life. The realm he inhabits belongs to a separate, suspended sphere of in-between spaces. He works with fellow villagers who use the language and meta-language with which they grew up. Although they now live in Italy, Samir does not even need to learn Italian in order to accomplish the daily shopping for the community. This in-betweenness represents for Samir a space characterized by fragmentation and invisibility that traps him in the margins of both Moroccan and Italian societies. Trapped in the identity of an immigrant, he is instead a true nomad, in the Braidottian sense, who wants to construct his unique identity in relation to the languages and the cultures of the two social contexts in which he has inscribed or is inscribing himself.[11] This can only be achieved by acquiring both physical and cultural mobility between the geographical locations that represent his past and his present. However, he cannot establish a relation with Italian culture without learning the language. He does so by listening to language tapes while taking care of his daily chores. The dialogues he hears on tape are in Italian, but take place in the United States between a hypothetical Mrs Bell, an American, and a Mr Rossi, an Italian immigrant. The tapes, which provide an effective satire of language-acquisition materials, help construct language learning on Samir's part as a way to narrate parallel stories of otherness that have been silenced within the dominant culture that Samir inhabits. The fictional Mr Rossi is an immigrant from Calabria who tangos with the American Mrs Bell in order to learn English. In an ironic and comical mode, Benhadj implicitly establishes a dialogue between Italian migration to the United States and the contemporary migration to Italy. He also lampoons the stereotype of the tangoing 'Latin lover.'

Benhadj articulates the stereotypes employed against Italian Americans and recycled within an Italian context to be used against new migrants. He creates fluid boundaries between identity constructions that connect the past and the present within an Italian history of migration to and from the peninsula. If the Italian dominant culture can be exposed as containing, inscribed within itself, a narrative of otherness connected to processes of migration, Samir's identity construction can be created in relation to the historically repressed otherness of being Italian in the United States. Benhadj forces his audience to set its gaze on an other who is telling the audience's story and using it to create a self in relation to the invisible otherness of the spectators: 'you who are looking at me, you who are telling my story,' in Cavarero's words. The relationship established between Samir and Mr Rossi – that is, between the immigrant from Morocco who looks like the immigrant from Italy and the Italian American who looks like Samir – cannot be erased even by the comical situation presented in the oneiric sequences. This film responds to the audience's need to relate to the narrative on the screen precisely by problematizing it, and performing the process of 'recolouring' the dominant culture that the spectators embody. The white gaze, or the complexity of white gazes, that focuses on Samir's game of otherness and sameness is implicated in the narrative itself. The process of recolouring, in fact, is performed in Benhadj's film thanks to an interplay of gazes. The audience looks at Samir and expects to watch his story. Samir displaces the audience's privileged position. He becomes the one who gazes at the audience and tells the viewers' story while inscribing himself in a revision of the imaginary narrative on national identity.

The re-articulation of the concept of distance between sameness and otherness is grounded, in Benhadj's work, in the construction of a relational context in which the separation between those who are the subjects and those who are the objects, those who watch and those who are watched, is blurred, and privileged positions are challenged. Carlo Ginzburg has theorized, outside of any gender-study context, the importance of the 'outside observer' who employs distance as a strategy to revise what has been construed as the familiar. *Occhiacci di legno: nove riflessioni sulla distanza* (*Big, Bad Wooden Eyes: Nine Reflections on Distance*, 1998)[12] reveals the 'other's' ability to uncover aspects of the dominant's (hi)story that have been repressed, and deliberately erased. However, Ginzburg abandons his observer in his entrapment as other, indispensable as agent of a destabilizing narrative on hegemonic positioning, but also locked in his identity as an observer. As in Cavarero's theoretical articulations, Benhadj's film moves away from discussions that assign agency to only one side of a traditional dichotomy. The focus is not on the other *or* the same, the dominant *or* the subordinate, but rather on the other *and* the same, the dominant *and* the subordinate that can become agents in the construction of relational selves in which the identities of the observer and the observed cannot be imagined as separate.

Later in the narrative, Samir's relational self also highlights those 'cultural disturbances' that cannot be erased because, by rejecting in-betweenness and a fragmented identity, Samir searches for a nomadic identity that can relate simultaneously to Moroccan and Italian cultures on the same plane and at the same time. This emphasis on agency, on the ability to tell his story and others' stories, turns Samir into both a storyteller and a storytaker. The practical fulfilment of his desire presents itself when Yussef, the son of a village chief who functions as a go-between between the migrants in Italy and their families in Morocco, dies of a heart attack. As the chief's son, he embodied that mobility Samir wants to appropriate: our young protagonist promotes his own nomination as a replacement for Yussef. Turned down as community driver because of his young age, Samir takes, against community will, Yussef's car, loaded with presents for the families and begins his trip back to Morocco.

Samir's reverse journey back to Morocco, through France and Spain, is complicated by the presence of an Italian travelling companion: Maria.[13] She is pregnant, unmarried, and absorbed in pressing problems that make her see this trip as an escape from the location where all her troubles began. Cultural disturbances dominate the relationship between Samir and Maria. In order to find shelter from torrential rain, for example, Maria enters an abandoned church. She feels comfortable there and invites Samir to join her, but he resists entering a Catholic shrine that has religious images hanging on its walls. In contrast, Maria sees the church as the place that contains both the narrative of her past (the film has a flashback of her first communion) and of her unhappy present. Standing in front of the picture of the Virgin Mary, Maria finds both her namesake and a representation of troubled motherhood that speaks to her. Maria sleeps inside the church, while Samir remains in the car, which had once belonged to Yussef.

'"Who am I,"' writes Cavarero 'is a question that only a unique being can sensibly pronounce. Its response, as all narrators know, lies in the *classic rule of storytelling*.'[14] The construction of the relational self is grounded in the possibility of 'recognizing one's own life story narrated by somebody else.'[15] Cavarero adds: 'The identity of the self, crystallized in the story, is totally constituted by the relations of her appearance to others in the world, because, even in autobiography, "the story told through the convention of first-person narrative is always a story which both discovers and creates the relation of self with the world in which it can appear to others, knowing itself only in that appearance."'[16]

If Samir could establish such a relationship with the audience at the beginning of his story, the same process fails in the construction of the relationship between Samir and Maria, which is based on difference and separation. While Samir revisits Morocco through Western eyes, Maria's, she is unable to see and experience Morocco through the eyes of a Moroccan. She is trapped in her own unvoiced story and unmalleable self. Yet, the function of the character of Maria is to destroy any illusion that it is possible in a process of return to find exactly what one has left behind. Changed by the experience of leaving, Samir is a different subject who can experience Morocco anew, filtering such experience through the new self shaped by migration. The presence of Maria in this trip is particularly relevant, as she is the tangible impediment to 'experiencing home' in any familiar way. Leaving and returning become, therefore, according to the feminist thinker Manuela Fraire, 'a journey to knowledge and not simply a necessity of repetition.'[17] There is no linearity in Samir's nomadic journey. He traces a spiral-like movement that Fraire describes: 'If you imagine walking on a spiral, you have the impression of remaining on the same spot, but in reality you are at a different altitude. You will never again be on the spot where you started, nor you will ever return to the same point.'[18]

Maria instead travels along a more linear journey of discovery as a tourist. It is not surprising that a love relationship cannot be constructed between Maria and Samir even in the creation of 'what' they are. Being a migrant means negotiating a public identity defined by identity papers that declare one's identity as documented or undocumented, one's presence as legal or illegal on the national territory, and one's right to achieve visibility within the public sphere of everyday life. Samir always knows where his personal documents are, aware that mobility through borders is a conquered privilege for those who come from the south of the world. Maria takes mobility for granted and she rummages at the bottom of her bag to find her identity papers, unaware of the discourse implied in documenting one's identity. She emerges as a character in separate biographical fragments that only at the end is she able to articulate as a story. In the final sequences of the film, Maria leaves Morocco and Samir finds a letter from her at the hotel where she was staying. The happy ending lies in her acquired ability to narrate, which creates the possibility of a revised narration of their encounter in the future in which Maria could extend her narrative to include Samir's life as well.

Samir achieves his dream of total mobility and of a nomadic existence between Italy and Morocco, which means, borrowing Bill Ashcroft's words, that Samir 'makes [him]self "at home" in motion rather than in place.'[19] This also involves acquiring an imaginary identity that rejects the traditional fictive architectures of national identities. His arrival at the village, loaded with presents, makes him the protagonist of a fairy-tale narrative in which his return 'home' in his nomadic trajectory allows him to reach both his goals, of transforming his identity locked in the role of immigrant in Italy and caregiver in his community, and of revising the perception that the members of his original village, those who migrated and those who stayed behind, had of him.

What appears problematic in this film is the fact that nomadism becomes a male prerogative. Samir is able to acquire that freedom of movement that Maria cannot afford because she is weighed down by her unwanted pregnancy, by contingent problems, and by the psychological turmoil of becoming a single mother. Nomadism is therefore marked as male and out of reach even for a native Italian woman. Thus, the impossibility of a love story also lies in other inequalities. On the one hand, Maria is secure in her documented first-world identity, while, on the other, she is trapped by the inequalities between genders that still plague that First World. Samir could successfully tell the story of other men's migrations by 'becoming' the Italian American man from Calabria. Samir's and Maria's respective stories are instead marked by a difference that has no development in Benhadj's film.

Cavarero's idea that in the 'perspective of reading others' stories, the distinction between biography and autobiography is not important any more' is particularly relevant in the context of this film and of migration culture in particular.[20] Rachid Benhadj, an Algerian film director who has worked in Italy for many years, tells the story of a fictional character who is a migrant, but in a very different position from the one occupied by the director within Italian society. The idea of indirectly telling one's story through somebody else's life narrative is the theoretical framework that has marked the transition between the autobiographical narratives by migrants written in the early nineties and later texts on migration experiences. This shift toward the construction of a relational self characterizes Benhadj's work, whether he is talking about Italy, Algeria, or another country.

Benhadj's films often revolve around women and gender issues. His film *Mirka* (1999) focuses on women and Bosnia's ethnic cleansing. At the centre of this narrative, are a rape and a pregnancy: 'The film is dedicated to women,' states Benhadj. 'History repeats itself against women. They are victims of violence and rape in war and in emergency situations.'[21] Mirka is a boy who suddenly shows up in an isolated mountain village carrying a piece of embroidery, a tattered pattern of thread that is, however, still recognizable as the work of a local woman. Woven within the threads is a family's story, a boy's life, and a country's history. Mirka embodies what had been repressed and erased, and his presence unsettles a whole village. Kalsan, a seamstress, witnessed the rape of her daughter and the subsequent birth of a child. While the rest of the village participated in a collective, and silenced, act of infanticide, erasing the visible consequences of rape as warfare and 'genetic cleansing,' Kalsan lacked the courage to kill Mirka. As a consequence, he had come back looking for his mother, Elena. Benhadj addresses the historical present and the recent conflict in the former Yugoslavia, by focusing not on the act of rape but on the consequences of such a rape on a 'who,' gendered as woman, mother, and victim, and on her relation to her mother, an entire village, a country, and war. *Mirka* is a powerful commentary on the 'whatness' that lies at the centre of ethnic cleansing and of discourses on racial identity. In addition, what Mirka embodies talks back to Italian history and the present divisions along genetic lines that separate northerners and southerners, natives and migrants.

Cavarero's discussion on relational selves revolves around gender issues and, in particular, around women's narrative relationships with each other grounded in the practice of consciousness-raising, the literacy programs in Italy in the 1970s, and the work of Hannah Arendt. I have arbitrarily employed her philosophy of narration in a post-colonial context that is only touched upon in *Tu che mi guardi, tu che mi racconti* with regard to Elsa Joubert's *Poppie Nongena*, the narrative of another woman's autobiography. Cavarero mentions this book because it embodies the translation into practice of a theoretical articulation of a storytelling that also narrates the experience of the listener. The writer is a white South African woman; the storyteller is a black South African. The story was written in Afrikaans so that the family of the storyteller could understand it, and only later was the text translated into English. Aware of the 'risks of cultural colonization and appropriation' that can take place in such a relationship, Cavarero does not, however, explore at length the limitations of these collaborations with linguistic and cultural experts.[22] This issue directly concerns the Italian situation, where collaborations between linguistic experts and migrant writers have marked the beginning of migrants' writing in Italy. Both the role of the native culture experts and the narratives about migrants by non-minority writers have complicated the context of migration writing in Italian. This is particularly evident in the context of filmmaking as it is an expensive medium more accessible to non-minority filmmakers.

Dichotomies, however, always impede discussions, and it is only by analysing both minority and non-minority filmmaking that such dichotomies can be challenged. It is in a non-separatist context that exercises in identity construction can take place and reveal the close interconnection between self and other. This approach validates my appropriation of Cavarero's framework in gender studies as a tool for reading the strategies of self-identification by minority and non-minority intellectuals within a hyphenated context beyond gender issues. In this theoretical debate the 'who' emerges as the privileged protagonist as speaker and subject, but the 'what' cannot be ignored. A special project, carried out by the Italian state-owned television channels (RAI), identifies the strategies employed in talking about migration as a 'what' and immigrants as others who demand to be defined according to who they are. In analysing the French case, Alec Hargreaves stresses that state-controlled television broadcasting has not devoted much air time to the representation of immigrants and immigration.[23] The same could be said about Italian television, which has, instead, portrayed the immigration 'emergency' and 'invasion' of immigrants in the discourses of news broadcasters. In 1997, RAI commissioned Pier Giorgio and Marco Bellocchio and their production company, Filmalbatros, to make four films in a series entitled *Un altro paese nei miei occhi* (*Another Country in My Eyes*).[24] Until then, RAI had paid little attention to migrations, allowing programs such as *Non solo nero* (*Not Only Black*; a news and information program for immigrants) to broadcast for a number of years, then disappear during one of many restructuring turnovers at RAI.[25] The token immigrant appeared in other programs: an African man plays the regular host in a program devoted to soccer and, frequently, black women as half-naked exotic items appear in innumerable programs with little content but plenty of 'whatness' in the form of exposed female body parts. The films produced by Filmalbatros were criticized as an unnecessary expense for RAI and were broadcast late at night, which in Italian is called *seconda serata*, that is, after midnight when few people can view the broadcast. Benhadj's *L'albero dei destini sospesi* was one of the four films financed by RAI. The others were *Di cielo in cielo* (*From One Sky to the Other*, 1997) directed by Roberto Giannarelli; *L'appartamento* (*The Apartment*, 1997), directed by Francesca Pirani; and *Torino Boys* (1997), by Marco and Antonio Manetti. Together, the series represents a partially successful attempt, as they reached a small audience, to investigate migrants' lives between and in different cultures from the point of view of both minority and non-minority filmmakers.

Di cielo in cielo tells the story of Hassan Itab and his unique identity. In a previous film/documentary *Il viaggio di Hassan* (*Hassan's Trip*, 1996), Maurizio Jannelli and Virginia Onorato narrated the story of a young Palestianian man, Hassan Itab, who had been imprisoned in Italy after exploding a bomb at the British Airways office in Rome in 1986. Hassan Itab wrote his autobiography while in jail and narrated his life devoted to fighting for the Palestinian cause. Giannarelli films Itab's narrative of self-identification by allowing him to speak at length about his life and choices. The director portrays Itab as a man who, after serving his sentence, must inscribe himself within a culture he has not really known because a return to his past identity is no longer acceptable to him. This film about identity construction, violence, war, incarceration, and migrancy is grounded in the assumption that 'neither the points of departure nor those of arrival are immutable or certain.'[26]

Relational paradigms in identity construction allow the exploration of the complexity of different migrations, of the concept of origin, and of destination cultures. Hassan Itab leaves his land as an embodiment of whatness. In fact, since he was a child he was trained to fight, to function as a means for a cause. His autobiography, the documentary about his life, and Giannarelli's film text all focus on Itab's construction of his conflictual relation with the 'whatness' represented by Western culture and people. Conflict is based on a macroeconomics of identity that reduces identity itself to representations of whatness and, again, to simplistic and dangerous dichotomies. For Itab, the West is identified as complicit with the forces that killed his family in the refugee camp of Shatila. He travelled to Italy in order to place the West in the position of victim and to do unto Western identities what had been done to his family. The West, however, soon reveals its complex illegibility to Itab who, once in Italy, carries out his terrorist mission and, captured, expects the 'West' to execute him. His 'West' turns out to be Italy, where there is no death penalty and where the sixteen-year-old Itab is legally a minor. Sentenced to years in prison, he comes in contact with the complexity of what constitute the West. He meets Italian terrorists, guilty of 'whatness,' of having killed those who embodied that power they wanted to undermine.

Fragmenting the West into individual representations of whoness allows Itab to understand the tensions and conflicts within the monolithic entity he had tried to attack. His encounter with the incarcerated Italian terrorists allows him to learn Italian and enough of Italian culture to motivate him to tell his story and inscribe his own 'whoness' within a complex and fragmented Western culture. The relational context thus established spills into a larger context, documented in the film *Il viaggio di Hassan,* when years later Itab is granted supervised freedom and can get a job in a cafeteria outside prison, where he must return at night. After living for years within Italian culture, although a very special margin of Italian culture, Itab cannot perform the ideological and physical trip back to a country where his strife originated. This shift in alliances is not grounded in new causes but rather in having inhabited a relational context in which his story also told, in part, the story of Italian terrorists. His point of departure turns out to be the beginning of a process that changes Itab from terrorist to migrant. Looking at him and telling his story has allowed Maurizio Jannelli (who met Itab in prison) to explore his own terrorist past and to create a connection with Italy's internal history of terrorism. The subtext is a powerful reminder that during the *anni di piombo,* the years of lead (1969–85), even Italian terrorists were treated as a 'what,' an inexplicable and temporary degeneration within Italian culture. Only much later, at the time when Hassan Itab was incarcerated, did Italians start to investigate the roots of terrorists' choices, finding their origin deep within the structure of Italian history and culture.

The Manetti brothers' *Torino Boys,* whose original title is in English, portrays a community of young Nigerians in Turin and attempts to document the issues that are relevant to such a community and to its age group. Working with non-professional actors, the directors investigate the life of a younger generation of migrants whose culture has much in common with the youth cultures of the West. Intended as the portrait of a group more than of individual identities, the film acquires at times the characteristics of a documentary, but fails to involve the viewer in the narrative. The film confirms the separation between characters and viewers and in doing so objectifies its subjects. It ends up portraying charmingly exotic characters and reproducing old strategies of representations of otherness.

It is instead particularly useful to focus on Francesca Pirani's *L'appartamento* in order to continue my discussion of the role that feminist theory is playing in creating the framework for discussing migration in contemporary Italian culture. If Benhadj moves his experimentation in the representation of strangeness from Algeria to Italy, to Morocco and the former Yugoslavia, Pirani circumscribes otherness in a very enclosed and, at times, claustrophobic space. The protagonists in Pirani's film live in Rome but originate from Egypt and eastern Europe. Layla comes from the former Yugoslavia, where she was a school teacher, but cleans apartments in her exile in Italy. The director focuses on her loneliness and on the economic struggles that occupy most of her time. Emotions caused by displacement and marginality are at the centre of a narrative that eloquently portrays the tragedy of involuntary exile experienced by a woman. Gender issues are subtly treated by Pirani as part of a complex system of relations connecting two different cultures.

An apartment becomes the tangible location of difference and foreignness shared by two strangers for a limited amount of time. The male protagonist, an undocumented Egyptian called Mahmud, encounters Layla while he is on the run. The viewer is confronted, at the beginning of the film, with the representation of a stereotype: an immigrant committing a crime. He snatches a baby from a cradle and sneaks out of the institution where the child lived while waiting for adoption. The plot does not give any plausible explanation for what is happening on the screen, and the viewer follows the protagonist's wandering in search of shelter and a place to hide. The viewer also follows his/her own deductive path, understanding what is happening using his/her own baggage of a preconceived notion of migrants. Mahmud sees a wealthy family leave for a vacation. He breaks into their apartment and begins taking care of the baby. In the apartment he encounters the 'cleaning lady,' Layla, who reluctantly allows him to stay for the night. The plot develops in one day and one night. It is a night of storytelling between Mahmud and Layla. They do not belong to the upper-class area of Rome nor in that rich apartment. They both have to come to terms with their identity as others who are watched by 'those who belong' and must protect their wealth. The police intervene, called by a nosy neighbour who has seen a stranger in the apartment, and the Egyptian man is arrested for trespassing. However, the baby girl remains in the apartment, and the 'cleaning lady' is left with her. She already knows the story he has told her: the child is his daughter, born from a relationship with an Italian woman who refused to raise her, to give her his name, and left her in an orphanage. He had to kidnap the child in order to raise her: as an undocumented immigrant without a home he could not be granted custody. The short truce found in the apartment is only temporary and the ending leaves us with a powerful image of a present in which otherness can only be defined by problematizing it and the future is being constructed by a young woman and a baby girl thrown together as strangers but also as reflections of each other's difference. Layla is, in fact, a Muslim woman from hard-hit Mostar who left her family there and embraced the safety and loneliness of exile.[27]

In her essay 'Who Engenders Politics?' Cavarero clarifies her position vis-à-vis English-speaking feminism and postmodernism and her theorization of 'whoness' and 'whatness.' She stresses that distancing herself from the widespread interest in 'multiple subjectivity' does not mean being 'an across-the-board antiquated, European, essentialist, metaphysical thinker.'[28] Cavarero's revisionist approach to both metaphysics and postmodernism is based on a concrete metaphor inviting us to 'mix the tools, use them maliciously and betray them intentionally.'[29] In the construction of her theoretical approach to the 'self,' Cavarero returns to Woolf's need for 'a room of one's own' that seems not to be sufficient any more, as 'it seems that we can want more: a house of so many rooms, perhaps even a mobile home, or even so many houses as to be able to go from one to the other.'[30] Yet, at the centre of even a nomadic abode there is always 'the self which renders the metaphor efficacious.'[31]

Cavarero's discussion of the centrality of the self in relation to a place of habitation is particularly appropriate in talking about Pirani's 'apartment.' Mahmud and Layla originate from a somewhere else, live in temporary dwellings identified only as a space to sleep, but also create a home in an apartment to which they do not belong. At the beginning of the film, both protagonists are seen as 'whats': Mahmud, like many other Egyptians in Italy, works in a pizza parlor. He has several duties: he makes pizzas, thus becoming the creator and manipulator of what often stands for Italian culture itself, at least outside of Italy. He cleans the floor of the restaurant just as Layla moves from offices to homes to clean other people's empty spaces. The first thirty minutes of the film are almost totally without dialogue as the audience follows the actions that define both people as immigrants working menial jobs. As immigrants, they inhabit margins where they live without contact with people, in a vacuum signified by their generic identity. It is within the space of the apartment that their story can be told to each other and to the audience, as their temporary appropriation of a space in which to exist validates them as unique individuals whose identity is irrepeatable. Who they are is impossible to separate from their story, and that story cannot be left behind after the audience has finished 'visiting' the apartment and listening to their narrations. When Mahmud gets arrested, Layla remains with the child to become the protagonist of another story of her identity that develops in a home not of her own, just as most stories of migrants develop in a new location, a new land.

There is a danger, however, in moving from Layla's and Mahmud's stories to 'other' stories, for what is at stake is the singularity of each narrative and each self. The 'story,' explains Cavarero,

> is not something that gets added to the uniqueness of the who, as if this who could be separated from his/her story (and therefore from his/her life, from his/her existence), or as if the 'who' could be the substance ... to whom a story happens. On the contrary, the who is not a substance at all: he or she is simply someone that always has a face and a name. It is someone who consists of his/her life and his/her story. He or she is an unrepeatable existing being whose identity coincides perfectly with that lived life that is his/her story.[32]

Identity here coincides with 'life story' according to Cavarero and allows the separation for Layla and Mahmud, like for many others, from a collective identity construction as migrants, Egyptians, and eastern Europeans.[33]

The 'who' that finds a home in *L'appartamento* is 'expositive and relational.'[34] Following Hannah Arendt, Cavarero concludes that 'who you are consists in the embodied uniqueness that, here and now, appears to me as I look at you.'[35] Mahmud and Layla construct an encounter in which language is not at the centre. It completes their stories that are already told by the relationship established even before explanations are needed. As Cavarero states, the 'uniqueness of [their] existing being[s] presents itself as reciprocal spectacle.'[36] In this 'spectacular ontology' in which 'Being and Appearing coincide,' Mahmud and Layla's stories embody unique identities witnessed by each other and, at the same time, by an audience.[37] Cinema becomes here the ideal location where 'embodied uniqueness announces itself by itself to others' sight, always, for whomever, and inevitably.'[38]

Mahmud's story has little importance, however, in a legal narrative of his identity. Who he is is secondary to what he is: an undocumented migrant trespassing in this new land and in the apartment. The consequence is that he is forcibly removed, reduced to being a one that is the reflection of many others who are viewed as being the same. While climbing down the stairs escorted by the police, Mahmud is not Mahmud any more: he is the man who should not be there. He is forced go back to a generic somewhere, just as one of the women who witnesses his arrest angrily states.[39] This 'here' and 'there' are impossible to define because they are general categories sanctioned by law, and at the same time they are too essentialistic to mean anything in the story of a relational self. In addressing the issue of 'who engenders politics,' Cavarero reminds us that the 'entire political tradition ... continues to address itself to an abstract subject and ask what is it?'[40] Within the language of the law, Mahmud is an illegal immigrant, the un-named father of a child who officially cannot be considered his own, and a criminal who has forfeited his right to live within a 'democratic' country. He has become part of Dal Lago's non-people, the faceless entities that the law produces and politics manipulate: 'Politics never looks its subjects in the face.'[41] The 'who' always has a face, a name, and a story according to Cavarero. In *L'appartamento* Mahmud's face, name, and story exist before he becomes a problem person that the law has to 'handle' and discipline. The police intervene, once his appearance has been interpreted by the neighbour as the appearance of an other who breaks and enters into her life and her neighbour's apartment. Mahmud must abandon the status as a 'who' acquired in the temporary respite enjoyed with Layla.

'Existence,' states Cavarero, 'is always relational,' and in 'exposing who I am, such an identity is constituted by the plural glances of others looking at me: it is an identity rooted in contextual and reciprocal relationships.'[42] Exposed to Layla's glance Mahmud could move from a 'what' to a man who Layla can befriend because she recognizes her story in his story. Layla becomes, in Mahmud's eyes, first a cleaning lady who has the power to report him and turn him into an undocumented 'what,' and later a self in relation to whom his identity can be told in its completeness. 'In sum,' concludes Cavarero, 'who comes, then, is the embodied uniqueness of the existing being as he or she appears to the reciprocal sight of others.'[43] Cavarero encourages, therefore, a politics of relations grounded in the uniqueness of each story told in the context of other stories.

The Language of the 'What' and of the 'Who'

In 1989, a short documentary entitled *Stranieri tra noi* (*Strangers Among Us*) explored the physical and cultural locations of strangeness and foreignness in Italy at the time when the legal debate over immigration was at a turning point because of pending immigration laws (Legge Martelli).[44] At the centre of this visual narrative is Pap Khouma – his story, his life, and his ideas. He is interviewed throughout the documentary, and narrates both his arrival in Italy as an undocumented immigrant and his struggle to survive in Italy, where he later became a spokesperson for the Senegalese community. The interviewer plays a discreet role as a listener. Employed as an educational tool in schools, *Stranieri tra noi* marked Pap Khouma's experience in Italy by allowing him to become visible through exposure outside the Senegalese community he represented. In the documentary his body occupies a 'space' that deliberately provokes the audience. On the one hand, Khouma uses a conciliatory tone and words to talk about his experience in Italy. On the other, images of Milan introduce his discourse and clearly locate Khouma within the geographic and cultural landscape of an Italian city. His unerasable presence claims the right to inscribe his story in a specific cultural context, and the right to belong. The experience with the documentary motivated Pap Khouma to explore other narrative forms that would allow him to experiment with both the oral tradition with which he was familiar and the demands of the Italian narrative tradition, in which he wanted to inscribe his voice. The resulting autobiographical text, *I Am an Elephant Salesman*, was published in 1990 by Pap Khouma and Oreste Pivetta.

Saidou Moussa Ba started from the opposite point of departure in his acts of cultural hybridizations, by moving from the novel to film. The stress in Ba's work is on agency in artistic production, on active intervention in the construction of meaning and paradigms. *La promessa di Hamadi* (1991) begins with a chant modelled on the Senegalese oral tradition and tells of the journey of two brothers from Senegal to Italy. The story is narrated by a dead man, the older brother, who dies before his younger brother arrives in Italy looking for him. By engaging in acts of cultural translation, both Khouma and Ba are able to construct their identities as mediators between past and present cultural identities. They confront issues of fragmentation and in-betweenness connected to both their 'whatness' as immigrants, Senegalese, black, and their 'whoness.' Cavarero insists that 'in fact, you who are here and appear to me as unique, you are obviously someone, you are one. Uniqueness carries with it unity.'[45]

Ba focuses on the representation of a migrant identity experienced as a postmodern dissemination that never reaches unity since it is connected to different cultural contexts.[46] This self lacks a reader who can create a unitary story and brings into discussion the illegibility of what an identity appears to be. In his film *Waalo fendo* (*La, où la terre gèle*, 1997), Ba claims for himself the position of the migrant who stresses the importance of a separation from the new culture in which he is living. He wants to privilege a non-Western culture and a life shared with a community that has experienced migration. This proclaimed need for separation from Italians stresses difference, the impossibility of a dialogue, and the insurmountable rupture between the lives of the natives and non-natives. One is monolithically Italian, the other is shaped by non-Western cultures, an education in French culture, and the experience of migration. This investigation in strategies of separation goes against the cultural practices that define Saidou Moussa Ba. He co-authors his books with Alessandro Micheletti and investigates the construction of a self as other by exploring the inherent otherness of being Italian. The story of *La memoria di A.* (1995) describes a young Italian man who practises discrimination within his homeland and is victimized by it outside of his homeland. The novels and the film appear contradictory. However, rather than embracing a separatist agenda in his film, Ba wants to remind us of the need to confront issues of fragmentation and whatness as practice because they dominate the discourses that reach large audiences.

According to Ba, language is a fragmenting agent. Non-Western languages remain outside the cultural range of most Western people. The migrant carries the responsibility of articulating the signifying bridge between contexts and becomes author of a fragmented translation that is both linguistic and cultural. For Ba, translation becomes a border that he crosses and re-crosses repeatedly, changing the language – and therefore the culture – that sits at the centre of the text created by his acts of translation. Such acts attempt, often successfully, to create a relational connection between characteristics that define both what and who he is. Ba is a Peul, fluent in Pulaar, Wolof, and French, and at ease in Italian, which for him is the language of co-authoring. In his collaboration with Alessandro Micheletti, Ba has written two novels; he insists that he wishes to pursue their collaboration in future projects. Italian is the language in which he has become a teacher, a playwright, an author, and an actor; it is the language in which he authors his daily life. Languages have become his way of unsettling borders, as his collaboration with the theatre group Ravenna Teatro now frequently takes him back to Dakar. The film *Waalo fendo* embodies his revisionist agenda, which looks at translation as a necessary cultural act that permeates daily life. Ba rejects any attempt to privilege one dominant language into which all other languages must be translated. Even while living and writing in Italy, he works on the possibility of destabilizing the dominant linguistic location of Italian.

Waalo fendo is a film originating from a cross-national, cross-cultural collaboration.[47] Saidou Moussa Ba wrote the script and was the actor-protagonist of the film. Mohamed Soudani, an Algerian living in Switzerland, directed the film with Italian, Swiss, and French funding. The story narrated is closely linked to the plot in Ba's first novel, *La promessa di Hamadi*. Neither seeks to be an autobiographical text; however, they focus on migration experiences in Italy. At the centre of this film there is a man, his story, and, in the end, his death, but above all there is language. The film is in Wolof and Pulaar with French subtitles. The choice of creating a film for a Western audience in a non-Western language radically changes the terms of the cultural relationship between North and South, and shifts the attention from the linguistic hybridizations brought by colonial languages to a reversal of roles. Ba and Soudani also articulate the possibility of creating a film for a European audience and grounding it in the ideology of language found in Ousmane Sembene's work in film: that is, using the non-Western language as subject in the narrative and subordinating the translation into a European language to, literally, a marginal script on the screen.[48] As Laura Mulvay affirms in her discussion of Sembene's work: 'The cinema can speak across the divisions created by illiteracy and language and is, therefore, a perfect mechanism for a cultural dialectic. It can participate in the oral cultural tradition; it can produce a culture in which the Wolof language plays a major role; and it can bring Wolof [and Pulaar, in Ba's case] into the modernity of the post-colonial.'[49]

In 'The Alchemy of English,' Braj Kachru analyses the impact of English in Asia, as it 'has provided a linguistic tool and a sociopolitical dimension very different from those available through native linguistic tools and traditions. A non-native writer in English functions in two traditions. In psychological terms, such a multilingual role calls for adjustment.'[50] Exposing an audience to the unfamiliar sounds of Wolof, Ba and Soudani demand an adjustment on the part of European viewers, who are confronted by the familiar, easily legible landscape of urban Milan, which is destabilized by the story of a migration as expressed in the language of the migrant.[51] In one of our conversations (13 February 1998), Ba justified the motivation behind this linguistic choice by stressing that this story is about migrants and that the actors portraying them feel 'comfortable' with languages other than Italian. It is their story, their life, and turning it into Italian would make the narrative artificial. In addition, this film was created with the express purpose of being marketable in Italy, France, and Switzerland; therefore, the foreignness of the text is a unifying rather than a separating element between the different audiences, who are confronted with the same displacement of a linguistic centre. Broadcast by Swiss and French television, this film has also reached Ba's family in Senegal and has crossed the linguistic cultural boundaries between Europe and Africa. It embodies the possibility of a return home that involves an intellectual journey without demanding a Manichean choice between past and present.[52]

Waalo Fendo also comes after Ba's experience as an interpreter of Italian texts about migrants. As an actor, Ba performed with Piero Mazzarella, a well-known Italian actor, in *La tempesta* (1993), a play by Emilio Tadini that intertwines the life stories of a black migrant and an old Italian man. Tadini's text is a space shared by two different identities at the margins; it offers a valuable commentary on contemporary life in a Western world where old people and 'new' migrants embody peripheral identities. In *Waalo fendo* the cinematic narrative space is filled by a character apparently similar to Tadini's character, whom, however, Tadini named 'il Nero,' a generic 'what,' in his play. In Ba and Soudani's film, the screen hosts the 'whoness' of the black protagonist, his voice, his language, his life, and his marginal identity, not as fragments of an identity but as interdependent parts of a unity that constitutes his whoness. Ba's work is based on a non-exclusionary pattern of collaborations and experimentations among genres. In addition, his ongoing collaboration with Micheletti is complemented by his collaboration with Soudani, an Algerian living in Switzerland with whom Ba can move from theatre to film and from fiction to script writing. This collaboration among migrant intellectuals destabilizes the inevitable hierarchical relationship that is established between the linguistic expert and the migrant writer.

In his acting, novels, film scripts, and plays, Ba experiments with translating his own experience into texts that are never completely autobiographical. He is a true multilingual nomad who hides his identity in *Waalo fendo*, which uncovers the mechanisms and strategies inherent in presenting a life in exile in the original language. Ba's native tongue is Pulaar, not Wolof. Khouma has noted that while he is Wolof, and only speaks Wolof, Ba can move easily between the two languages, and from there to French and Italian. This interplay between revealing and concealing one's identity is at the basis of Ba's narrative construction, which never becomes openly autobiographical, but is rather a fragmented combination of his life story and other people's experiences. However, Ba stresses the presence of an 'accent' when he speaks Wolof, and insists that his identity as a Peul is easily recognizable by other Senegalese. His stress on his foreignness, even within the boundaries of the familiar languages, establishes this film as an exercise in linguistic transgressions that destabilize the separations between original and adoptive languages. The linguistic and cultural 'accent' is already a structural component of his Senegalese identity that was constructed before and outside of the dislocation created by the act of migration.[53] While Wolof is the language more often used in this film project, the title of the film is in Pulaar, which is also the language employed in some exchanges between characters in the film. This film, which represents a visual and visible location of strangeness for Western viewers, also offers a complex interplay of linguistic texts for Pulaar and Wolof speakers. The stress on the illegibility of difference for a European audience connotes the need to create a film that crosses the boundaries between audiences' cultural and linguistic identities. The film contains a plurality of texts according to the 'reading' abilities of the viewers. In *Waalo fendo*, a Western world signified by Pulaar, Wolof, and Italian words, Ba and Soudani succeed in constructing a cultural accent that can be re-translated back into the cultural context where Ba's migration began.

Film is the medium in which the accent, inscribed in the grammatical imprecisions in migrants' texts, acquires additional meaning. The sound of accented voices adds to the grammatical variants that migrants write in their novels and short stories. Words, in fact, count for both their 'semantic value' *and* their 'phonetic substance.'[54] Speaking with an accent therefore means thinking with an accent and expressing that difference through a sound that is an agent of change, a mark of uniqueness. In her book *A più voci: filosofia dell'espressione vocale* (*Many Voices: A Philosophy of Vocal Expression*, 2003), Cavarero continues her exploration of the concept of uniqueness, focusing on the role of the individual voice. The voice allows the vocalization of a uniqueness that involves a communication of that uniqueness in 'relation to another uniqueness.'[55] That aural uniqueness points toward an individual cultural embodiment that finds a privileged space in film. In fact, the voice highlights the physical presence of the body from which it originates. In Cavarero's words: '[T]he voice echoes the human condition of uniqueness.'[56] In film the voice and the body acquire volume and size, they become the focus of the audience's attention because, as Cavarero states, 'the voice of the person who speaks is always different from all the other voices, even if the words enounced are the same.'[57] The voice originating from one specific body marks the uniqueness of that individual and underscores the singular being and his/her difference. That 'phone' in Italophone that appeared inadequate to describe migrants' writing in an Italian destination culture acquires in film a new signification. It points in fact to the 'relational value of the voice.'[58] The linguistic experimentations enacted by Ba focus on sound to communicate difference inscribed in a Milanese landscape and an aural familiarity inscribed in an unfamiliar landscape for Senegalese audiences. Disconnected from any semantic value of words, the sound embodies relational difference.

The relationship between voice and word involves drawing into the discussion theoretical approaches to orality that lead to a revisionist agenda in creating historical narratives, in particular, a history of migration to Italy narrated through the individual voices of migrants. Ba's first novel began with a *griot* chant in order to inscribe the cultural voice of orality in a narrative in Italian. *Waalo fendo* explores the oral tradition by representing the narrative as told by a collective voice embodied by two narrators: Teo, who is the friend of Yaro (the main character, played by Ba), and Demba, Yaro's brother, who survives at the end of the narrative while Yaro dies. A *griot* who sings the Senegalese diaspora is also inscribed in the narrative of the film, which moves from Italy to Senegal. Through repeated flashbacks, it moves back again to Senegal, and bears witness to the complex acts of leaving a country to move toward *Waalo fendo*, the land where the earth freezes. In these repeated and destabilizing shifts between two continents, the film teases the audience by employing the same stereotypes that the West has constructed about Africa. They are voiced by different characters, who in Wolof or Pulaar pronounce generalizations that are familiar to a Western audience. In their individual enunciations they create a relational connection with Europeans that ironically describes the same process of constructing essentializing stereotypes. Before leaving the village, an old man asks Demba to take a letter to the old man's son, who migrated to 'waalo fendo,' where the earth freezes. It is a letter with no precise address: in *Waalo fendo*, the West becomes the generic entity that Africa is in Orientalist discourses.

It is the migrant who has the privileged position of bearing witness to different worlds and to the transitions or mediations between the different cultural contexts. Yaro stands up for his rights and fights the people who want to exploit the migrants. He constructs a life with his Italian friends who help him in a difficult situation, but he still sets boundaries to his belonging to *Waalo fendo*. In a dialogue between siblings, Yaro reprimands Demba for being attracted to a white woman, a friend whom Yaro sees only as an obstacle to Demba's construction of an independent identity in Italy. As in many French films by minority filmmakers, Ba has focused in part on 'the immigrant as victim and [has] taken a pessimistic line on the possibility of integration.'[59] In this context, the linguistic and cultural experts found in the country of migration are represented as obstacles, not facilitators, in the process of redefining one's identity in translation.

In an Italian national context in which identity cards are issued in one language only and can bestow the right to belong to a Western country, Ba plays with the concept of legal identity cast in Italian by scrambling identity papers and using many languages to do so. The result is the description of a journey from Senegal to Italy, where the main protagonist cannot survive. In Italy, Yaro inscribes his diversity within the already fragmented sense of Italianness that permeates contemporary Italian culture. He mocks Umberto Bossi and his northern separatist agenda ('La Savania libera, noi della Savania libera marceremo su Roma'), by replacing the slogan 'Padania libera' (Free Padania) with 'Savania libera.' He also draws Italian historical memories into the equation, threatening a 'black march' on Rome that mocks Mussolini's black shirts' march of 1922. Ba conflates fascist rhetoric with contemporary xenophobic discourses and creates an explicit discourse on ideological continuity between present and past in Italy. These film segments address an Italian audience and temporarily interrupt the 'European' and 'non-European' dialogue that is both Ba and the director's main agenda. Appropriating and manipulating slogans that belong to Italian culture and language scrambles the hierarchy of relationships because Ba, an 'other,' can voice a revision of a Western historical narrative, but Yaro is killed at the end.

The protagonists of *Waalo fendo* are closely connected with particular migration issues in Italy, and their life in the West is marked by experiences developed in confronting Italian culture, society, language, and intolerance. Italy becomes, therefore, the location in which their new identities are being shaped in that initial moment when the country of migration is completely new and uncharted. At the end of the film, Yaro disappears as a guide for the newcomers. His death represents the disappearance of a separatist way of reading and approaching a new culture. His heroic death in the name of an ideal is replaced by a new movement, a new journey on other people's terms, people who become independent interpreters. After Yaro's death, the final shots of the film focus on a moving streetcar and reintroduce the concept of the cultural and geographical journey that even his death cannot interrupt. By moving away from a representation of the immigrant solely as victim, Ba and Soudani separate themselves from a certain kind of French cinema that portrays 'ethnic minorities in subordinate roles as the (relative) helpless victims of aggression,' which 'can be hardly empowering for minority audiences' and the viewers in Senegal.[60]

Minor Identities: Linking 'Whatness' and 'Whoness'

In 1997, Mohsen Melliti co-directed with Massimo Guglielmi a film project entitled *Verso casa*.[61] Made for the Italian state television, *Verso casa* documents the trip back home of a number of Moroccans who board a bus at the central station in Milan and return 'home' for disparate reasons, travelling by bus through France and Spain. The camera follows them into their Moroccan homes and investigates the difficult processes of return to what was once home but can no longer be defined as such. A very successful project, Melliti and Guglielmi's documentary contributes to a discussion on separations and borders in the emergence of migrant voices within Italian culture.[62]

Accessibility within dissemination, intended as nomadism and not fragmentation, is the aim of the authors who are documenting the location of 'strangeness' as the 'irremovable' strangeness of being different' within fortress Europe.[63] This search for an exploration of the 'what' and the 'who' is located both in the country where their migration originated and where migration took them. The location of 'strangeness' resides both in the destination culture that they inhabit and in the attempt to re-inscribe their selves within the pre-migration familiar context. Strangeness becomes a marker for the changes in both who and what they are. Wanting to debate the issue of their cultural location, filmmakers confront the concept of cultural borders by searching for a creative space that can be linguistically – as is the case for Ba and Soudani – and thematically appealing to large, geographically disseminated audiences that represent their past and present. It is in this context that Bhabha's 'strangeness of being different' can be explored as a convergence of Cavarero's articulation of the concept of 'whoness' and 'whatness.'[64] 'Whatness' occupies a privileged position in the rhetoric contained in many public discourses on migration. What both native and non-native authors and filmmakers explore is how to inscribe such a popular and successful rhetoric in complex discourses that are not so easy to manipulate and that allow for 'whoness' to surface.

Directly and indirectly influenced by migrants' experimentations with Italian culture and by the innovative projects of migrant authors, native Italian filmmakers have confronted issues of 'whatness,' 'whoness,' fragmentation, strangeness, and hybridity. Giovanni Maderna's *Jahilia* locates itself at the intersection of different cultures. Inspired by Flannery O'Connor's *The Life You Save May Be Your Own* (1953), Maderna replaces the main character in the American short story with a devout Muslim from northern Africa who lives in Italy. The story unfolds similarly to O'Connor's: a man arrives at a farm run by two women. The mother is well off and has raised a daughter (named Antonia in Maderna's film) who appears to have mental problems. In O'Connor's narrative the man is a con artist who covets their car and succeeds in getting it. Marrying the daughter leads to the revelation that the man only wanted to take advantage of the women.

In Maderna's version, by contrast, there is an attempt to link two identities at the margins. At the centre of the narrative is a migrant, who has only a dirty towel as his prayer mat. He reveals that his name is Jalal and he comes from Morocco, but also manipulates his own identity and the stereotypical generic constructions about his self that the West has constructed regarding being Moroccan. In an exchange with Antonia's mother, he could truthfully reveal his name and country of origin. He could also say that he is Tunisian and has a different name because, through stereotyping, Italians invite such an interplay of identity constructions. There is no better representation of the 'whatness' of being a migrant than Maderna's brief representation of Jalal's understanding of his location within Italian culture.

Following the plot in O'Connor's short story, Jalal covets an old car that reminds him of his work in a car factory in Morocco. To own it, he must marry Antonia, which changes the terms of O'Connor's story, as Jalal is not the one controlling the rules of the exchange. The narrative ends when the new couple leaves in the car after the wedding ceremony. The final shots narrate their silence, the impossibility of communication between them, underlined by the loud music he has chosen and by her quiet desperation. In this old car, which once belonged to Antonia's father and that Jalal repaired with Antonia's mother's money, the newly-weds listen to an old popular song, Patty Pravo's *Sentimento*, which tells them that happiness is somewhere else, beyond hypothetical stars and in a geographic location that only exists in imagination.

This final twist, which modifies O'Connor's unhappy ending, shows the influence of other European films that focus on migration. In particular, Maderna's film enters into dialogue with Fassbinder's *Angst Essen Seele auf* (1974), in which a young northern African develops a relationship with a much older German woman. Inspired by O'Connor's story and influenced by Fassbinder's film, Maderna's *Jahilia* absorbs a number of international influences that move the discussion on migration outside Italian borders. Maderna's international influences also remind us of Pap Khouma's German autobiographical model and place a film about migration at the crossroads of a global dialogue on migrant identities. These encounters at the margins within the narrative structure of Maderna's short film point to the difficult transition between whatness and whoness when identity is grounded in difference, whether it is that of a Muslim migrant or a simple-minded young woman handed over by her mother to a man who promises to remain and work on their farm. Making disparate representations of difference intersect, undermining stereotypes, and connecting to constructions of alterity outside the boundaries of a national literature and film production are strategies at the centre of Maderna's film, which functions as an eloquent manifesto for a young generation of native filmmakers.[65]

The manipulation of stereotypes that qualify as the 'whatness' that needs to be challenged is a constant concern for many native filmmakers. Stefano Incerti's *Prima del tramonto* (*Before Sunset*, 1999) takes place in southern Italy and deals with the relationship of a northern African immigrant with Italian organized crime. Incerti hired actor Said Taghmaoui, who plays the main character in Benhadj's film *L'albero dei destini sospesi*.[66] Alì, Incerti's protagonist, is Moroccan and is going to marry the daughter of the local Mafia boss. However, Alì is in love with Assia, a Moroccan woman, who embodies his unerasable connections to a past before migration. In fact, the conversations between Alì and Assia are always performed in Arabic. Together they decide to wait until sunset on Alì's wedding day to elope. Alì does not show up at his own wedding, setting in motion the events of the plot. He is presented as a waiter, as a social climber who is going to marry the local rich, connected woman. In the opening shots, while he is preparing for his wedding, his insistence on articulating a conversation with his mother only in a Western language reinforces the image of his apparent wholesale transition into Western culture. Alì responds either in Italian or French to his mother's questions in Arabic. He is the embodiment of the migrant who wants to assimilate even by erasing a language that represents part of his identity and by marrying into the local Mafia family. Bringing the Mafia into a discussion of migration is problematic. The purpose is to bring into play, ironically, the stereotype of the criminalized migrant vis-à-vis native organized crime. In addition, integration here becomes an ethical question, for it involves selling out by joining the native criminals.

Incerti manipulates stereotypes of Italianness and makes Alì part of an unglamorized portrayal of the Mafia. The plot unfolds in a generic location in the south of Italy where a big commercial billboard becomes a recurring image. All the characters transit by a large advertisement, placed along a beach road, of a model wearing the latest bikini, called 'Agadir.' The exoticized location and the objectified naked body of the model embody for the audience the familiar that Incerti erodes by exposing the ruthlessness, the mediocrity, and, strangely, the unglamorized 'normality' of organized crime. From voluntary accomplice, or maybe aspiring accomplice, Alì becomes victim and self-destructive emulator. As the bodies pile up and the *mafiosi* kill and in turn are killed by Albanians they have tried to rob, Alì tries to escape from the consequences of his choice. He survives, and Assia is killed, but, unable to escape, he internalizes the patterns of violence that victimize him and dies while attempting to rob the local post office. His killer is neither a *mafioso* nor a policeman, but rather a postal employee who uses the robbery to execute his boss with Alì's gun. In the end 'whoness' escapes the reach of both the native Italians and Alì. What remains is an unglamorized pulp fiction that revises a genre by borrowing from the Hollywood tradition and leaves the audience trapped in representations of a 'whatness' that reveals its limitations.

What a few contemporary Italian films affirm is the impossibility of going beyond whatness that allows only for tragedy to be performed on the screen. Such is the case with *Article 2* (1993), a film by Maurizio Zaccaro. The article 2 in the title is that article of the Italian constitution that recognizes freedom of religion. Said, the film's protagonist, is a bricklayer from Algeria who has two wives: Mulika is taking care of his elderly parents in northern Africa, Fatma lives with him in Milan. Trouble begins when Mulika joins him in Italy. The act of reconciling what he is with the set rules and laws in the host country ends in tragedy. Freedom of religion is guaranteed, but monogamy is the rule in the Western country where Said is a migrant. Only his accidental death while working resolves the dilemma, and he is returned to Algeria in a coffin marked by a cross. A theoretical investigation privileging 'whoness' in discussing diversity clashes with contingency and the limitations of laws that cannot answer to the challenges that migration offers. Even Cavarero's feminist elaboration of the concept of 'whoness' may be challenged by the problem of reconciling Italian women's long fight for legal and social 'whoness' with the rights of a Muslim man that could be achieved at the expense of women's rights.

And Then There Is the Unerasable 'What'

The complexity of a discourse on the translation into practice of the right to 'whoness' is kept at a distance in popular programs offered on Italian television and 'enjoyed' by large audiences. While the films that I have privileged have been seen by a comparatively small group of people, commercial channels have been busy reproducing a portrayal of 'whatness' that recycles all stereotypes of racial inferiority and an unerasable strangeness that excludes the migrant other from any discourse on the identity of contemporary Italian culture. The universal category of a specific kind of 'what,' the immigrant as a problem to be erased, imbues the popular daily programs on television. Many more people have seen Gigi Proietti's *Un nero per casa* (*Black and Underfoot*, 1998), a film for television produced and broadcast by Canale 5 and an excruciatingly pathetic attempt to 'deal' with alterity through stereotyping, than Benhadj's complex *L'albero dei destini sospesi.*[67] When watching television, people are constantly faced with the insurmountable separations between black and white that even a miracle in Milan could not 'heal.'

Channel 5 is part of the Mediaset empire owned by Silvio Berlusconi, who has also enjoyed a political career that led to his becoming prime minister. *Un nero per casa* is a film that eloquently summarizes his network's position vis-à-vis immigration. The film was broadcast on prime time on 7 December 1998. The opening shots of the film introduce the main character, an architect, Lorenzo Paradisi, played by a well-known Italian actor/comedian, Gigi Proietti. The actor addresses the viewers directly, establishing a familiar link between himself and the audience. Lorenzo is a reasonably wealthy man whose roots lies in the south of Italy, via his parents' migration to Rome in the 1950s. His house is filled with African artefacts that his wife collects. His relationship with his daughter, Valentina, is artificially devoid of conflict. Lorenzo is supposed to represent the socially mobile Italian who has embraced democratic ideals and defines himself as anti-racist. His hypocrisy is soon revealed. The film seems to state that Italians, represented by Lorenzo, find themselves agreeing with more conservative ideals, that is, directly and indirectly, with Berlusconi's ideological stance.

Inspired by the well-known American film *Guess Who's Coming to Dinner* (1967) directed by Stanley Kramer, *Un nero per casa* narrates the love story between the sixteen-year-old Valentina and a black immigrant man, Mori. The black man is signified by a name, Moors, that functions as a flash card. Liberata, the Paradisis' black maid, is named 'liberated,' just to make sure that the viewers do not see her as a domestic 'slave' in the heavenly home of the Paradisis.[68] She is the Italian translation of Hollywood's most racist portrayal of black people. Liberata speaks in infinitives and is the naive, faithful, and grateful servant who demonstrates her deep attachment to her blond mistresses. At the beginning of the film, Valentina brings home Mori, introducing him as her boyfriend, and Liberata becomes flustered because there is a black man who is sitting at the table with her white employers. She gets scared and jumps as if seeing a ghost, and drops the birthday cake, supplying comic relief at her own expense. Irony inevitably seeps into the description and analysis of such a plot as it frustratingly recycles comedic strategies that belong to a tradition of obsolete racial representations, yet these successfully resurface on Italian television in prime time.

Mori, of course, is a *vu cumprà*, a street vendor who has fooled the beautiful, good, and blond Valentina into believing that he is a prince. To be sure, Valentina is in love and wants to know Mori's world. She even chooses an African hairdo for herself. Her trip to an African hairdresser introduces her and the viewers to a culture represented by people who break into dancing at the least provocation. Lorenzo Paradisi wants to break up the couple. Consequently, Valentina thinks of suicide, and Mori relieves his heartache by, of course, playing the drum. Valentina's father learns that he is not as open minded as he thought he was, but 'learns' to like the African people he encounters, and heals his daughter's heartache by bringing Mori back to her. He even saves the day by preventing Mori and his family's eviction from the building in which they live. The happy ending is supplied not by the fact that Lorenzo now allows Valentina to see Mori, but by Mori's choice to move somewhere further North with his family, maybe France or Germany, outside of the Italian national boundaries and the familial environment of the viewers. It is only by making Mori expendable that the Paradisis can triumph, complacent in their liberalism and rewarded by the disappearance of a man who is not a prince, is not rich, is just black. The presence of the African man and of blackness have to be erased from the plot unless being black means being Liberata, the maid, trapped in a role controlled by the Paradisis.

'Whatness' reveals itself to be the normative paradigms on which racism is constructed: Mori is black, a street vendor, a generic African, and a sure threat to a white, wealthy, nuclear family whose members represent the viewers, the majority, and the threatened norm. Promoted with the label 'G.P.,' which indicates that the film is also appropriate for children (on Italian television, the rating appears as a green circle with a stylized little boy in its middle), *Un nero per casa* becomes the model for interracial relations that is deemed appropriate to teach the future generation of adults and voters. 'Whatness,' the 'normality' of whiteness, and the rights of the majority define what is popular on prime time. Revisionary voices are still relegated by conservative debates to a *seconda serata*, which declares the invisibility of innovative representations of the multiple and irrepeatable migrant subjectivities.

Amelio and Bertolucci

A clear separation emerges in film production between what is popular and grounded in 'whatness' and what is not well distributed but represents the complex relation between 'whatness' and 'whoness.' Two contemporary Italian filmmakers, Gianni Amelio and Bernardo Bertolucci, have succeeded in both bridging opposites and reaching wide audiences with their sophisticated representations of 'whoness.' Amelio's *Lamerica* (1994) focuses on Albanian migration to Italy at the beginning of the 1990s. The film shows that for Albanian migrants Italy represents what 'America' was for Italian emigrants of past generations: a geographical location, but above all an imagined promised land of hope and opportunity. Amelio grounds his film in a 'sameness' that links old and new migrations. Such a connection can only be established by narrating 'whoness,' the unique experience of individuals in stories about migration and in the history of the identities that perform such migrations.

In *Lamerica,* two native Italians, Fiore and Gino, travel to Albania to take advantage of the fall of the local regime and the subsequent economic and social upheaval. They present themselves as Western moguls whose money is what a poor country like Albania needs, but in reality they are plotting a scam that would only benefit themselves.[69] Their purpose is to obtain international funding to establish a shoe factory that will never actually exist. Once in Albania, Fiore and Gino need to find a local nominal owner of their enterprise. They find the ideal associate in Spiro Tozaj, who after years in prison and forced labour has lost his individuality and awareness of historical time. Gino departs and leaves Fiore to deal with bureaucratic details and finalize the transactions, and the scam. Spiro, however, is an unwilling accomplice whose generic identity as an Albanian hides a complex past. He tries to run away, setting in motion for Fiore a journey that takes him from Tirana, to the mountains, and gradually strips him of the gadgets, the clothes, and the car that identify him as Italian. Reduced to travelling with the Albanians who want to escape from their country, Fiore can only survive if he establishes a dialogue with the local people and loses his privileged position in his relationship with Spiro.

The film begins with documentary material from the 1939 Italian occupation of Albania, defined as a colonialist act that 'brings civilization' to an inferior population. The new Italians, embodied in Gino and Fiore, reveal themselves to be the ideological heirs of the old colonialism. They hide behind a thinly veiled rhetoric of economic imperialism: they present themselves as the Western saviours of an inferior economy (and culture). In reality, they are busy exploiting a country for their own interest. Everything has changed and, at the same time, nothing has changed in a historical pattern that fails because of the 'insignificant' presence of a 'what,' an Albanian who was destined to be a tool in the Italians' scam. Once the illiterate old Spiro begins to lead Fiore through the hellish circles of a poor country, unsettling details about his identity emerge. He turns out to be a Sicilian soldier who was trapped in Albania during the Second World War.[70] His strong Sicilian accent and memories of his former life introduce Spiro/Antonio as Fiore's alter ego: Fiore is Sicilian, a new Sicilian willing to victimize people who could have been himself in a different place and at a different time in history.

Sameness emerges as the dominant paradigm defining Spiro/Antonio and Fiore, and consequently the Albanians who want, by any means, to escape from their present conditions. Once an Albanian government representative that Fiore has not been able to bribe deprives him of his Italian passport, Fiore has no means to construct separations and boundaries between himself and the others, between being Sicilian now and being Sicilian then, and being Albanian in the 1990s. It is in this moment of loss of identity that Fiore embodies the historical memory of being Italian, and paradoxically emerges as a 'who' whose attempts to hide behind whatness and its symbols fail. Fiore can only head for Tirana's port and board an overcrowded ship that iconographically mirrors the ships boarded in the past by Italians who headed to the new world. Fiore questions what constitutes a national identity or the right to an identity that places a man in a privileged position vis-à-vis *les damnés de la terre*.[71] Spiro, who still thinks it is the 1940s, and that he is a young man, confuses the issue even more. He expects that the ship he has boarded with Fiore will reach America. Albania has become Sicily for him and Italy is America, *Lamerica*. Identities and geographical destinations are scrambled, turning the same into the other and the other into the same in a process of hybridization grounded in the representation of 'whoness.'

For both Fiore and Spiro the destination is Italy, an 'Italy' that is America for the Albanians who, by watching Italian television in their country, have internalized the media representations of a glamorized and commercialized national culture. Fiore, Spiro/Antonio, and the Albanians travel on a ship that carries the name of 'Partizani,' the wartime resistance fighters, a name that has symbolized for Italians a mythical struggle against fascism and a 'new' beginning. Amelio appropriately chooses a name that reminds the viewers of resistance. This concept of resistance as the motor and means of migration suggests that even fragmented acts of talking back defy constructions of whatness. The Albanians expect a new beginning in Italy, but they will experience a *reductio ad unum* by becoming a 'what' in their European America.

Critically acclaimed, *Lamerica* is a powerful model in representations of migrants, origins, and the historical past. By displacing his Italian protagonist from his place of belonging – Italy – to a place of unbelonging – Albania, Amelio has explored processes of identity construction outside what is familiar for both the protagonists and the audience. He concludes his film with shots of the overcrowded ship, floating in an in-between space that is neither Italy nor Albania. The open-endedness of the film turns a story of migration into an epic journey in which the whoness and whatness of both native Italians and migrants cannot be separated.

Four years after the release of *Lamerica,* Gianni Amelio continued to develop its plot with unexpected results in another film: *Come ridevano* (*How They Laughed,* 1998) begins with the arrival of the Sicilian Giovanni at a train station in Turin. These two films demand being read intertextually as they articulate a revisionist approach to past and present histories of identity construction in Italian culture. Enrico Lo Verso, who plays Fiore in *Lamerica,* also plays Giovanni in *Come ridevano.* In *Lamerica* Fiore is the arrogant Western imperialist, but Lo Verso also plays the 'Albanian' in *Come ridevano,* a film on internal migrations in the late 1950s and early 1960s. Giovanni arrives in Turin to join his younger brother, Pietro, who had been sent up north to fulfil Giovanni's expectations of social mobility through education. However, the consequences of the geographical separation between the brothers complicates their relationship. Pietro waits for his brother at the station but hides when he sees Giovanni leave the train with a crowd of other Sicilian migrants. The dapper Pietro is as ashamed of Giovanni as Fiore was in discovering that Spiro/Antonio was an 'Albanian' who turned out to be as Sicilian as himself. *Come ridevano* further develops the construction of irremovable connections between sameness and difference, but the narrative loses its effectiveness by focusing on the complicated relationship between the two brothers. Giovanni ends up becoming a shady character who kills a man, and Pietro sacrifices his life by taking responsibility for the murder committed by Giovanni. *Come ridevano* was neither a commercial nor a critical success. Interpreted as a sequel to *Lamerica,* however, *Come ridevano* becomes an important document on the essentializing power of whatness and on the necessity of uncovering whoness by narrating unique stories about individual subjects of migration.

Amelio's films are about men's migrations. It is not surprising that female characters have corollary roles in most Italian films that focus on multicultural issues. Bernardo Bertolucci is, surprisingly, an exception to the tradition of telling men's stories first. He is interested in the encounter of identities at the margins and on the revision of hierarchical relations. His *L'assedio* (distributed in the United States with the title *Besieged*, 1998) moves away from any attempt to construct a discourse on collective identities such as Italian, migrant, same, or other by focusing on the 'whoness' embodied in the uniqueness of the film's two protagonists: Kinsky and Shandurai, played respectively by David Thewliss and Thandie Newton.[72] Inspired by a 1985 short story, 'The Siege,' by the English writer James Lasdun, Bertolucci moves the location of the story from England to Rome, where the two protagonists meet.[73] The director names the African character Shandurai, exoticizing the more ordinary Marietta in Lasdun's story. Fortunately, Bertolucci remains faithful to the original story of an African woman, a political refugee, attending medical school in the West, and of Mr Kinsky, who has enjoyed a privileged aristocratic life, but is not emotionally equipped for a life outside his chamber music and his students who come for private tutoring. The plot is a *kammerspiel* between Shandurai as Kinsky's maid – a student, a persecution survivor, a migrant, a wife whose husband is in an African jail for political reasons – and Kinsky, who is in love with Shandurai. His emotional immaturity allows Kinsky to attempt an awkward courtship that the woman initially rejects. Finally, exasperated, she dictates the conditions for accepting his love. Shandurai asks Kinsky to get her husband out of prison and he sets in motion events that will free her husband but leave him destitute.

Kinsky's willingness to risk his privileged economical condition and change his identity and status within a Western context establishes the framework that allows for an attraction to develop between the two protagonists. Played by using dialogue very sparingly, the love story develops through love tokens given by Kinsky to Shandurai thanks to a dumb-waiter that connects her maid's room and his elegant apartment. It is a silent courtship mediated by objects, piano music, and incomprehensions. However, the hierarchical separation between upstairs and downstairs slowly crumbles as Shandurai, who cleans Kinsky's apartment, witnesses the disappearance of his art works and his antique furniture and objects, which are sold to pay for her husband's freedom. It is up to her to understand why her employer's apartment is being emptied out as nothing is explained openly. Closeness develops through a gradual change in the way Shandurai understands Kinsky's 'strangeness.' The point of contact is in the 'strangeness of being different' for both the woman and the man, even though Shandurai has experienced the tragedy of history and Kinsky's tragedy is his own emotional and social inadequacy. At the centre of the plot is a detailed psychological investigation of the protagonists grounded in an interest in 'who' they are outside of any social, economic, and racial label. An interracial relationship does not, in the context, stand for any larger discourses on such an issue. Its conflicted and ambiguous happy ending concerns only the two protagonists and does not attempt to deal with larger questions about difference. In fact, Shandurai's husband is finally released from prison thanks to Kinsky's money. He travels to Italy, but Kinsky and Shandurai do not open the door when he rings the bell of their, now shared, apartment.

This film has signified a change for Bertolucci who, before making *L'assedio*, had devoted himself to epics such as *L'ultimo imperatore* (*The Last Emperor*, 1987) and to obsessively scopophilic films such as *Io ballo da sola* (*Stealing Beauty*, 1996). In contrast, *L'assedio* could be considered a low-budget project that Bertolucci executed after the idea was developed by his wife, director Clare Peploe, who was involved in writing the script.[74] Bertolucci and Peploe's discreet investigation of 'whoness' in *Besieged* contrasts with the title of the film itself. Defined in the press in over-codified terms as an invasion, a siege, an emergency, migration becomes in Bertolucci's work a relational matter. The 'embodied uniqueness' of both Shandurai and Kinsky reveals itself as they are looking at each other.[75] Expositive and relational, their 'whoness' is recognized as 'the uniqueness of the existing being [that] presents itself as reciprocal spectacle.'[76] The unrepeatability of beings embodied by Kinsky and Shandurai transforms a discourse on an undefined mass into the story of singular identities that find in film the ideal medium to be 'exposed, external, visible, and manifest.'[77] The audience functions as a witness to such an 'embodied uniqueness' that 'appears to me as I look at you.'[78] In economic and pragmatic terms, since Bertolucci is an icon in international filmmaking, his work can reach larger audiences and repeat his story about 'whoness' that connects an English story to a southern European context, and also to an African narrative of oppression, making uniqueness and singularity global and local at the same time.[79]

Conclusion

The construction of 'whoness' in films about migration provides the possibility of reading a number of films as a concerted attempt to talk back to a rigid construction of the 'whatness' that each migrant inhabits. Films as cultural products contribute to a form of weak resistance against the irremovable prescriptiveness of legal narratives that allow and forbid without granting the right to representation to the subjects of migration. The validity of these acts of resistance lies in the construction of a framework on which future directors can ground their work. It is the future work of other filmmakers that can enact the validity of these initial forms of weak resistance. Complementary to literary constructions of many different embodiments of 'whoness,' film has had the responsibility of constructing a language made of images that responds to the representations of migrants that crowd the television screen every day.

Replacing the representation of an invasion of undocumented, strange, and threatening people often guilty of crimes with narratives about lives of migrants that are at the same time 'same and different' from those of native Italians has been the agenda of many native and non-native filmmakers. They contribute to the possible construction of a map of the processes of cultural hybridization necessary to create a destination culture based on inclusion, not exclusion. Their success depends on the future use of their cultural constructions and on the legal and financial limitations imposed on the creativity of filmmakers. I am referring to the cuts that the *governo* Berlusconi enacted in the Fall of 2002 that limited the partial financing of films with public funding, and to his personal control over private and public television, and newspapers, that belong to his financial empire. Film and television productions are at an impasse: a crossroads of representations cannot be performed if *Un nero per casa* becomes the model for prime-time commercial television. Small-circulation films talk back to the racist portrayal inherent in *Un nero per casa,* but they cannot have any impact on audiences if they are kept out of the mainstream broadcasting channels. This pessimistic forecast for the future of representations of otherness is somewhat mitigated by large-distribution films such as *Lamerica* or *L'assedio,* which create powerful commercial models that challenge representations of difference marked by negative connotations and racist stereotypes.

There is a need, therefore, to explore the relationship between discursive practices in cultural products such as literature and film and the strategies employed by bureaucracy to script migrant identity. This involves analysing the struggle over language and the tropes that are mobilized in time of crisis and are particularly pronounced when migration becomes the emergency to confront. Privileging the space of literature and film is a political move that authorizes the precedence of processes of self-identification. However, such authority validated in the context of literary criticism must confront the problematic space of legal discourse and the majority's defensive rhetoric.

Cavarero's articulation of concepts such as 'whoness' and 'whatness' points toward problematic processes of individuation outside textual specificity and into the problematic context of politics. Her rejection of fragmentation of and in identity reclaims uniqueness and unity as a political stance. It is a philosophy of narration that also claims the individuation of uniqueness in politics. The application of Cavarero's categories of whoness and whatness in the analysis of film narratives is not a re-adoption on my part of an old liberal rhetoric about the fact that we are all unique, but rather a positioning of embodiments of otherness as unique subjects that demand recognition in other public discourses as they claim a position, a space, and a representation. It is therefore necessary to explore the role of the construction of narratable selves in literature and film vis-à-vis the creation of rigid models of alterity that laws and politics impose as dominant.

CHAPTER FOUR

The Laws of Migration

Accanto alle patrie immaginate, vi sono poi quelle reali ...

Remo Bodei[1]

La stabilità della legge consiste nella rete delle interpretazioni che l'hanno via via incarnata nella storia.

Gianni Vattimo[2]

Laws and Culture

In her discussion on the need to privilege unfragmented 'whoness' instead of 'whatness,' Adriana Cavarero creates a category of uniqueness. That uniqueness is a constitutive element in the creation of an 'identity as life story' that must inevitably confront the language of politics and of law making.[3] According to Cavarero, a 'political model constructs its form by constructing at the same time its subject.'[4] It is an 'abstract subject' that renders even a democracy a system grounded on 'politics that speak the language of the what.'[5] Articulating a discourse on difference and individual needs in such a system would change the nature of politics: 'Politics never looks its subjects in the face. For if it looked them in the face, if it took an interest in that spectacular ontology where existing beings appear face-to-face, it would have to renounce a language that, with infinite internal variations, goes back to the 'whatifying' foundation of its own disciplinary statute.'[6] Within politics, the law functions by employing the language of the 'what'; that is, it functions by ignoring that uniqueness at the centre of 'whoness.' Immigration laws aim to regulate and guarantee, to allow and forbid; they function by placing at their centre a subject whose fluid identities change more rapidly than the monolithic body of the law itself can acknowledge. Both the law and politics concern themselves with categories and with the migrant as a 'what' that shares characteristics with other embodiments of 'whatness' and with them become a subject under the law. In particular, the evolution of migration laws in Italy is a history of both deliberate and involuntary misinterpretations of what migration is and who the subjects in migration are. Legal interpretations of migrant identities and political concerns about contemporary 'invasions' deal with migration in anachronistic terms by taking care of the contingent problems that, however, quickly change and necessitate new legislative measures. Migration laws function in a time frame that deals solely with today: they become difficult to modify and are already obsolete the moment they are implemented. They insist on a perception of migration as a temporary phenomenon, while migration is a global issue spanning the past, the present, and the future.

In a discourse on migration and culture, it is useful to look at the tensions that precede the creation of migration laws and the pressures that drive the political agendas of lawmakers. For instance, party lines clash with the contingent need of importing a labour force that can guarantee production in areas such as the north-east of Italy. Umberto Bossi, the leader of the Northern League party, has grounded the ideology of his party on xenophobia, on the economic and genetic superiority of Northern Italy, and on the demonization of the Roman administrative power. His federalist agenda is formulated in protectionist terms: it demands the separation of the North from the rest of the peninsula and goes hand in hand with the demand for stricter measures concerning immigration. Thanks to the establishment of his 'green shirts,' combined with strategies of public oratory based on shouting, Bossi's agenda has appealed to a number of northerners who have accepted his alarmist messages. Bossi appears as the defender of the wealth that the North has accumulated and that – in Bossi's rhetoric – immigrants threaten. To understand the appeal of Bossi's rhetoric, one must go back to the history of places such as the north-east of Italy. In only the past thirty years, this area has shifted from being an economically depressed region, which until the 1970s generated emigration, to being a place now called (often ironically) the Italian economic 'locomotive.' For instance, at the beginning of the third millennium, Vicenza and its neighbouring areas alone export yearly as much as the whole country of Greece. The industries that produce textiles, leather goods, and food in the North, however, could not function without the labour force that immigrants constitute. That those native Italians relying on migrant workers to keep production at such successful levels are also the ones who have bought into Bossi's anti-immigration policy is a phenomenon without a rational explanation. The result is an attempt to perceive the migrant as a worker who should erase 'itself' after the hours of production as 'it' can only be accepted as a 'what' in order to be efficiently used. Bossi's success is grounded on deliberate support for the functionality of such a paradox. The migrant exists to produce in a cultural and legal context that restricts his/her right to integrate outside the workspace. Consequently, his or her duty to produce is accompanied by a duty not to reproduce, have a family, and occupy a cultural space.

The dichotomies between belonging and cultural foreignness, rich and poor, outsider and insider resurface here, but only tell part of the complex story of migrations within an Italian context. In her book *Il sorpasso* (*Overtaking*), Miriam Mafai analyses the economic miracle that took place in Italy in the late 1950s and early 1960s. In order to perform such a miracle, states Mafai, southern Italians migrated to the urban Italian north instead of choosing to migrate to more northern European countries. Often called *Marocchini* (Moroccans) at the time, some southern Italians chose to migrate within the national boundaries because they were unable to obtain the necessary documentation to expatriate. Mafai reminds us that without the *certificato di buona condotta* (the certificate of good behaviour) issued by the parish priest, the migrant became a suspect individual, the carrier of potentially revolutionary ideas, and his or her demands for a passport were considered suspicious. These were the years in which Italy had to prove its alliance to the United States' political and economic directives, years in which Clare Boothe Luce was the American ambassador in Italy, and Communism was THE threat to fight. When expatriation was impossible, internal migration became the other option that turned the Italian *Marocchini* into undocumented migrants. 'These Italians arrived from the South are in fact "illegal,"' writes Mafai.[7] A fascist law of 1939 issued to take a stance against 'urbanization' and in favour of a rural economy 'deprives Italian citizens of the right to choose freely where to reside.'[8] Although the law became unconstitutional since it went against the rights guaranteed by the 1948 Italian constitution, it was still enforceable. It certainly had consequences for the lives of the protagonists of the internal migration in the late 1950s and early 1960s, consequences that are very familiar to today's migrants. Mafai also reminds us that if the internal migrant could not obtain the certificate of residence in the city where he/she had migrated, the migrant could not be legally employed. This allowed some employers to take advantage of the undocumented employees because these 'foreigners' in their own land accepted exploitative employment contracts. The alternative was, Mafai argues, to be 'expelled' and sent back to their towns of residence.

In the years of the economic miracle, the press often presented internal migrants as either savages or potential criminals who disrupted the respectable lives of Milanese or Torinese citizens. Politicians tried, on the one hand, to have the 1939 law revoked but, on the other, struggled with the fact that if the Italian *Marocchini* could acquire residency in one of the industrial cities where they migrated, they would be entitled to vote in local elections. Politicians, therefore, would have had to confront important issues for migrants such as their exploitation in the job market and discrimination in the housing market, problems that are familiar to today's immigrants. There are many parallels that can be drawn between past internal migrations and recent immigrations to Italy. Southern Italians were often welcomed as foreigners who, as Mafai stresses, were seen as exotic and uncivilized others: 'It seems that two or three of the new tenants sleep in one bed. That is true as they use the beds in turns. One sleeps in the bed while his fellow countryman is at work and vice versa. It seems that they don't know how to use the bathroom and that they grow basil in the bidet.'[9] The rhetorical and legal strategies employed against the subjects of internal migration in the late 1950s and early 1960s were a dress rehearsal for the legal and cultural discourses articulated to confront more recent migrations. The same rhetoric and parallel stereotypes have been employed in Italian culture against two different sets of migrants: the 'domestic' migrant protagonists of the Italian economic boom and more recent immigrants from abroad. Their being 'uncivilized,' either because they allegedly grow basil in the bathtub or live in overcrowded dwellings where they own time-shares on the same bed, seems to be the recyclable stereotype. Fluid applications of essentializing formulas have created continuity between past and present anxieties about migrations and migrants.

Italy, Migration, 2002

Within Europe, as of 2002, Italy has one of the lowest concentrations of migrants. About one and a half million people are documented migrants. Statistics vary in evaluating the number of undocumented people present on Italian soil. The national newspaper *Corriere della sera*, in 2002, estimated there were 300,000 undocumented migrants present in Italy.[10] Corrado Bonifazi, demographer at the Centro Nazionale di Ricerca (National Research Centre), asserts that the largest group of documented migrants come from Morocco, followed by Albania, the Philippines, Romania,[11] China, Tunisia, the former Yugoslavia, Senegal, Egypt, and Sri Lanka.[12] The immigrant communities in which men are more numerous than women are those from Egypt, Bangladesh, Pakistan, Algeria, and Senegal. This last case is remarkable since the Senegalese group was one of the earliest communities to migrate to Italy and is still characterized by short-term migration. More women than men are present in migrant communities originating from the Dominican Republic, Russia, Brazil, Colombia, and Ethiopia. Giovanna Meneghel Bellencin reports that 46.8 per cent of migrants in Italy are women.[13] A large number of immigrant women are employed in domestic work and in the care of children and the elderly.[14] In centre north of Italy migrants constitute 3.2% of the population; in the north-east they form 3.1%; the figure increases to 3.7% in the centre of Italy and decreases dramatically in the south, where migrants form 1.1% of the population. In Rome, migrants constitute 5.4% of the local population; in Prato, near Florence, where a large Chinese community has settled, they form 4.8%; and in Milan they form 4.7% of the local population.[15] Statistics reveal that most migrants live in the centre and the north of Italy where the economy is stronger and only a small percentage works in agriculture in the south. Data and qualitative interdisciplinary research are fundamental in defusing the widespread attitude of emergency that colours discussions on migration. Such an interdisciplinary approach opens the possibility of defining the characteristics of migrations to Italy that constitute the motor of change and hybridization in the future of Italian identities.

The web of distribution of migrants and their communities is complicated by two phenomena that coexist in the Italian and European context. One consists of the presence of ethnic concentrations within individual regions: for instance, in Piedmont, Moroccans concentrate in Biella, Albanians in Casale, and Romanians in Turin, creating an ethnic landscape that redefines the political and geographical profile of a region.[16] In Lombardy, Indians live in the Cremonese province, where they often take care of cattle. People from Ghana and Senegal favour the province of Brescia. These groups and organized communities often experience a type of migration, characterized by stability, that extends into the future, involving future generations. The second phenomenon is marked by an instability that involves mobility from one location to the next, in which migration is fragmented into transmigrations dictated by global trends, but also by the lack of structures that can create economic conditions tying the migrant to a specific locale.

As of 2002, Lombardy is the region that attracts the largest number of migrants, followed by Lazio and Veneto.[17] In each region, migrants have transformed the territory. In Veneto, according to Graziano Rotondi, they have revitalized, by settling in, those areas abandoned during earlier e-migrations of native Italians.[18] In Brescia, by contrast, as in many other areas in Italy, migrants concentrate in historical centres, and their presence is used as an indicator of *degrado urbano* (urban blight) as they often accept living conditions rejected by native Italians. Lacking meeting places, besides the religious spaces that migrants have carved out of already existing locations, migrants have occupied specific public areas, often squares, that make their communities visible. They have redesigned and adjusted the use of public space within Italian society to their needs. The proliferation of migrant street vendors, window washers, and flower sellers has also reinterpreted the cultural meaning of city streets, turning them into locations of entrepreneurial activity often stuck in an economy of survival. Therefore, there is a need to articulate a complex approach to discussing how the changing urban face belies a wider change in Italian identity construction. Academics are seeking a method to analyse such changes by appropriating and modifying theoretical approaches borrowed from other Western contexts.

Following Michael Conzen's work on ethnic landscapes, the Italian geographer and literary critic Davide Papotti has focused his work on changed perceptions of the urban space populated by successful ethnic restaurants and modified by the appearance of religious symbols such as the controversial construction of mosques.[19] Papotti explores the changes in the sensorial perceptions of what constitutes contemporary Italian cities and what characterizes the evolution of an Italian identity vis-à-vis migration. His research is particularly relevant to this discussion of law and migration because he employs both the language of the 'what,' in data and the quantitative analysis of what constitutes migration from the point of view of demography and economics, and the language of 'whoness' that interests humanists. By embracing Marc Augé's invitation to re-learn how to think about urban space vis-à-vis the presence of spatially located embodiments of otherness, Papotti attempts to bridge two approaches and formulate a possible future direction of interdisciplinary research in Italian migration studies.[20] His interest in analysing both the politics of ethnic exclusion within an urban landscape and the cultural dynamics within ethnic landscapes represents an ambitious project that defines the role of the academic confronting migration issues. Following Augé's assertion that 'if immigrants alarm the 'natives' so much (often in a very abstract way), it is perhaps because first of all they demonstrate the relativity of certainties inscribed in the soil,' Papotti urges that we analyse what constitutes the majority's cultural identity and find the source of its fear of the other.[21] The fallacy of an original homogeneous cultural identity grounds Papotti's and most academic approaches to Italian migration studies, which borrow from the theoretical approaches in other cultural and linguistic contexts, but still need a unique set of theoretical paradigms that interpret the specific Italian case. It is from an interdisciplinary approach, to which Papotti and others actively contribute, that an innovative approach to Italian migration studies can be developed. In his book *Colonial Desire: Hybridity in Theory, Culture, and Race* (1995), Robert Young asserts that culture develops as 'a dialectical process, inscribing and expelling its own alterity.'[22] The study of Italian culture vis-à-vis migration and alterity has to ground itself in a synchronic and diachronic analysis of the interpretation of sameness and otherness that pre-dates the focus on immigration. By analysing, for instance, the urban space modified by internal migrations in the 1960s and 1970s and the subsequent use of such a space, the studies can identify how much Italian culture has first attempted to expel, and then has inscribed within itself, its internal alterity. The constant and tangible mutability of cultural self-definitions, which are based on distinctions between self and other, lie at the centre of academic investigations; however, at the margins of political and popular media-based analysis, a rhetoric still remains in place that stresses 'expulsion' and thus relegates any possibility of 'inscription' to restrictive and limiting strategies of assimilation.

Unfortunately, the proliferation of complex academic investigations regarding the phenomenon of migration to Italy does not highly impact the political discourses on migration, which tend to define migration simply as a 'problem.' Antonio Ragonesi of the *Associazione Nazionale Comuni Italiani* publicly appealed to academics and requested their intervention to educate the politicians who are assigned to deal with migration issues. Ragonesi made his appeal at the conference *Mobilità geografica in Italia* (Geographical Mobility in Italy) that was held at the Università degli Studi di Trieste in March 2002.[23] His proposal followed generic and uninformed pronouncements by Daniela Carlà, the general director of the Immigration Office, a branch of the Ministry on Welfare headed by Roberto (Bobo) Maroni, a representative of the Northern League Party, who was appointed to that office during the tenure of the *governo* Berlusconi. Carlà's main concern was to endorse publicly a bill on immigration proposed by Umberto Bossi, the leader of the Northern League, and by Gianfranco Fini, leader of the post-fascist party, who had been steering the discussion on migration toward increased on restrictions and on the criminalization of migration. The proposed bill argued for a politics of entry visas connected to labour contracts that, once expired, would automatically cause the visa to expire. Such a bill gave disproportionate power to employers who could then dictate the terms of contract renewals because the migrants would have no leverage in the negotiations. It also potentially privileged migrations as seasonal, that is, as temporary. This would place residency and citizenship out of reach for the 'ideal' migrant, that is, a 'non-person,' a 'what.'[24] The Bossi-Fini bill leads the discussion on migration back to terms very familiar to the restrictive 1939 laws on mobility that fascism had embraced and post-war Italian industrialists had exploited.

The Press and the Law

The texts of the laws become accessible to people through newspapers and magazines that summarize and simplify technical legal language. Created under the ideological influence of the parties in power, laws are subject to an additional ideological manipulation on the part of newspapers. These, in addition, employ sensational language that reduces issues contained in the laws to headlines that stand for the laws themselves. This reduction by summarizing and interpreting has translated immigration laws regulating the lives and the bodies of migrants into alarmist messages that fuel the processes of scapegoating that are aimed at victimizing migrants.

In the winter and spring of 2002, for instance, the reactionary immigration bill proposed by Bossi and Fini was being discussed before a vote, and the press reported on both the main and the corollary debates on immigration. *La Repubblica*, a newspaper with a reputation for its intellectual approach to issues, published an article entitled 'Più difficile espellere i clandestini' ('It Is Growing Harder to Expel Illegal Immigrants'). The headline was preceded by writing in smaller print: 'Decreto urgente dal governo e firmato da Ciampi, anticipando l'approvazione della legge Bossi-Fini' ('Urgent Decree Issued by the Government, Signed by Ciampi, Anticipating the Approval of the Bossi-Fini Law'), and was followed by a subtitle: 'Dopo l'ordine del questore, due giorni per il sì del magistrato' ('After the Stamp of Approval by the Chief of Police, Two Days for the Approval from the Magistrate').[25] Squeezed between a short article about the biggest octopus ever fished, one on the beginning of Easter vacation traffic, and a luxury-car advertisement, the article on immigration described 'the problem' that was spoiling an otherwise happy day marked by a big fish, a vacation, and a dream car. Two pictures illustrated the article on the urgent decree: one of Bossi, the other of two black young men guarded by three policemen. Defined by key words such as 'urgency,' 'expulsion,' 'chief of police,' 'magistrate,' the discussion on migration, even in a news source reputed for its centre-left intellectual engagement, becomes a criminal emergency to be solved by erasing the presence of undesirables through deportation.

In February 2002, Berlusconi's minister of defence, Antonio Martino, proposed making use of immigrants by enlisting them in the Italian army. An article in the widely circulating *Corriere della sera* printed this quote from a politician as a headline: 'Sì agli stranieri nell'Esercito, penso a una brigata di albanesi' ('Yes to Foreigners in the Army, I Am Thinking of an Albanian Brigade').[26] The grammatical error of capitalizing the word army, but not Albanians, indicates a hierarchy of signification in this discussion. The headline presented a way in which a law could make immigrants 'useful' by replacing native Italians in the armed forces. In the same article, the post-fascist Luigi Ramponi reminded readers that if Italians have to enlist foreigners they should choose Eritrean soldiers, who served as colonial forces in the conquest of countries such as Libya. The *ascari* (colonial troops), in fact, fought in the Italian army in the conquest of Ethiopia, for in 1935 Eritrea had been an Italian colony for decades. This horrifying proposal was made possible by a political context created by Berlusconi's reactionary administration, then trickled down to daily commuters through headlines that reproduced a simplistic representation of contemporary migration to Italy and of the issues deriving from a changing Italy.

The re-inscription of the discussion on immigration within a colonialist context was the framework for a public debate on contemporary migration issues and invited the employment of a rhetoric that led Italy back to the fascist era. In the same issue of the *Corriere della sera*, a history of the employment of *ascari* through the centuries appeared next to the discussion on the future of the Italian army.[27] Aware of the offensively outrageous nature of the terms in which the discussion on migration was being framed, the *Corriere della sera* also printed on the same pages an article titled 'Quando "criminale" era il marchio affibbiato ai nostri emigranti' ('When Our Emigrants Were Branded as Criminals').[28] Presenting this issue in his article as the return of the repressed, Gian Antonio Stella discussed the rhetoric employed in Switzerland, France, and the United States to talk about Italian migrants in the first half of the twentieth century. He insisted on highlighting an Italian identity that has been methodically erased from official histories of Italy. However, this call for a revision of the narrative of the Italian past was undermined by the illustrations in the article that portrayed Albanian immigrants in Italy and repressed the visualization of Italians that looked, in their migration, exactly like today's migrants to Italy. Even while softening the racist discourses about migration surrounding the legal debate on a new bill, the performance of what I call a process of recolouring – that is, of dismantling the carefully crafted construction of an Italian whiteness – cannot take place in full view by placing pictures of Italian e-migrants and immigrants to Italy side by side. Unfortunately, it is not the uncovering of the identity of Italians as others that influences the process of law making.

The immigration bill proposed and promoted in 2001–2 by Bossi and Fini (which became law in 2002) articulated itself in opposition to the previous laws in its attempt to create an even more rigid legal structure to contain immigration. It catered to the artificial perception of a European invasion perpetrated by both documented and undocumented migrants. This bill proposed that quotas of immigrants would be decided every November for the following year and restricted the criteria for receiving a *permesso di soggiorno* (temporary residence visa). Seasonal residence visas would be valid for nine months and any other form of visa would be issued in connection with an employment contract. Immigrants with permanent jobs could obtain a two-year renewable visa. The employers would also be required to pay for the expenses of repatriating the migrant if necessary. By tying a migrant to one specific contract, this bill assigned enormous power to the employer, who had the freedom to dictate the terms of a contract renewal that, if refused, could result in the deportation of the migrant. In a short story 'Identità trasversa' ('Transversal Identity,' 2002), Kossi Komla-Ebri lets one of his characters interpret the cruel absurdity of the Bossi-Fini law on employment:

> I haven't had a job for almost two months because the firm I worked for went bankrupt. A man who cannot feed his family isn't a man. Every day I get up and my feet wander tirelessly through streets and gates without finding any solution. If we've thought of going back it is because this law doesn't give us any way out. I should go home and wait to be called to come back to Italy. I know that this is an absurd law, just as no one would buy a knife if it were hidden in its sheathe. But this is their country and they make the law. We have no choice.[29]

The character criticizes a segment of the Bossi-Fini bill, which with limited revisions became law in 2002. The law establishes immigration quotas and limits employers' ability to select their workers. It would be like buying a knife without checking its blade. Komla-Ebri responds to the criminalization of the migrant so prevalent in the media by employing – with irony – this violent imagery. He also focuses on the paradox of a law that does not work even for those employers for which the law has been created. Being able to select employees and to be selected seems to be a basic market element that the Bossi-Fini law has ignored.

According to the Bossi-Fini law, an employer has to guarantee housing for the immigrant, who would in turn take responsibility for paying the rent. Because of the shortage of housing in Italy, demanding that the employer provide housing is an open invitation to developing inadequate temporary living facilities for migrants, for contributing to their subsequent ghettoization, and to slum-lording by employers. The original bill penalized any landlord who did not report housing a 'foreigner' to the local police by fining him or her up to 1100 euros. Once again, migration presented itself as a police issue in the text of the law and the migrant was an entity to be policed by native people whose relationship with the 'others' is regulated by official public-security reports.

This same bill, which handed the police the power to manage the micro-relations between landlord and migrant, assigned to the Navy the duty to patrol the Italian coasts against illegal immigration.[30] While people-trafficking was and is a lucrative business to be stopped at all costs, employing not only the police but also the armed forces would turn migration into a defence issue and the act of migrating a potential national-security issue.[31] Also, employing the military to halt people-trafficking suggests that the main 'victim' is the threatened nation and not the often desperate people who are being exploited by the traffickers. Employing the army to regulate migration is a temptation to which many countries, included the United States, have at times surrendered.[32] However, within the Italian context that has experienced both emigration and immigration it acquires additional meaning. The first article of the Constitution defines Italy as 'una Repubblica democratica, fondata sul lavoro' ('a democratic Republic founded on work'). Article 35, 'riconosce la libertà di emigrazione ... e tutela il lavoro italiano all'estero' ('recognizes the freedom to emigrate ... and protects Italian workers abroad'). One of the rights of an Italian citizen is to find work outside of Italy if he or she cannot find it in his/her own country, where work is a founding republican principle, which suggests that Italian citizens have a constitutional right to emigrate.

I would add that migration is not only the right of a specific individual carrying a specific passport, but rather a human right that allows a person to search for an acceptable life and occupation. It follows that, in principle, regulating access to a country means defending privilege against human rights. This is a pattern that is common to Western countries. For instance, according to the United States' Constitution, any American has the right to pursue life, liberty and happiness. It seems discriminatory not to accept that migration is the human right of people whose survival, and not only happiness, depends on relocation. Employing the army to regulate access to the West openly announces the intention of defending privilege against human rights. The additional paradox that deserves a mention is that if immigrants are enlisted in the Italian armed forces, they may end up occupying the contradictory position of being both the 'problem' and, simultaneously, the means employed to fight that same problem, as embodied by other migrants who attempt to enter Italy. These soldiers would find themselves in a position similar to that of the colonial *ascari* who fought other Africans to defend Italian colonial interests.

My polemical tone points in the direction of a post-nation perspective that, however, finds no voice in the ideologically marked discussions on immigration laws. Post-nation issues have marked the discussions on a unified Europe, although these discussions are always framed by a respect for arbitrary borders, which according to the

Northern League, co-signer of the Bossi-Fini law, should be reproduced even within national boundaries. In a discussion on contemporary Italy, a post-nation discourse needs to be approached by taking into consideration the tension toward fragmented particularities that demand separation between an internal North and South in order to privilege a North that must be part of Europe, but not part of Italy any more. Partially approved in March/April 2004 in the form of additional decisional powers delegated to individual regions, this regional fragmentation has been called 'devolution' even in Italian. The act of employing an English word embodies cultural dilemmas that the term itself is used to describe: the act of devolving involves a proliferation of minor borders that separate regions within a unified Italy. Moreover, while the term points to the need of moving beyond any territorial boundaries, it is used at the same time to define specific Italian micro-nationalisms. In turn, what comes back to unify the regional differences is the need felt even by a separatist party to have a national law that protects regions and the nation from immigration.

The original Bossi-Fini bill attempted to decrease the number of undocumented migrants in Italy by proposing incarceration of up to four years for the undocumented migrant who, after being expelled, crossed the Italian border again without proper documentation. Given that the reasons that prompted the migrants to enter Italy in the first place would not necessarily have disappeared at the time of the expulsion, of course, he/she would attempt to retrace his/her steps. Expulsion for administrative reasons functions in a space of disconnection: the outside into which the migrant should be expelled is separate and unconnected from the forbidden place of the national territory. Besides the biblical undertones inherent in the act of expelling somebody from an elective location, expulsion functions according to outdated concepts of national boundaries and nation states that are not completely separate from that outside space into which the migrant has to disappear.

Using the Navy and more severe punishments to fight 'illegal' immigration to Italy is, anyway, a losing battle because of the geographical location of the Italian peninsula. Because of its 5000 miles of coastline, Italy, and by extension Europe, cannot become impenetrable fortresses against global migratory movements, even if the rhetoric surrounding the aggressive barricading against potential migratory invasions plays an important part in contemporary electoral and political arenas. Migration remains in Italy either a military or a police issue, rather than an administrative one, to such a degree that even the most routine renewal of procedures of a documented migrant's papers are handled at a police station. The Bossi-Fini law augmented the jurisdiction of police stations by further developing already existing, special offices responsible for all procedures relating to the short- and long-term employment of documented migrants and family reunification. By restricting migrants' access to reduced-rent apartments in *alloggi popolari* (housing build in part by public funding), the original bill attempted to deliver the coup de grâce to migrants' rights to re-establish a nuclear family and therefore effect a long-term migration to Italy. Later, the Bossi-Fini law rescinded other previous policies that allowed family reunifications.

This law interpreted documented migration as a temporary privilege. On the one hand, it allows a person to apply for a permanent resident visa after six years of documented residence in Italy while, on the other, rendering it much more difficult for the family of the migrant to join him or her in Italy. Under the Bossi-Fini law, parents may join a son or daughter only if there are no other children in the country of origin who can potentially support them, and a child who is not a minor cannot join a migrant parent in Italy. Restricting family reunification reveals the ideological stance of this law, which interprets migration as an acceptable phenomenon only in so far as it is exploitable and useful in developing the local economy. It articulates the concept of the ideal migrant as a single individual whose ties to Italy are temporary and can easily be severed.

From the point of view of the Bossi-Fini law, migration ought to be temporary as it concerns the Italian economic present and not the Italian cultural future. This law refuses to confront the global phenomenon of migration and the causes that motivate it and focuses on temporary solutions. Once again, the Bossi-Fini law ignored the issue of political asylum. Italy has signed all the international agreements on political refugees, but has never created appropriate laws. Although in the rest of Europe a judge can decide on an application for political asylum, in Italy it is still a *prefetto*, that is, a representative of the political authority, but also a member of the police, who makes such a decision. In the end, the access to the *polis* is regulated by police, as the problematic representative body of a society. In addition, with the Bossi-Fini law people who apply for political asylum have to live in generic 'centri di accoglienza temporanea' (which are in fact detainment centres) that do not cater to their special needs. Surprisingly, the same law improved the law protecting minors.[33] Previously, undocumented minors could be expelled when they turned eighteen. With the new law, they were granted a stay permit provided that they could prove that they have been in Italy for three years, which is often very hard to prove as most of them enter Italy as undocumented migrants. It was one of the few exceptions in which the Bossi-Fini law did not emphasize the temporariness of visas.

Discussions and attempts to 'regularize' workers continue to fail or remain incomplete because the submerged economy of illegal workers has traditionally served the Italian economy very well. The rhetoric of regularization is effective in the electoral arena, but clashes with the economic structures that have exploited migrants with great profit. On 1 March 2002 the financial newspaper *Il Sole 24 Ore* devoted a front-page section to several articles commenting on the Bossi-Fini bill.[34] Particular attention was paid to the amnesty that would follow the approval of the proposed text of the law and would document a number of immigrants living and working in Italy in what is called in Italian *mercato nero*.[35] Besides the predictable negative racial marking of such an expression, the *mercato nero* has been endemic to the history of the Italian labour market and epidemic with regard to the migrants' labour force. This practice of exploitation has been visible with any amnesty that followed an immigration law issued in Italy since 1986. The official number of undocumented migrants who could become documented following the Bossi-Fini law was 43,000.

Usually reliable in its yearly dossier on migration, the Catholic association Caritas predicted 200,000–300,000 applications for documentation. Hiring immigrants is a lucrative practice for employers: in northern Italy irregular workers numbered 1,316,000 in 1999; in Central Italy 1,719,000; and in the South 1,451,000.[36] These figures, which highlight the exploitation of both natives and non-natives, contain a large number of migrants including domestic workers. Housework and the care of the aged, children, or the sick had special mention in the Bossi-Fini law, under which families would be allowed one non-native *collaboratrice domestica*, or COLF, per family with acceptable exceptions for families with special needs. Minister for Equal Opportunities Barbara Fiammeri stated that 'regularizing' domestic workers was 'reasonable' because 'employing immigrant women for domestic work [most domestic workers are women] is a reality for many families and not a luxury any more, but rather a necessity.'[37] Indirectly declaring the failure of the Italian health and welfare system, the minister defined immigration as the only solution to maintain the Western lifestyle to which native Italians have become accustomed. In these articles published in the most prestigious financial newspaper in Italian, what becomes apparent is that Berlusconi's conservative government was rhetorically fighting illegal immigration while, at the same time, being conscious that illegal migration has been a very productive pillar of the contemporary Western economy.

In March 2002 Livia Turco, one of the authors of the 1998 Turco-Napolitano immigration law, expressed her opposition to the Bossi-Fini bill.[38] The Turco-Napolitano law, approved under the tenure of a centre-left administration, confronted considerable opposition because it attempted to align Italy's immigration laws with more strict regulations in the rest of 'fortress Europe.' Turco, a member of the Democratici di Sinistra, an opposition party to the Berlusconi administration, expressed her disagreement with the Bossi-Fini legislative bill in *l'Unità,* originally the communist Italian newspaper, and now still a voice from the left. First of all, she questioned the new policy that would declare the gradual death of the national programs for political refugees. Stating that the new measures were an attack on the constitutional right of political asylum, Turco pointed to the meagre number of refugees in Italy: 8000, compared to the 40,000–50,000 present in France and Germany.[39] According to Turco, disseminating panic vis-à-vis immigration issues is the mission of the Berlusconi administration, although the previous centre-left administrations had, at times, employed the same alarmist rhetoric.[40]

The centre-left newspaper *la Repubblica,* on the front page of its 12 March 2002 issue, contributed to the discussion on the Bossi-Fini law by stressing the criticism voiced by the Catholic church.[41] It added a lengthy article on the tragedies that have marked the trafficking of undocumented migrants who attempted to cross the Mediterranean in unfit vessels.[42] In the hope that another report on the tragic death of migrants would create a grass-roots opposition to the bill, the articles in *la Repubblica* employed language that defined the episode as a 'slaughter' and the people as victims of a new slave trade.[43] On page 2, banking on the impact that tragedies have on the public, the newspaper printed a pie chart showing that 50 per cent of Italians interviewed opposed the Bossi-Fini bill, while 39 per cent still believed the bill was adequate for dealing with migration issues. Thanks to an interview in the same newspaper issue, the Church contributed to the discussion: 'An Accusation from [Cardinal] Ruini against the Government: "Immigration, Erroneous Law."'[44] The Catholic magazine *Famiglia Cristiana* elaborated further on the tragedies at sea and commented on the use of the Navy as an immigration deterrent: an earlier shipwreck near Otranto had, in fact, been caused by a ship of the Italian navy.[45] The article reported that even the minister of Defence, Antonio Martino, had issued a statement declaring that war ships were too big to stop the small and already damaged boats carrying migrants without creating additional danger for the people on board.[46]

The Catholic church expressed its opposition to the Bossi-Fini bill by criticizing the strict connection between legality and work contracts that created a catch-22: 'an immigrant cannot have a contract if he/she is not documented, he/she cannot be documented if he/she does not have a work contract.'[47] An article entitled 'Uomini o topi' ('Men or Mice'), published in *Famiglia Cristiana*, quoted the bishop of Caltanisetta, Alfredo Maria Garsia, expressing the Church's disagreement with the positions on immigration contained in the Bossi-Fini bill.[48] The bishop attacked the bill's position on family reunification, which would corrode the priority of family values as it only allowed minors to join the family in the new country. He criticized the lack of 'an organic asylum law' and the shortsightedness of the bill.[49] Another article highlighted the rhetorical paradox contained in Bossi's crusades against the alleged invasions of undocumented migrants:

> But Umberto Bossi, the Minister of Reforms, runs wild with his hard line against illegal immigrants and resorts to metaphors from the high Middle Ages: 'Without firmness, immigration will be uncontrollable. Hordes would arrive and hordes sweep away everything they find. They impose their rules and their religions. They impose their history and erase ours.' The barbaric allusions are much loved by the leader of the Carroccio [Northern League]. Yet at the recent congress of the League, held at the Palaforum in Assago, there was a club of young members of the Northern League from Cinisello Balsamo, called 'Celtic Horde.' I wonder if they have changed their name in the meantime.[50]

The Church representatives vocally opposed the racist rhetoric behind the Bossi-Fini law, but even the Catholic church's work with the migrants has been highly criticized. In his book *Chiamatemi Alì*, Mohamed Bouchane remembers the pressure exercised by some priests who offered assistance in exchange for conversion. Such testimonies reveal the potential limitation of the Church's role in immigration debates if its attempt is to transform the migrant's 'whatness' into a Catholic 'whoness' that can be interpreted as a Catholic 'whatness' subject to institutional manipulations.

Dated July 2002, the Bossi-Fini law went into effect in September 2002.[51] Its most visible innovation consisted of two separate kits of documentation: one for the regularization of COLF, that is, domestic workers, or *badanti* (people taking care of the elderly and children), and the other for all employees. Such kits could be collected at post offices, where they could also be returned by 10 November 2002.[52] The complex operation of filling in the forms was facilitated by instructional material distributed by the press and by advertisements on televisions that also supplied web sites, addresses, and telephone numbers. The language used to describe the changes brought about by the law employed terms such as the *emersione* (surfacing) of people who work *in nero* (in black, i.e., illegally). The minister of welfare, Roberto Maroni, emphasized that the regularization of employees could be carried out thanks to long-term contracts that could be onerous for employers. Dissent for such a limiting formulation of the new law came from the minister of interior and allowed for a more discretionary interpretation of the law.[53] At a juncture in time when the traditional Italian *posto fisso* was disappearing from the job market, Maroni's reform demanded what the market could not offer any longer. The Northern Leaguers of the Italian north-east also protested against those same restrictions for which their leader Bossi had been fighting. The protest was motivated by the fact that the apple harvest around Trento was in danger because 'useful' Polish seasonal workers had not received a work permit in time.[54] In the end, the members of the Northern League party, who had authored the law, declared the Bossi-Fini law's failure to cater to the needs of Northern League voters.

The regularization of undocumented workers turned, of course, into an amnesty for which the administration tried to establish quotas that conflicted with the more restrictive measures that the Northern League supported. A compromise was reached when Bossi's party accepted the high number of regularizations expected if such regularizations in excess would be subtracted from the quota established for the following year. However, given the fact that in September 2002 no quotas for the following year had been established, the agreement only nominally appeared to establish rigid rules about immigrations.[55]

During the debates on the Bossi-Fini law, the press reported on the increased number of boat people who had reached the Italian southern coast in 2002 as undocumented migrants and on the tragedy of people-smuggling that often ends in death.[56] The Italian coast guard often devoted their time to collecting the corpses whose *emersione* around the Sicilian coast represented an eloquent visual contrast to the social emersion of undocumented workers sanctioned by the new law. Silvio Berlusconi treated the tragedy as an added expense for the Italian state and suggested that 'per raccogliere dei cadaveri i pedalò vanno bene' ('paddle boats are adequate to fish out corpses').[57] The same articles also focused on the paradox between creating laws for a country in which pluricultural migrants live and the attempt on the part of the minister of education, Letizia Moratti, to make the cross a mandatory symbol on the classroom walls in state schools.[58] By ministerial decree, the cross would have had to hang in all classrooms. As it contradicted the most recent Lateran Pacts signed by Bettino Craxi in the mid-eighties, this new decree raised an uproar in defence of the separation between Church and State and was temporarily shelved.[59] The press had the role of reporting on the contradictory and, at times, outrageous decisions of the Berlusconi administration, without forgetting to focus on trivialities such as the election of Miss Africa in Italy, won by the Ethiopian Tezeta Abraham Admassu.[60] Visibility of the other, is in this context, acceptable if it is a product of acculturation (acceptance of Western female objectification, i.e., pageants) and of non-integration (African women have their own pageant).

My analysis of the ideological voices connected to political parties, and identified in various widely distributed newspapers and magazines, reveals how separate such discussions often are from the contingent issues concerning migration. It is not reductive to stress how the issues of immigration confronted by political institutions are disconnected from the issues facing the immigrants themselves. Institutions focus on the needs of the majority and the usefulness of a mass of migrants deprived of their individuality. Debates about migration carried out by political parties ignore data and fuel political agendas and feuds in a rhetoric that is disconnected both from articulations of what is necessary to regulate immigration and from what immigration means for the Italian economy and culture. A statement from Giancarlo Giorgetti, secretary of the Northern League party and political heir to Bossi, illustrates the disconnectedness of politics from concerns about migrations: 'The landing of undocumented migrants in Catania is the result of an operation run by people-smugglers connected to mafia organizations. These organizations get thousands of dollars for each passenger. This casts doubt on the poverty of these people because they can spend tens of millions of lira for a trip to the *Bel-paese*.'[61] Why the country would need strict immigration laws to stop wealthy migrants from entering Italy is a logical mystery and another example of the contradictory rhetoric created to deal with migration issues in the political arena.

The language contained in the quotation is an example of the circularity of the moves present in political discourses that speak to themselves and not to the problems of migration and the connected multicultural developments. A specific conservative rhetoric dialogues with an opposing political rhetoric in a legal verbal game. The resulting language of the law identifies a 'straniero' (a foreigner) as an invader who, unable to vote, remains outside of the political arena. As a result, a law constructed in a contingent political juncture speaks very loudly of the ideological position for which the law was originally written, but ignores the agents of migration and their impact on the local culture. In the end, even the law forms a circular dialogue with another law that was created under a different administration and its political/rhetorical moves, creating a sense of disconnectedness that requires retracing the evolution of the relationship between immigration laws and Italian culture.[62]

The circularity of the law is also complicated by intrinsic ambiguities vis-à-vis ideological affiliations. In 1998 the Turco-Napolitano law, which originated from a centre-left administration, established *centri di permanenza temporanea* where migrants would be kept for up to sixty days while awaiting a solution to a decision on their expulsion case. These concentration centres, highly criticized even in 1998, were later (winter 2004) accused of practices that violated human rights. For instance, without their knowledge, migrants were fed drugs hidden in food and drinks in order to prevent organized disruptions in the centres. As predicted, these centres eventually violated the rights of individuals and, from the outset, contradicted the traditional ideological values of the left. In October 2003 Alleanza Nazionale, which had co-authored the Bossi-Fini law, proposed a bill that would allow documented migrants to vote in administrative elections after living in Italy for at least six years. D'Alema, leader of the Democratici di Sinistra, responded by stating that such a bill had already been designed by his party in 2001. Alleanza Nazionale proposed a bill that was inconsistent with its own ideological affiliation and the restrictive nature of the immigration law it had created, and upset the Northern League, which had co-signed that same immigration law.[63] The ideological contradictions intrinsic in the writing of the law make its *iter* non-linear. Its complexity, therefore, requires the tracing of the history of immigration laws in Italy.[64]

Iter Iuridicus: Italian Immigration Laws

My lengthy discussion of a specific immigration bill, which could quite probably be replaced or modified by the time this book is published, is justified by the fact that I do not believe that the overarching terms employed in legal and political discussions on migration can change very rapidly. Examining the specific Bossi-Fini law with its attendant social implications is also useful in highlighting the Italian case, which shares characteristics with immigration in the rest of Europe, and, at the same time, has differences that become evident in tracing the history of Italian immigration laws.

In 1997 David Christiansen eloquently summarized the genealogy of immigration laws in Italy in an article for the *Georgetown Immigration Law Journal*.[65] He begins by analysing the decree issued by Mussolini in 1931 that required foreigners to declare their presence in Italy to a police station that could issue a 'permesso di soggiorno,' or stay-permit. The fact that during Mussolini's time this decree would be entitled 'Approval of the Laws of *Public Security*' (my emphasis) reveals that at a time of extreme dictatorship, alien presences become suspicious and are automatically an issue concerning public security. Foreigners had to self-report their presence in Italy and their movements throughout the peninsula. At a time when Mussolini was concerned more with emigration of Italians than the meagre presence of foreigners in Italy, 'aliens could be deported for criminal convictions, for failure to comply with reporting and identification requirements or for reasons concerning "the public order," including lack of sufficient means of support. Finally, the re-entry of a previously deported alien was punishable by a prison sentence of two to six months and subsequent re-deportation.'[66] Although Mussolini's dictatorship collapsed in 1943 and ended in 1945, the legal paradigms employed in dealing with immigrations today remain inscribed within the categories of public security, safety, and order. The mediation between migrant and country of migration have remained in the hands of the police. Until 1986 when a new set of immigration laws were approved, 'immigration regulations were dictated by the fascist law on public security and by a long series of administrative acts.'[67] According to the fascist law, it was the responsibility of the employer to report the hiring and firing of a foreign employee, which gave considerable power to the employer and set a trend that still marks contemporary regulations. In the decades following the end of the Second World War, Italy issued 'provisions restricting the prolonged stay of aliens, the regulations essentially forbade legal migration. At the same time, however, aliens could easily enter Italy either with tourist visas or by covertly crossing the porous Italian borders.'[68] Christensen states that the subsequent policy of non-deportation and the already flowering black market economy created 'an illegal employment alternative,' and 'the number of illegal aliens multiplied.'[69]

Christensen summarizes the regulations and administrative decrees until 1986 when the first comprehensive set of immigration laws was finally approved. By 1970 foreigners had to acquire an entry visa and *permesso di soggiorno* from an Italian Consulate. Migration was seen as only a temporary issue (and the Bossi-Fini law has not changed its approach thirty years later, even though migration has revealed itself to be *not* just a temporary issue). Even refugees were only allowed temporary entry visas and 'labor regulations [already] favored Italian and European Community citizens over aliens from other countries.'[70] Very few provisions were being made for foreigners seeking self-employment. Reciprocity regulations required that the country of origin of the foreigners had to offer the same rights to Italian citizens, without taking into consideration the different economic conditions between the country of departure and that of arrival. An anecdote can illustrate this point clearly: Tunisia and Italy had no reciprocity agreements, thus Italians were not supposed to own property in Tunisia, nor could even a legal migrant from Tunisia buy a house or an apartment in Italy. However, when former Prime Minister Bettino Craxi fled Italy to avoid prosecution for corruption in the early 1990s, he moved to Hammamet, where he purchased an enviable sprawl that legally he should never have been allowed to own. The necessity for bilateral agreements was revoked with the Turco-Napolitano bill of 1998.

Starting from 1963, various Italian administrations issued 'a long series of ministerial circulars that significantly restricted the ability of aliens to work in Italy.'[71] This restrictive approach is still in force in the Bossi and Fini bill, which states that an immigrant could enter the country if the employer guaranteed a job and no Italian could fill that position. Once the visa expired it could be renewed by proving full-time employment. If the immigrant was fired he or she was required to leave the country immediately. Of course, this regulation increased the percentage of undocumented employment: migrants would not leave the country after losing the first documented job.

In 1979 and 1982, in order to remedy the undocumented presence of an increasing number of people, the lawmakers issued the first *sanatorie*. In the age of AIDS, the use of such medical terminology in a legal debate is disturbing and suggests that immigration is a potential disease. On the first page of his article, Christensen employs the unfortunate term 'sanitation' to translate *sanatoria* into English. It is, however, a more literal translation than the term 'amnesty' that I employ in my discussion. Thus, within the very text of the law, words used to define migration and migrants (indirectly) refer to the protagonists of migration as contaminating agents that could make the body of the nation ill. That this language is present in the legal vocabulary reveals the widespread acceptance of migration as a lethal disease awaiting a cure.[72] The connections between migration and illness have become all the more powerful because immigration officers like the ones at the Questura Centrale in Rome (Via Genova 2) in 2002 started wearing white gowns, giving a police station the appearance of a hospital. White-gowned officers carrying stacks of immigration folders were not an unusual sight at that Questura. They looked busy nursing, collecting the history of the contamination, and scribbling the country back to health. The decision, probably created by ministerial circular, to issue white gowns was prompted by the Bossi-Fini's bill requirements that migrants' documentation would include their fingerprints and that immigration agents had to protect themselves from the (even metaphorical) stains that the ink could create on their clothes. Therefore, white gowns were employed for the protection of the people in charge of the operation, and the law succeeded in assigning a very specific and visible meaning to the process of documenting. Christiana De Caldas Brito's short story 'Io, polpastrello 5.423' ('I Am Fingertip Number 5,423') describes with humour an invasion of fingertips in Italy that obediently show up to be fingerprinted.[73] The chaos that the crowd of fingers causes at a police station is nothing compared with the chaos caused by the absence of those fingertips from their daily jobs. Life as usual can be restored only when all the fingers can go back to work by disobeying the law. Mocking the law and the language used for the construction of regulations, Brito protests the bureaucratic procedures that inefficiently attempt to document migrants and relegate them to the status of an infection.

Sanatorie are temporary remedies to keep the increase in undocumented workers – that is, the 'progression of the disease' – under control: 'The 1979 program was minor in scope, applying only to aliens employed illegally as domestics and to illegal aliens who had entered Italy prior to December 12, 1979 for non-work reasons and who were seeking employment as domestics.'[74] This says a great deal about the economical and cultural transformations taking place in Italy and within the Italian family. The entrance of larger and larger numbers of women into the workforce created a need for underpaid and overworked people who would replace the underpaid and overworked female members of families who were seeking roles beyond the traditional ones. In the words of David Christensen, the 1982 amnesty was '[a] broader program [that] offered legal status to illegal aliens employed as subordinates in any sector of the Italian economy who had entered [Italy] before December 31, 1981 ... The results of both amnesty programs, though, were considered limited, as bureaucratic inefficiencies and lack of publicity resulted in the legalization of only a small percentage of Italy's illegal aliens.'[75] Italy's pattern of temporary political solutions and shortsightedness concerning the future is evident in the use of amnesties that would later become a habit in the convoluted *iter* of immigration laws. The 1980s were marked by increased illegal employment of immigrants. Christensen estimates that in 1983, the 'black market may account for as much as one fifth of the Italian economy.'[75] Even after taking into consideration that native Italians are not strangers to undocumented employment, external migrants replaced internal migrants in supplying convenient cheap labour.

In his autobiographical best-seller *Io, venditore di elefanti* (1990), Pap Khouma narrates both the limited, underpaid, and undocumented jobs he found in Italy and the way in which immigrants evaded deportation. In the 1980s, Khouma states, immigrants would travel without their documents, and declare an identity using names from their original language that the Italian police would not understand. When they would receive an order of expulsion under that 'foreign' name, the immigrant would dump the expulsion order in the garbage can nearest to the police station and continue their undocumented lives in Italy. Identity cards and a Western system of naming was undermined by the use of languages foreign to the bureaucratic system employed in tracing foreign presences on the Italian soil. *Fogli di via* (expulsion orders) increased the bureaucratic workload and failed to make expulsion an efficient way to deal with immigration. In 1998 the Turco-

Napolitano law allowed the creation of centres where migrants who appealed the expulsion order were detained. Considering the historically frightening connotations involved in the establishment of detention camps, an uncharted legal territory, and the slow pace of Italian justice, this solution creates a questionable precedent awaiting a complex resolution. Of course the Bossi-Fini law complicated the issue even further by extending the term for detention in these centres to sixty days.

Vaifra Palanca states that the first 'important' immigration law in Italy was approved in 1986 and called the 'Foschi law.'[77] Grounded in article 1 of the Italian constitution, which defines Italy as a republic founded on work, the 1986 immigration law has an 'impostazione fortemente lavoristica' (is mainly concerned with labour issues).[78] This law declared equal rights for documented immigrant workers and their families and native Italians, and the migrants' right to representation. However, after declaring equal treatment, this law established an additional 1 per cent income tax for immigrant workers, with the funds earmarked for deportations. This law ratified the right to family reunification, articulated the need to establish quotas of documented immigrants to be allowed entry into Italy, and removed the controversial provision that a stay-visa automatically expired if an immigrant lost his/her job. Unfortunately, it lacked a vision for the future of the country vis-à-vis immigration. Christensen adds:

> Rather than being approved before a plenary session, Law 943/86 became a law after committees of the Senate and the House approved a backroom deal between the Christian Democrats and Communists, who favored the legislation, and the neo-fascist MSI [Movimento Sociale Italiano] party which initially dissented. Thus, it was not until 1989, with the passage of the Martelli Law, that Italy enjoyed its first public legislative debate over immigration.[79]

The failure to understand the impact that immigration would have on the future of a strong Italian economy and of a changing culture and the failure of legislators who were unable or unwilling to understand the phenomenon precipitated additional undocumented immigration to Italy. The number of undocumented workers increased considerably in the late 1980s, which was accompanied by the first racist episodes of violence against immigrants. In their book *La memoria di A.* (1990), Saidou Moussa Ba and Alessandro Micheletti narrated the true story of

Jerry Masslo, an immigrant from South Africa who had thought Italy would be a safer country than his native land. His 1989 murder brought to the surface the widespread alarmist attitude against the invading hordes of Africa's poor and the fear of a threat to Italy's traditional way of life. Of course, this racist rhetoric found fertile ground with the Italian extreme right-wing parties, which used it as a springboard for their electoral successes at the beginning of the third millennium. Alarmism was also sustained by the consequences that unregulated migration had on the role that Italy attempted to play in the formation of a unified Europe. As Christensen argues:

> Italy's inability to curb the growth of illegal immigration made its association with the Schengen group problematic because the other signatories to the agreement did not want to open their borders to Italy's illegal immigrants. Consequently, although Italy ratified the Schengen accord in November 1990, the borders between Italy and its neighboring Schengen Group partners remain closed due in part to Italy's profound illegal immigration problem.[80]

Of course, instead of politicians focusing on their failures in dealing with immigration issues over the previous two decades, immigration was cast as the obstacle that impeded Italy's full participation in the first step to European unification. Instead of assuming a mediating role between the demands of restricting immigration from other European countries and the demands of Italy's unique position as a crossroads in the Mediterranean, Italy firmly defined itself as a member of the First World that has to defend itself against immigration.

However, a few of the Italian immigration laws reveal inherent tensions originating from an attempt to create a compromise between a well-established left-wing tradition of ideological solidarity with the oppressed and the protectionist stance of rich industrialized countries. Pap Khouma, who arrived in Italy after realizing that France and its established immigrant communities had rejected any new immigration, experienced the emancipatory stance in Italy's 1990 immigration law. In his novel, Khouma writes at length about the 1990 Martelli law. An undocumented street vendor in Milan, his protagonist remembers seeing posters advertising the new law and the subsequent *sanatoria*. Because of his knowledge of Italian, he seized this opportunity provided by the well-publicized law and spread the news throughout his community. This law achieved visibility via street posters that the 1986 one had not even tried to attain. Khouma emphasizes the ability of the migrant to interpret the legal narratives about new laws in order to modify his or her own irregular identity within Italy. It is an ability grounded in the acquisition of a new language that would allow mediation between immigration agents and the migrants themselves. Because of his knowledge of Italian, Khouma in fact became the mediating agent first for the small community with which he was living and later for the Senegalese community in Lombardy. The need to occupy an interpretative position vis-à-vis legal and culture texts has also resulted in the proliferation of newspapers in foreign languages that mediate between the law and the migrant in interpreting the procedures of regularization of the new Bossi-Fini law of 2002. In September of that year, an attachment to the financial newspaper *Il Sole 24 Ore* explained the new law in Italian. The Albanian *Bota Shqiptare*, the Arabic *Nur, Il Tempo EuropaCina*, and the Rumanian *Gazeta Romaneasca* were a few among the eleven Roman newspapers that explained the new regularization procedures to migrants in other languages.[81] Echoing the long tradition of Italian newspapers published all over the world by Italian migrants in the world, contemporary migrants in Italy appropriated a space that is familiar to an Italian tradition.[82] Once more, they bring to the fore the tensions inherent in transforming a country of emigrants into a country of immigration.

According to Christensen, in 1990 the Vice–Prime Minister Claudio Martelli 'advocated a "tolerant" law, recognizing Italy's "duty to help the development of the South of the world and to welcome its population in Italy."'[83] For the Italian reader, the name of Claudio Martelli is closely connected to that of Bettino Craxi, the man who led the Socialist party to power in Italy and to its demise in the early 1990s. The corruption of the Craxi administration notwithstanding, Martelli's approach to the creation of a new immigration law in 1989–90 was grounded in the core principles of the Italian left and focused on the subaltern masses rather than the interests of a defensive majority. He was willing to set aside alarmist rhetoric to institute a rather liberal immigration statute at a time when the rest of Europe was transforming itself into a fortress. The Martelli law embodied the attempt to remain faithful, even through a time of political compromise, to the ideals of equality that had been a founding principle of the Italian left. At that juncture, marked historically by the collapse of the Berlin Wall and the crises of the European left-wing parties, the Italian left attempted to translate into the law some of its theoretical core principles. Wiped away by scandals and by the post–Berlin Wall redefinition of left-wing ideologies connected to party lines, the Martelli law remains one of the last (although flawed) legacies originating from the Italian left in the first Republic.[84]

Loud opposition to the Martelli law came from the right, in particular from the small Republican party, which was exploiting the widespread anti-immigrant sentiment. This, of course, affected the final version of the Martelli law. After politicians curbed its more liberal tendencies, the Martelli law, or Law 39/90, was approved. This law 'disfavor[ed] the poor and other undesirable classes of aliens' so no huddled masses could be granted entry to Italy unless they could prove they had a sponsor or a job contract.[85] The new law relied, in fact, on old regulations concerning both entry visas for immigrants and their stay in Italy. However, the renewal of a stay-permit became more flexible, as it was not strictly linked to a work contract: the immigrant had to demonstrate that he/she was earning an income that was equal to a state pension. In addition, in order to cater to possible changes in a migrant's status, the Martelli law allowed some flexibility in changing visas (i.e., from a work visa to a study visa). Although deportation remained regulated according to previous laws, the Martelli law introduced the right of asylum for persecuted people. The law was grounded in the Geneva Convention of 1951, ratified by Italy in July 1954.

Finally, the Martelli law deliberately distanced itself from the 1931 fascist law by repealing portions of it. It recognized the plight of refugees, continued the practice of periodic amnesties, and took into consideration, for the first time, the rights of self-employed immigrants, although only for those immigrants whose country of origin recognized the same rights for Italian citizens. It ratified the process for acquisition of Italian citizenship for both incoming immigrants and descendants of Italian migrants abroad. Finally, it introduced norms regulating the entry visas for family reunification, thus creating an identity for migrants not only as a workforce, but also as carriers of a culture whose human rights should not be violated.

Even with the increased fines and stricter deportation regulations, which were intended to decrease undocumented migration to Italy, the number of undocumented migrants increased. At the beginning of the 1990s, changed historical and economic conditions in countries such as Albania, the fall of the Berlin Wall, the final demise of the separation of East and West, African wars, and the Kurds' flight from persecution brought additional waves of migration that probably no immigration law, however comprehensive, could have confronted. In the early 1990s, acts of racist violence in Italy escalated and prompted the creation of 'urgent' laws against racial, ethnic, and religious discrimination. These 1993 laws declared the state's right to prosecute those who incite violence and who discriminate for racial, ethnic, or religious reasons. They forbade the creation of any movement, association, or group that promotes discrimination and racial violence, and they increased the sentence for crimes inspired by racial hatred. Fifty-five years after the promulgation of the fascist racial laws, Italy finally issued a complete legal text in opposition to the 1938 legal act that discriminated against the Jewish minority in Italy and legally penalized miscegenation in Italy and the Italian colonies.

In 1995, the Dini decree responded to pressures from parties such as Bossi's Northern League to establish stricter deportation regulations and attempted to appease the *Democratici di sinistra*, which opposed such regulations, by granting a new amnesty. The Dini decree added new laws for seasonal workers, severe sanctions for people-smugglers, and 'a penalty of up to six months incarceration for the failure of aliens to provide police with proper identification.'[86] The subversive game of supplying false identities described by Khouma was officially over and was replaced by a criminalization of 'undocumentation.' What was formerly an administrative issue became a crime leading to incarceration. Alessandro Dal Lago affirms that the 1995 Dini decree allowed the deportation of migrants guilty of misdemeanours without allowing them the possibility of an appeal. He adds that 'the decree has constituted a turnaround in legal and cultural policy in Italy. In fact, it transferred to the police the handling of real and imaginary micro-conflicts created by immigration'[87] However, in trying to curb the number of undocumented migrants, this decree failed as the ones before it had. The Dini decree revealed its inadequacy and the need for a new legal debate that would reflect the developments in global migration movements.

The Turco-Napolitano, or 40/98, law and the legislative decree 286/98 established new quotas for people allowed to enter Italy legally, attempted to fight undocumented immigration, and tried to introduce the right to vote for documented immigrants.[88] However, that would have involved a revision of article 48 of the Italian Constitution, declaring that 'sono elettori tutti i cittadini' (all voters are citizens), which makes citizenship the *conditio sine qua non* for voting in both national and local elections. In an attempt to protect minors (children of immigrants) the law expanded the family-reunification right to unmarried parents, supplied basic health services for minors, and protected their right to an education.[89] The Turco-Napolitano law introduced measures to protect the victims of trafficking, such as prostitutes, whose trips to Italy were paid by the people who would then exploit and enslave them. Discrimination based on religion, race, or national origin became punishable by law so that employers or landlords could not discriminate against immigrants. Even though the law originated from the centre-left administration in power, the new bill continued developing the restrictive measures in previous laws by establishing a *fermo amministrativo*, that is, an administrative arrest for people who could not be immediately expelled (if their case is under appeal, for instance). The 286/98 decree reaffirmed a *politica delle espulsioni*, according to Dal Lago, 'and introduced internment camps, deceptively called "centres for temporary stay," for foreigners awaiting expulsion.'[90] This measure would prevent migrants expecting extradition from going underground among other undocumented migrants. At the same time, this law attempted to remain faithful, at least in part, to the principles behind the original Martelli law, as it addressed human rights such as education, legal and civil representation, health services, and humanitarian asylum for refugees.

Carlo Brusa underlines how the 1998 law contained two different and traceable geographies: one of exclusion and one of social citizenship. The geographies of exclusion are those processes that discriminate among immigrants according to directives determined by the text of the law. Such geographies do not concern European citizens, but rather those who attempt to enter the country without proper documentation and those who are alleged criminals: 'The "geographies" of exclusion culminate in rejections at the borders of foreigners who are without the required documentation to enter the territory of the State (art. 9) and in deportations, in the name of public order or state security, of illegal immigrants or immigrants with prison records.'[91] The notion of investigating the law that constructs, in geographical terms, imagined communities allows the creation of the concept of geographies of social citizenship, which Brusa borrows from Tesfahuney's work in migration studies.[92] Even if the law determines what rights make up social citizenship (health, pension, unemployment, housing, education), such rights still confront contingent problems. For instance, the law guarantees that documented migrants have the same right as Italian citizens to obtain low-income housing. However, because of a shortage of housing, native Italians loudly protested, and politicians responded to voters' indignation, preventing the law from being translated into practice. Even within a geography of inclusion, social citizenship can often remain an unreachable goal, and that very unobtainability then turns into law at the hands of right-wing politicians such as Bossi and Fini.

As recently as 1996, Guido Bolaffi considered the Italian right a minor player in political issues concerning immigration:

> With regard to immigration, it would be unjust and ungenerous if we did not recognize that up to now the Italian right has behaved with relative moderation and prudence, in spite of its guilty involvement in serious episodes of xenophobic intolerance. It is an anomaly that has been left relatively uninvestigated as the limited research on the subject show. Many attributed the reason for such an anomaly to the right-wing parties' fear of returning to a political ghetto where the old (*sic*) fascist roots had trapped them, adding the prudent influence of the Catholic culture on an authoritative section of their electorate, and the relative weight that xenophobia has on their ideology.
>
> This is a combination of factors that makes it difficult, if not actually prohibitive, for the Italian right to think of using the question of immigration to its advantage, turning to the populist cynicism employed by le Pen in France or by Haider in Austria.[93]

Bolaffi's optimism was fuelled by the conviction that the Catholic church could play an important role in mediating extremisms and that the Italian model could avoid the frightening renaissance of the power of right-wing fanaticism. However, he had not taken into consideration that collaboration between Catholic volunteer organizations and government administrations could not replace the rhetorical strategies of scapegoating that are as enormously successful in Italy as in France or Austria. He also did not expect the electoral success that the right would have in the new millennium with the return of Berlusconi as prime minister and the increased popularity of politicians like Le Pen in France.[94] In 2001, Bolaffi's optimism confronted the legislative failure of dealing with immigration. He argued that '[i]mmigration must be kept out of the electoral and political arenas, meaning that its manipulation by political parties can seriously damage democratic laws.'[95] This utopic approach to solving the problems of a new multicultural country displaces the political debate and generates electoral campaigns that find parties on opposite warring sides. Bolaffi himself recognized the failure of the political institution to create 'a new social pact, *between us and them* [original emphasis], that consists of rights and duties, a pact that can grant those immigrants who so desire and deserve to move from the condition of being foreigners to the condition of becoming new citizens.'[96] However, a new social pact based on dichotomies of 'us-ness' and 'them-ness' is again doomed to failure and ends up being trapped in the right-wing discourses that it attempted to challenge.

In his book *L'immigrazione straniera in Italia* (*Foreign Immigrations to Italy*, 1998), Corrado Bonifazi stresses that policy-making with regard to migration has had to mediate pressures from contrasting parties, which has resulted in the contradictions inherent in, for instance, the Dini decree. In the 1990s, the collapse of traditional political parties and the disappearance of the political currents that had guided Italy's politics since the end of the Second World War were, according to Bonifazi, among the reasons why the Italian model of immigration policy-making was based on emergency procedures and laws that took care of present issues and ignored the future development of the phenomenon. Like the rest of Europe, Italy was and is mainly concerned with fluxes of irregular migration. Even after recognizing that undocumented migrations cannot be completely controlled, Bonifazi suggests that continuing a policy of collaboration with the main countries from which migrations originate (Albania and Maghreb, in the Italian case) could help Italy and Europe. One must also remember, however, that the money that migrants send to their families abroad always exceeds the amount of financial aid that Western countries allocate for developing countries. In addition, money sent to families is directly administered by their members, while money received by individual governments is often mishandled.

Eliminating unreasonably strict measures linking family reunification and the renewal of stay-permits for migrants already present in Italy could prevent documented migrants from becoming undocumented. While in theory Italy has legislated and financed programs aimed at acculturating migrants, programs that respect migrants' cultural identities, the translation into practice of such projects has either failed or revealed methodological problems in teaching a language and a culture. The opposition between 'us' and 'them,' superior and inferior cultures, continues to plague Italy and other Western cultures.

Law and Literature

The actual voice of the subject of migration – the immigrant – is noticeably absent from the circular process by which laws governing migration are formed and filtered. Laws connect with or react to previous ideological stances that informed the creation of other laws that, in turn, often responded or conformed to the rhetoric of political campaigns that were in dialogue with specific translations of the law communicated via the press. Even if representation appears as an important element in decrees and bills, the migrant remains silent, as his/her voice is enclosed in a space of otherness that inhabits the interstices of both the public and the private spheres. The problem of appropriating a space that can talk back to the text of the laws that regulate one's life and body is at the centre of the first narratives that immigrants wrote in Italian. By using texts as a way to 'talk back,' immigrant writers concur with Bourdieu's assertion:

> It is possible to resist the violence that is exerted daily, with a clear conscience, on television, on the radio and in the newspapers, through verbal reflexes, stereotyped images and conventional words, and the effect of habituation that it produces, imperceptibly raising, throughout the whole population, the threshold of tolerance of racist insults and contempt reducing critical defenses against pre-logical thought and verbal confusion ..., insidiously reinforcing all the habits of thought and behavior inherited. [97]

After the well-publicized Martelli law of 1990, a number of undocumented migrants wrote themselves into public existence by telling their life stories. Pap Khouma, just to mention the best-known example, narrated his role as community mediator in *Io, venditore di elefanti.* He was able, because of his knowledge of Italian, to interpret the posters and disseminate the news of the amnesty that could grant other Senegalese immigrants legal status. The right to acquire visibility allowed them to construct their lives outside the parameters of 'illegality,' and rid themselves of the constant fear of the *carabinieri* (police).

Often accused of being removed from the tangible problems of life, literature embodies here the only alternative to specific parameters in public representations. Literature initiates a discourse in which the migrant is not only the 'foreigner' that appears in the law, but also a speaking subject beyond the role of cipher in numerical immigration quotas. While the law confronts migration and the migrant as problems, treating people as problems, Mohamed Bouchane writes of the problems inherent in being a migrant, but places the roots of such problems within a host culture that wants to defend itself from difference (*Chiamatemi Alì*). A bricklayer, Mohamed is renamed Mario, but rejects this christening by claiming for himself the name Alì, easier for Italians to pronounce as it appears in the orientalist versions of Middle Eastern tales. The problem for him lies in the exploitation of his work, in the rigidity of the work structures that make it difficult for him to find time to pray, and in the impossibility of finding a place to live.

Once again, I need to reiterate a fundamental issue that surfaces frequently when talking about migration literature. Traditional Italianists would downgrade the texts written by migrants to being non-literary expressions of autobiographical or semi-autobiographical experiences that have no place in a canonical classification of the narratives that define Italian literature. This protectionist approach to literary studies has a place in very normative approaches to aesthetics and runs the risk of limiting the role of literature in interpreting the culture in which it interacts. If we consider Benetta Jules-Rosette's statement that 'literature reflects society on many different levels,' migrants' uncanonical literary exercises become the key to revealing the connections between Italian culture, law, and literary expression, at a particular junction in time.[98] In his studies on second-generation migration literature in France, Alec Hargreaves has both investigated the connections between social experiences and literary expression and warned against making them simplistically.[99] However, if we return to my own identification of migrants' writing as an act of talking back, literature authored in the past ten years by Pap Khouma, Saidou Moussa Ba, and all the authors who followed accomplishes the goal of narrating selves that decriminalize migration. Collectively, they supply an alternative rhetoric that places migration outside the realm of protectionist discourses that demand regulations and boundaries. Out of line and out of bounds, they are in contempt of both literary canons and regulatory legal measures. In literature, migrants object to being an 'object' in legal discourses. The initial texts that narrated first-hand experiences of migration took the liberty of writing otherness from within a linguistic context that defined immigrants as foreigners. Dominant identity politics that assign to the migrant the ability to speak in broken Italian find themselves challenged in Salah Methnani's *Immigrato*. Methnani came to Italy with a university degree in languages and learned Italian rapidly, which made him suspicious to native Italians who rejected heterogeneity in migrants and preferred to imagine them as a homogeneous, 'inferior' cultural mass. He internalized such identity politics in order to simplify his daily struggle for survival and spoke in broken Italian, but talked back to such an imposition with an autobiographical narrative that placed his linguistic abilities in plain sight and in dialogue with other narratives. Migrant authors appropriate the foreign language in which laws that regulate migrants' lives are written. That language serves the purpose of constructing narrative transgressions and of creating representations that challenge the text of the law and its finality in shaping the limiting roles that the immigrants can embody. The literature that migrants write is, therefore, in dialogue with the cultural constructions they find in place in Italy and questions the future of a culture that legally attempts to exclude or dramatically contain difference.

In cultural studies, we can investigate the 'social power of popular forms of textuality' that supply a plurality of meanings for what the law has tried to rigidly regulate.[100] Salah Methnani recounts in cathartic tones his internalization of the concept of migrant as a criminal and his becoming involved in drugs. He fulfils the expectations of a socially reinforced stereotype of the migrant primarily as a potential criminal. Narrating his self as breaking the law, he absorbs a stereotype and places it in a context that also contains a plurality of other identities that he embodies. Rosemary Coombe asserts that 'if law is central to hegemonic processes, it is also a key resource in counter-hegemonic struggles.'[101] Texts written by migrants internalize the assumption of a migrant's criminal potential and of the legal criminalization of migration that is always an issue of public security, but they inscribe that experience within a life story that cannot dehumanize the migrant to a reductive entity to be expelled, but deals with the 'whoness' of the individual who is in trouble with the law.

Within this context, the law functions as another text that can be talked back to, that can be toyed with, and that can be used literally and manipulated. If the law places the migrant in a passive position because his/her presence is accepted only conditionally, the literary narrative of a migration experience imagines the possibility of depriving the law, the police, or the *carabinieri* of agency. This is particularly relevant in texts authored by immigrants in prison. Yousef Wakkas repeatedly participated in the Eks&Tra literary award for immigrant writers and submitted his pieces from prison. He wrote about the violence involved in crossing those borders that cannot be legally crossed and of the experience of breaking the law by fragmenting the grammatical rules of the Italian language and talking back to linguistic laws.[102] Writing from prison involves occupying the position of the migrant who has fulfilled all the negative expectations about the role of the other within Italian society. What the migrant writer accomplishes from his prison cell is to remain an agent in the construction of his own 'whoness' that talks back to that 'whatness': prisoner, criminal, prostitute, other, which is only a part of who he or she is.[103] In a land that has known terrorism, Hassan Itab's autobiographical text written in prison talks with Italian history and describes the process of becoming a fighter for the Palestinian cause. In *La tana della iena* (*The Hyena's Den*) Itab tells of his life as a Palestinian boy, as a terrorist, and as a prisoner in Italy. He embraces autobiography to exist outside of the texts created both by newspaper reports and by criminal records. Complementing his 'whatness,' which is his identity described in articles and documents, his autobiography vindicates a right to 'whoness' on which he can construct his life after prison. Jadelin Mabiala Gangbo practised a narrative form that pushed the boundaries in the representation of violence, describing migrants as criminals in his novels and making them untamable by the rules of a dominant culture. Wakkas, Itab, and Gangbo script the crime of breaking and entering into Italian culture and the public sphere of literature.[104] The construction of 'whoness' in literary texts that embody the crime of writing and the crime within writing highlights the illusionary nature of any construct that attempts to create a totally controllable 'whatness.'

Interpreting the law becomes therefore a strategy for constructing a dialogue that challenges positions of power. It places the author of the text, the migrant, in the position of an agent able to imagine a manipulation, through interpretation, of legal regulations that have placed him/her in the position of object. Within immigration laws the migrant, repeatedly defined as *straniero* ('foreigner,' but in Italian also 'stranger'), remains trapped in a text that defines itself always as definitive but, in actuality, embodies an inevitable temporariness evidenced by the frequency with which Italian immigration laws have been created.[105] In his *Acts of Resistance*, Bourdieu states that 'one still needs to rethink the question of the status of the foreigner in modern democracies, in other words of the frontiers which can legitimately be imposed on the movement of persons in worlds which, like our own, derive so much advantage from the circulation of persons and goods.'[106] That circular structure of discourse that involves a dialogue among legal texts, political discussion, party lines, and sensationalism in the press stands in opposition to the circulation of people, or at least of those people who qualify not only as foreigners but also as others. The identity of the 'stranger' in the law is rigidly defined, but still open to redefinition in the text of the next law. In fact, a law is the law until its absolutist stance is replaced by another legal text. 'Dragging' the law into a narrative context allows the migrant to acquire that agency which, being an alien without the right to vote and therefore the right to count, he/she cannot have. The literary space is a privileged context of creative manipulations that exposes the contingent and transient value of the word in the law and makes interpretation the connecting strategy between literature and law.

Consequently, such a connecting strategy invites a consideration of the law as a text to which the laws of literary criticism can apply. It is necessary to challenge the laws that define what literature is and reject definitions based on rigid aesthetic values. In addition, placing the law next to literature deprives the law of its aura of objectivity and universalism. Seeing the text of the law from the point of view of literature highlights the role of interpretation as the signifying link between legal and narrative constructions. In their book *Literary Criticism of Law* (2000), Binder and Weisberg argue that 'we should recognize that the literary is intrinsic to law in so far as law fashions the characters, personas, sensibilities, identities, myths, and traditions that compose our social world.'[107] In such a context 'law [is] a cultural datum and [we] can analyze legal processes as arenas for generating cultural meaning.'[108] Such meaning is traceable through the interpretative processes carried out by the press, which reads the text of the immigration laws as a way to create a rhetoric of emergency that sells in the publishing market. The political arena interprets and writes the law intertextually, that is, by creating a dialogue with other texts that are also party lines. The texts authored by the migrants set up an intertextual relation with the text of the law in order to undermine the normative legal textual structure and tell a different story from the one that the laws tell. Laws tell the story of a country's defence against unwelcome people in migration; immigrants' texts trace the history of migrants, their relation to the laws that regulate their access to Italy, and their 'whoness' that disappears in the law. Immigrants' writings also show the laws as limited texts, deprive them of their pretense of universality, and reveal the cultural anxieties that validate restrictive laws. Immigrants' texts critique and revise 'particular narratives embedded in law, and the identities and institutions these narratives enable.'[109] Thus, if the law attempts to construct itself as a closed text, migration literature is that intertextual tool that allows the reader to reread the normative and limiting laws about migration and to contest the way migrants are represented in them.

Stanley Fish's work on literature and law is particularly useful in interpreting the relationship between the two textual contexts. Migration laws in Italy attempt to create rigid definitions of the identities to which the migrants can aspire. Its rigidity, however, is subject to different 'interpretative authorities.'[110] One interpretative approach is performed by a set of readers who translate the law into practice: lawyers on the one hand and policemen on the other. In Italy the police's discretion in applying immigration laws has played a decisive role in regulating entrance to Italy. A chain of interpretation welcomes an interpretative approach from the press and the various religious and lay associations that explain the law on behalf of the migrants. Migrants' approaches to the law are, therefore, often mediated by other interpretative sources that separate the migrants' literary acts of talking back to the laws from the original texts of the law. These 'related forms' of interpretation condition the construction of acts of talking back authored by migrants who are interpretative agents within the constraints put in place by an intertextual structure of reading.[111] If 'interpretation is a *structure* of constraints ... which ... renders unavailable the independent or uninterpreted text and renders unimaginable the independent and freely interpreting reader,' then literary acts of talking back are both connected to other interpretative processes and impose alternative processes of identification of the subject/object within the law.[112] Consequently, migrants' literary efforts invite a rereading and a reinterpretation of legal texts and of representations of migrants in the texts of the law and in the press. The presence of migrants' texts also intervenes by interrupting the complicit and circular dialogue between dominant legal and journalistic discourses. In the act of writing, a migrant claims the equal role of interpretative authority.

This does not mean that literature can in any tangible way deprive the police of agency. Standing in line and applying for visas proves, without any doubt, where the power of translating the text of the law into practice lies. However, literature represents the position of the subject that is deprived of agency by standing in line, but not in writing a/his story. As Bill Ashcroft affirms, literature allows the portrayal of changing subject positions that opens up the 'horizon of place.'[113] While the law produces migrants through a prescriptive practice, literature legitimizes instability in the creation of the subject and its position in migration.

Nassera Chohra's autobiographical text is particularly relevant in a discussion on literature and law. Her *Volevo diventare bianca* (*I Wanted to Become White*) challenges any preconceived idea about the subjects of migration and the story of transmigration, for she delineates the latter as a non-linear process of multiple migrations that cross generations. Her autobiographical narrative contests any legal definition of migration and migrants as concepts connected to only one national context and one set of legal identity papers. While laws are still constructing a linear model suggesting that all migrations originate from 'one' country and end in 'another,' Chohra describes the journey of an Algerian French woman who leaves her native country, France, to perform another act of migration to Italy, where she arrives as a European citizen. Her re-migration and identity re-definition through languages and culture challenges any simplistic identification of otherness with citizenship and legal status. Her narrative is fraught with tension about belonging and not belonging to a cultural context in which she grew up, and with her unerasable difference through which her identity is defined by the Italians she encounters. However, 'how can we speak of immigrants,' writes Bourdieu, 'to refer to people who have not "emigrated" from anywhere and who are moreover described as "second generation?"'[114] Within a first generation of immigrant writings, Chohra inscribes the concerns and the identities of subsequent generations who embody the inherited experience of migration from their parents and resist any facile identification of themselves as complete outsiders to the European culture in which they came of age. Chohra's transmigration claims the right to a mobility granted to a majority in Europe and, at the same time, creates the context in which she can inscribe herself in a first generation of migrants in Italy, to which she belongs and from which she feels simultaneously at a distance.

In her very political text, Chohra unveils the problem of assigning normative identities: her 'Arabness' was always questioned in France, as the colour of her skin did not conform to the stereotype of what an Arab woman should look like, of what an Arab woman is. By performing themselves in texts, migrant writers moved the discourse on migrants from 'what' to 'who' they are, but their literary 'whoness' only occupies a narrative margin in Italian culture. From that margin they attempt to talk back to other texts, but their resistance can only be weak, as it reaches a limited number of readers. The subaltern can speak if conditions allow for his or her voice to emerge. However, the creation of immigrant voices does not go hand in hand with a creation of a reading public. Dozens of books belonging to different genres have talked back to the rigidity of the legal language and of its translation into practice, and to the language of the press and its stereotyping of migrants, but they have failed to develop a dialogue that can reach a large number of people.

My concern for the position of the law in the contemporary Italian culture is validated by two books published at the beginning of 2003. They frame the context in which my discussions on literature and law takes place and define what is at stake in opening a discussion on law, citizenship, rights, and difference at a specific time in history. The first book is Jacques Derrida's *Force de loi. Le 'Fondement mystique de l'autorité'* (1994), translated into Italian as *Forza di legge. Il 'fondamento mistico dell'autorità'* (*The Force of the Law. The 'Mystical Foundation of Authority,'* 2003). Following Montaigne, Derrida stresses the mystical (metaphysical) value of laws and, consequently, their disconnectedness from justice. To remove laws from such a position involves, according to Derrida, employing the tools of deconstruction and, above all, exercising the right to deconstruction as a form of justice. Subjecting the law to the rules of deconstruction demands a revision of traditional definitions and categories. It also involves a redefinition of the concept of authority and of democracy under the law. Published originally in 1994, Derrida's book was translated into Italian nine years later and became a striking commentary on the arbitrary value attributed to legal text. A decade after the *mani pulite* process, which uncovered the corruption of the Italian political system and parties, and the beginning of the Italian 'second republic,' Berlusconi succeeded in reinstating the right to immunity for himself and other elected officials. Berlusconi's tenure as prime minister has been marked by his attempts to rewrite laws in order to weaken texts that threatened his own power and wealth. His arbitrary approach to laws aimed to protect the political and economic influence of a selected number of people who had at one time or another collaborated with the *presidente del consiglio*. His very public act of weakening the position of authority of the law has removed any illusion about the absolute or universal value of the law, yet it has not stopped him from reclaiming the absolute position he had weakened for specific legal texts. In fact, with the Bossi-Fini law, Berlusconi's administration reclaimed for immigration laws a position of authoritative strength of which other legal texts had been deprived by Berlusconi himself.

The second book that supplies interpretative meaning to my analysis of contemporary Italian culture is Gianni Vattimo's *Nichilismo ed emancipazione: etica, politica, diritto* (*Nihilism and Emancipation: Ethics, Politics, Rights*, 2003).[115] Vattimo grounds his observations in Nietzsche and Heidegger, whose works were also fundamental in his earlier texts on postmodernism and the Italian 'weak thought.' For Vattimo, the subject in a postmodern society is somebody who is able 'to wander like a tourist in the garden of history. It is a someone who can look at cultures with an attention that is more aesthetical than "objective" and interested in truth.'[116] In dismantling absolutes, Vattimo also recognizes that in this garden of history 'respect for an other involves above all recognizing that *finitezza* that characterizes both of us and that excludes any possibility of a final overcoming of that opaqueness that everybody carries in himself/herself.'[117] In this garden of narratives and relative comprehension of otherness, the literature of migration and by migrants belongs to a new aesthetic approach to interpretation. Vattimo adds that postmodern civilization can be saved only aesthetically in a process that does not predicate a final and definitive truth. What is particularly relevant to my discourse is that Vattimo himself drags literature into his discussion. However, his literary categories are unreasonably rigid, as he divides them between the 'historically authentic' and 'novels.'[118] In his garden of interpretative fragmentations based on aesthetics, what is autobiographical is defined as being closer to that interpretative historical truth that he had previously rejected. However, the fragmentation that characterizes his approach to postmodernity negates such a rigid hierarchy in interpretative values. The emphasis is in fact on the 'carattere affabulatorio dell'interpretazione' ('the narrative character of interpretation') that marks the relationship with any object of interpretation: literature, law, or literature about the law.[119] Interpretation, according to Vattimo, 'always brings the interpreter into play.'[120] The interpreter becomes a subject that by the act of interpreting becomes also the object of interpretation. Applied to the interpretative value of migrants' literature, Vattimo's observation leads to theorizing a narrator who analyses a culture and, at the same time, his/her own ever-changing role within that culture. Consequently, a migrant's interpretation of the law places the creator of that interpretation at the centre of a legal text that has attempted to regulate the life of the migrant by depriving him/her of any interpretative agency. What Vattimo adds is that 'where we thought that there were principles of law there is only the arbitrariness of those who create laws or of those who interpret them.'[121] Interpretation is always *affabulazione*, that is, *finzione*, fiction, although such *finzioni* are hierarchically defined in order to create authorities that can privilege and impose selected interpretations of laws and rules: 'the *affabulazioni* are not all equal.'[122]

In the end, creative manipulation is often brought back to its weak position in which it can talk back, but not resist. This is the case of Jadelin Mabiala Gangbo's experience in his professional role as a writer. He grew up in Italy, became a writer and author of two books, but never a citizen or a permanent resident of Italy. Because the Bossi-Fini law issues stay-permits only if the person requesting the permit has a work contract, Jadelin Mabiala Gangbo as freelance author cannot acquire a stay-permit that could allow him to live in the country where, paradoxically, he has lived most of his life. He writes in Italian because that is the language in which he has been educated and that has constructed his identity. It is the law in this instance that, as a rigidly closed text, drags the author into its narrative structure and declares his expulsion. The limitations of theory are in this case tangible. At the same time, it is Gangbo's visible role as author published by one of the better-known publishers in Italy, Feltrinelli, that makes him the subject of a newspaper article (albeit a very short one) that, in turn, uncovers the incompleteness of the text of the law. Gangbo's experience becomes the location at which theories on the limitations of the law ground themselves and can engage in criticism of the status quo. What remains outside theory is Gangbo's body, experience, and isolation, which theory cannot protect from translations into practice of the law.

Law, Racism, Culture

My own theorization of a potential destination culture for both native and non-native Italians is grounded in the realization that if the subaltern speaks, he/she dialogues with an Italian tradition that has itself experienced migration. However, laws such as the one masterminded by the Northern Leaguer Umberto Bossi and the post-fascist Fini undermines the construction of a hybrid cultural future in which incoming and native traditions can move beyond hostility. A number of theorists have articulated diverse hypotheses about the cultural impasse between majority and minority in an Italian context. The current political and cultural context leads Laura Balbo and Luigi Manconi to articulate only the possibility of the construction of a *società poco razzista*, that is, a society in which racism cannot be erased but could be contained.[123] They focus on the pragmatic impossibility of solving tangible problems that connect the cultural to the political and the legal context. They cite the issue of polygamy as a test case for cultural conflict; while legal and at times the norm in some countries, once inscribed within the Italian context the practice of polygamy challenges the rights that women have struggled for centuries to obtain.[124] In his programmatic elaboration of a left-wing public agenda, even Gianni Vattimo articulates the difficulties in establishing a new 'patto di cittadinanza' ('pact of citizenship') grounded on 'a greater flexibility of our laws' without recognizing the right to traditional strategies of oppression such as ritual mutilations.[125] In exchange for that legal flexibility, migrants would have to renounce aspects of their tradition. However simplistic this sounds, it points in the direction of tangible problems. According to Balbo and Manconi, irreconcilable cultural differences are at the centre of any compromise and of legal mediations that position the rights of a majority at the centre of politics. The legal limitation to tolerance violates the liberal approach to minority rights that, in Will Kymlicka's words, 'requires *freedom within* the minority group, and *equality between* the minority and majority groups.'[126] Balbo and Manconi investigate concepts of a civil society that pragmatically envision the slow process of imperfect cohabitation, what they call *una società poco razzista*, as an alternative to the conflictual status quo.[127]

In his book *The New Racism in Europe* Jeffrey Cole reminds us that the Italy of which Balbo and Manconi talk is in itself very fragmented. He asserts that studies on migration have focused on migrants' contribution to Western economies on their 'institutionalized disadvantage,' and on 'anti-immigrant political movements' that portray immigrants as 'dangerous and threatening.'[128]

> Productive as these perspectives are, scholars have pursued them to the neglect of the important issue of how Europeans, on an every-day level, think about and treat immigrants, and the attendant ideologies of difference. I suggest that what is needed to complement research on inequality and political discourse is an ethnography that investigates how class and local history shape the ways people do and do not give expression to the entangled issues of immigration, race, and culture.[129]

Cole selected a poor neighbourhood in Palermo, Sicily, to carry out his investigations and realized 'too many concerned scholars on both sides of the Atlantic take for granted how Westerners think about and act with regard to race and immigration, how they give or do not give political expression to notions of difference and similarity, and how class, culture, and gender shape views and practices.'[130] In his observation of working-class, underprivileged Sicilians, Cole discovered that although they are afraid of the competition embodied by an immigrant workforce, few express racism toward the immigrants. What he discovered is ambivalence toward the new Italian lower class. It is an ambivalence marked by class insecurities and fear of competition, but at the same time by solidarity with the migrants' condition, combined with a reluctance to admit a shared experience of migration. In the end, Cole's ethnographic study diffuses the alarmist attitude both of the intellectuals, like me, who stress the racist attitudes displayed toward migrants and of others who construct a rhetoric of migration emergency. After analysing the reaction to migration from people of different social classes in other areas of Italy, Cole appears to support Balbo and Manconi's pragmatic articulation of a *società poco razzista* that tends to challenge any monolithic investigations of cultural and ideological reactions to immigration.

In both Balbo and Manconi's and Cole's texts, racism, or the many definitions of racism, reveals its rootedness in institutions and local culture, but also its inherent complexity.[131] Bourdieu argues that '[i]t is infinitely easier to take up a position for or against an idea, a value, a person, an institution or a situation, than analyze what it truly is in all its complexity. People are all the quicker to *take sides* on what journalists call "a problem of society" ... the more incapable they are of analysing and understanding its meaning, which is often quite contrary to ethnocentric intuition.'[132] For instance, immigrants themselves have adopted and manipulated reductive stereotypes about Italy's South. In *La promessa di Hamadi*, Saidou Moussa Ba narrates a stereotypical encounter with the Mafia and describes a Sicilian context in terms that are certainly familiar to Italian and American aficionados of crime-family narratives. Salah Methnani describes the dirt in southern Italy and the feeling he has of being in a new country that closely resembles northern Africa. These accounts borrow from a long-standing Italian stereotype that has discriminated against an Italian South defined as African.[133] In doing so they have invited their readers to shift their attention from what a migrant is to what constitutes being Italian and what models of Italianness the migrants internalize and reproduce. Dialogically, these texts contribute to the issues of racial identification with discourses on native Italians that talk back to native Italians' constructions of otherness that place the migrant outside of the discourse itself. By recycling stereotypes, migrant writers turn the process of generalization against the native Italians who generalize about migrants by attaching connotations of inferiority to otherness. Inscribing such a strategy within autobiographical narratives highlights two tensions: on the one hand, the appropriation of the right to self-definition in discursive paradigms that contain strategies of sameness *and* difference; on the other, the struggle against definitions of otherness imposed on migrants, and therefore an appropriation of the right to become an interpretative authority of the cultural context in which immigrants inscribe themselves. It is at this juncture that the act of talking back to racisms locates itself and acquires meaning.

Albert Memmi's text *Racism* (2000) is particularly useful in talking about autobiography as weak resistance to both institutionalized and daily practices of racism. Starting from the autobiographical, Memmi talks about heterophobia and ethnophobia as constitutive of racism intended as a structure, that is, as an artificial creation that legitimizes the superiority of whiteness. Discussing social relations and the politics of racism, Memmi explores the construction of institutional and political racism that can be combated only by educating people to fight it. By intertwining his personal narrative with a theoretical debate, he sets up a powerful model that migrant writers have also adopted in their autobiographical narratives. Unfortunately, this powerful model ends up being trapped in the margins of the publishing market and becomes a weak form of resistance.

In her book *Convivenza civile e xenofobia* (*Civil Cohabitation and Xenophobia*, 2000), Marcella Delle Donne explores the conflicts inherent in notions of citizenship and belonging vis-à-vis concepts of ethnicity that fragmented the Italian identity even before the arrival of immigrants. In her introduction entitled 'La ragione e le viscere' ('Reason and Guts'), she writes: 'The modern concept of citizenship takes shape in a public sphere grounded in a rational basis. The ethnic group that emerges in the space-time of a village is grounded in solidarity and parental relationships. Citizenship and ethnic group belong to different categories. The former corresponds to a mental order, the latter to a natural order.'[134] This dichotomy between mind and body, rational and natural, is something with which all feminists are familiar. It reappears again in discussions on racial difference and constructs separations and categorizations with which migrants are familiar. Citizenship and ethnic group become here two categories in a hierarchical structure that is biologically determined and therefore dangerously 'natural.' Such categories also point toward a separation between multiculturalism and a multiethnic society that caters to the fears of cultural contamination and theorizes the construction of separations along ethnic lines that always remain arbitrarily defined by a dominant majority. The 'mental order' upon which citizenship is supposed to be grounded reveals its own inherent flaw, for its foundations lie in political rhetorics of belonging and contingent battles for political influence that, according to Memmi, ultimately result in institutionalizing racism. Institutionalized discrimination becomes, therefore, one of the laws of migration that weakened acts of resistance can expose, but cannot efficiently undermine.

In both Memmi and Delle Donne the issue of the language we use in talking about migration is an invaluable tool for examining how words can be employed to reproduce anti-immigrant rhetoric even in academic environments. In Italy, where American political correctness is highly criticized and at times laughed at, terms such as 'nero' and 'negro' are still interchangeable, although the latter has negative connotations that the former does not. Federico Faloppa, who has authored one of the most recent texts on lexicon and alterity, *Lessico e alterità: la formulazione del 'diverso'* (2000), is an Italian academic who speaks from outside the borders of Italy, first as a graduate student in England and then as an academic in Spain. The failure of acts of talking back also informs some academic discourses that can supply intellectual credibility to anti-immigration rhetoric. In an article entitled 'Islam e Occidente, sintesi impossibile' ('Islam and the West: An Impossible Synthesis') the well-known anthropologist Ida Magli contributes to the discussion on 'integration' by analysing the concept of time in different cultures. She states that looking back at a culture's past involves investigating its concept of time. In Islamic cultures, she states, time is cyclical, connected to nature. For Jews time revolves around the concept of 'waiting,' removed from nature and informed by their relationship with the divine. Christian time, and consequently Western time, is marked by 'becoming,' that is, a tension toward freedom, action and conquest, including scientific exploration. Her classification of the concept of time is therefore based on irreconcilable cultural differences that lead her to state:

> It is from this conception of time that comes the impossibility of integrating western culture with any other culture, including Islamic culture of which we talk so much today ... Both the West that believes in Christianity and the secular West are grounded in 'becoming,' in being open to history, to the evolution of customs and ideas. The word 'integration,' often invoked as the possibility of cohabitation with other cultures, offends what characterizes the human species: the logical system of thought.[135]

This informed conservative discussion on difference is, therefore, marked by separation and a return to 'whatness,' which does not look the migrant in the face, as Cavarero would wish, but invokes again a concept of History that requires essentializations. This discourse places, once more, the 'monopoly of reason' in Western hands and leads the discussion back to 'the false universalism of the West,' to what Bourdieu calls 'the imperialism of the universal.'[136] While Ragonesi expressed his faith in intellectual discourses and invited academics to participate in the discussions that lead to the creation of immigration laws, Bourdieu expresses his scepticism with regard to the role of intellectuals in political life: 'I would like writers, artists, philosophers and scientists to be able to make their voice heard directly in all the areas of public life in which they are competent ... At present, it is often the logic of political life, that of denunciation and slander, "sloganization" and falsification of the adversary's thought, which extends into intellectual life.'[139] The failure of the language of intellectual discourse on otherness takes place when the carefully crafted discussion on the irreconcilability of difference that troubles Balbo and Manconi turns into an absolutist articulation of a Western culture whose difference involves processes of total separation and impossible dialectics between differences. The lack of dialogue brings the discussion back again to the absolutism in rhetorics that assigns to migration the role of 'the' problem in contemporary Italy. In fact, in his essay 'Is There a Neo-Racism?' Balibar argues that the 'category of immigration' has replaced the category of race.[138] In a 'racism without race' the 'dominant theme is not biological heredity but the insurmountability of cultural differences' and 'the harmfulness of abolishing frontiers.'[139] Therefore, dominant discourses complement, rather than challenge, the language of the law that is concerned with protecting the right of a majority but is unable to address simultaneously the rights of minorities, and of migrants in particular.

Conclusion

'Ora qui posso fare quasi tutto, quasi come un italiano' ('Here, Now I Can Do Almost Anything, Just Like an Italian') is the title of a life narrative contained in the volume *La terra in faccia* (*Dirt in Your Face*, 1991).[140] The quotation describes the unerasability of difference and the unattainability of equality. It also eloquently summarizes the condition of being a migrant under Italian law. Immigration laws in Italy have highlighted the concern of policy-makers to protect the rights of a majority who, however, capitalize on migrant workers. This is evident in the attention placed by politicians on the present embodiment of migration and in the lack of interest placed on its future developments – unless alarmist rhetoric about the endangered future of a majority counts as serious political attention. Laws have demonstrated their inadequacy in understanding migration as a problem, as an inevitable global movement, and as the inevitable motor of hybridization in the future of Italian culture.

The language of the law has reflected the contradictory policy constructed by various Italian administrations. In the early 1990s the politicians in power attempted to remain faithful to the Italian left-wing traditional ideals vis-à-vis migration and migrants. Later administrations have succeeded in aligning Italy with the rest of Europe in the construction of a fortress against migrants, but built on the work of the migrants themselves.[141] The texts and the language that document the transformations taking place in Italy reside outside the laws and their official interpretations. From the privileged position of literature, migrants have verbalized their presence within an Italian cultural context and have shaped identities that reveal the heterogeneity of the protagonists of migration and their role in shaping what Italian culture(s) are. Their literary efforts have talked back to problematic legal interpretations and have short-circuited the circularity of limiting cultural discourses on migration. In claiming a right to interpretation, migrant writers have placed the texts of the law on the same plane as their articulations of identities influenced by those legal narratives. They have opened the door for critics to analyse both legal texts about immigration and narratives of migration and subject them to the laws of literary criticism. Removing the law from this privileged position as a text has also involved questioning the 'whatness' that permeates public discourse on migration. The plurality of 'whoness' that allows a multiplicity of interpretative approaches to the identity of the migrant allows the articulation of agency as constitutive of the identity of readers of the legal texts. What has been impossible to create is a reading audience that can interpret the writers' eloquent intercultural constructions of identities and of revisionary politics of interpretation. Fortunately, migrants' literature can be employed in qualitative analysis that complements the quantitative research on migration. In fact, that literature documents the history of migration to Italy, narrated by its protagonists. It is necessary therefore to 'insure a voice for minorities' from a legal point of view, as Will Kymlicka explains, and pay attention to acts of talking back that although isolated can supply Eurocentred intellectuals with an informed history of migration.[144]

Migrants' literature, film, and artistic expressions, in general, are a form of cultural representation. Kept at a distance from administrative representation, immigrants have explored the interpretative and representative niches in a flawed democratic system in order to make their voices and agenda heard. They prove that the art of talking back is fundamental in the construction of a destination culture able to braid local and incoming cultures. They also prove that literature matters and becomes an unerasable space demanding a readership in order to move from being an act of talking back to becoming resistance.

As a reader, my own politics of interpretation of contemporary Italian culture and of the location of migrants' literature in it has been both theoretical and descriptive in order to explore the relevance of writing in the processes of cultural transformation taking place in Italy. In fact, I want to engender questions rather than offer conclusive solutions about future developments in the hybridization of Italian culture thanks to cultural constructions authored by immigrants and, let us not forget, native Italians. Migrants' texts seek to dialogue with a chain of interpretative strategies. Migrants' constructions of meaning in their narratives is grounded in the necessarily intercultural and interdisciplinary nature of their approach to Italian cultures. What I have attempted here, in particular, is to enact the relevance of literature in such a process; that is, to validate literary interpretative strategies as a tool for constructing representation (even a form of political representation) in interstitial cultural locations.

Conclusion

> Guarda, l'attuale invasione dell'Europa non é che un altro aspetto di quell'espansionismo. Più subdolo, però. Più infido. Perché a caratterizzarlo stavolta non sono i Kara Mustafa e i Lala Mustafa e gli Alì Pascià e i Solimano il Magnifico e i giannizzeri ... Sono anche gli immigrati che s'installano a casa nostra, e che senza alcun rispetto delle nostre leggi ci impongono le loro idee. Le loro usanze, il loro Dio. Sai quanti di loro vivono nel continente europeo cioè nel tratto che va dalla costa Atlantica alla catena degli Urali? Circa cinquantatré milioni.
>
> Oriana Fallaci[1]

> Ils se multiplient comme les rats. Si riproducono come topi.
>
> Fallaci[2]

Oriana Fallaci's *La forza della ragione* (*The Strength of Reason*, 2004) became a best-seller right after its publication and remained a very popular book in Italy for several months. The book warns Western readers that Muslims have invaded Europe, have transformed it into *Eurabia*, and are threatening 'western reason.' This 'reason' is the unitary logos of Western civilization that Fallaci wants to defend, even at the cost of her own life, as she asserts in the book. The populist statements contained in the book have been challenged, but no one can deny the commercial success that the book has had in Italy. At this particular moment in history, when a major Western military presence in a Muslim country has become an occupation, Fallaci redirects her own and her readers' attention to the invasion of immigrants and the colonization of the West on the part of Muslims. Her version of globalism sees Christian Europe conquered by cruel and uncivilized non-Western bodies. Fallaci's call to arms to defend Western reason against a particular kind of globalism finds a home in the agenda of Italian right-wing parties that have considerable influence in the Berlusconi administration. This fervour in defending Italy from cultural miscegenation stresses the unsurmountable 'difference' between 'us' and 'them,' returning to an interpretation of contemporary Italy based on dichotomies and on a Manichean interpretation of global culture. In this universe that reduces otherness to a threat, Fallaci claims for herself the privileged role of defender of Western values. In fact, she defines herself in Messianic terms: she is telling the only truth that becomes word in her text and turns her writings into the incarnation of a new crusade.

On 29 May 2004 the newspaper *la Repubblica* published an indirect response to Fallaci's apocalyptic denunciations.[3] An article entitled 'Qui ci vuole un euro-islam' ('We Need a Euro-Islam') contained an interview with Jürgen Habermas in which the philosopher suggested that instead of talking about nationalisms we should focus on 'patriotic constitutionalism.' Habermas focuses on the values inscribed in constitutions rather than on nationalistic particularisms that ought to lose their validity in a unified Europe. His position talks back to the protectionist strategies that Fallaci deems necessary in order to protect universal Christian values. Habermas instead privileges constitutional rights built on the particularities of European histories that take into consideration the differences inherent in European cultural traditions. Issues, such as polygamy, practised by some immigrants have created a discussion on rights guaranteed by the Italian constitution. In particular, Italy has recently confronted issues concerning the practice of women's sexual mutilation and unequal rights in a number of cultural traditions that are now present in Italy. It is crucial to ask the fundamental question of how to defend the rights acquired by women in Italy after decades of civil struggle and, at the same time, respect the demands of other traditions that would undermine those legal and cultural rights to equality and gender difference. Habermas's answer to such a question lies in the destruction of rigid separation and the creation of a political practice that leads to an expansion of Europe, to include Islamic countries, that can mediate a complex relationship between cultures.

Habermas posits that Turkey, as a member of a unified Europe, would embody the possibility of creating a 'Euro-Islam' that does not exclude the values of a European patriotic constitutionalism. The goal is hybridization and reconciliation between Western and non-Western traditions within the context of a newly unified Europe. In her concept of *Eurabia*, Fallaci constructs instead irreconcilable differences that find in the concept of 'fortress Europe' their main embodiment. A fortress Europe locks itself in a defensive system that wants to prevent immigrants from crossing its borders. The defensive tools at play are restrictive immigration laws, a criminalization of undocumented migrants, and the use of police to keep the crime of otherness from crossing national borders. In his concept of a 'Euro-Islam,' Habermas explores a much more complex articulation of European culture grounded in the rejection of those dichotomies that support Fallaci's argument. In fact, Habermas reminds us that the threat to European constitutional values comes more immediately from the West: 'What is foreign to us, in Europe, is the erasure of the separation between a political office and the conviction of the individual faith of whoever is in office. This is a separation that George Bush seems to find secondary. Politics must be free from religious connotations.'[4] Habermas's interpretation of a possible European future based on patriotic constitutionalism and on the construction of a 'Euro-Islam' appeared in the women's section of *la Repubblica* and, therefore, reached a smaller number of the daily's readers. Printed in the more 'ephemeral' women's section of a Friday issue, Habermas's interview was literally distanced from the regular 'culture page' of the newspaper. Such an editorial decision unfortunately strengthens Fallaci's authoritative position, and the position of all the alarmist discourses on difference and migration that find ample space in dailies.

Fallaci's best-selling demonization of one specific kind of otherness and of cultural embodiment demands scrutiny, particularly in that her conclusions hardly arise from a rigorous investigation of the processes of cultural hybridization. Habermas's complex and well-documented articulations of cultural and political redefinitions of European cultures point in the direction of transformations that are both local and global. However, it is Fallaci's apocalyptic text that is enjoying a widespread distribution thanks to the market strategies of a major publishing company. The result is that Fallaci's best-selling book fuels anxieties that interpellate (in an Althusserian sense) readers, who also internalize the facile rhetoric that has motivated the Bossi-Fini immigration law and the politics of scapegoating migrants. Other narratives, such as novels, short stories, and film, that talk back to a dominant alarmist rhetoric remain at the margins of the publishing and distribution market. Such a marginal position prevents them from resisting essentialising generalizations. In talking back to Fallaci's xenophobic texts, even this book can only claim a marginal position whose impact will remain 'academic.'

At times I have employed a polemical tone in order to deal with the specific case of Italy as a location of cultural hybridization and with the paradoxical contradictions in the way immigration has been confronted in the public sphere. Far from exhausting discussions on contemporary Italy, this book lays the groundwork for analysing the ongoing developments in Italian multiculturalism, developments that are already shifting as I write this conclusion. A discourse on contemporary Italian multiculturalism and cultural hybridizations is possible only if we consider such a discussion as a merely temporary evaluation of the unpredictable directions in which Italian culture is moving. Migrants' writings analysed in this book teach us that any teleological interpretation of migrants' literature does not do justice to its complexity. Post-migration and post-ethnic writings in fact demonstrate that even separations between native writers and migrant writers can only be temporary, and only relatively valid. Those borders established between linguistic experts and migrant writers shift and reflect the changing relation between local and incoming cultures.

Literary prizes for immigrant writers have attempted to encourage a dialogue between a local culture and migrants' writings. The result is that they have helped to call into question the validity of fragile preconceptions concerning the ownership of language and of a literary tradition. Therefore, migrants' writing highlights the impossibility of talking about Italian literature as a national literature, intended in traditional and canonical terms, and moves the discussion of a literature into an arena that interprets the production of culture and meaning more globally.

Any work on migrations to Italy and on cultural contaminations is germane to the discussion on globalisms and global migrations, and in particular to those on global cultures. Migrants' literature, film, and cultural production in general are the indicators of a new dialogue and relationship between an already multicultural Italian culture and other immigrating cultures. Therefore, from a global point of view, regulated by market strategies dictated by rich Western countries, migrants' literature redesigns a world map from below, from individual narrations of geographical displacements. In these texts the complexities and ambiguities of Western cultures are brought to the surface together with the complexities and ambiguities of the non-Western cultures from which migrants articulate the act of migrating. This double deterritorialization creates a very particular point of view from which migrants witness changes in cultures that mark the past and the present of the subjects of migration.

However, points of origin and arrival cannot be kept separated, as contemporary migration is marked by transmigration, a process that follows complex lines of repeated migration. Consequently, in migrants' stories the concept of home is redefined by removing it from localisms and particularisms in order to create 'invented homelands,' as Arjun Appaduraj terms them, that talk back to cultural protectionism and any definition of 'origins.'[5] Linearity is therefore not possible in works of imagination that articulate past and present synchronically and constitute one of the possible futures of hybridizations. Migrants' narratives are therefore literary representations of shifting viewpoints from which the complexity of acts of migration turns into the complexity of constructing cultural identities. As Appaduraj states: 'Few persons in the world today do not have a friend, relative or coworker who is not on the road to somewhere else or already coming home bearing stories and possibilities.'[6] It is in the process of telling stories that migrant writers trace the convoluted lines of transmigration and cultural construction that mark a global phenomenon in its localized embodiments of invented homelands.

Appaduraj's work is particularly useful in talking about migrants' cultural production as he sees a strict connection between migration and imagination, since 'diasporas bring the force of imagination, as both memory and desire, into the lives of many ordinary people, into mythographies different from the disciplines of myth and ritual of the classic sort.'[7] The stories that are being created and the new mythographies that constitute migrants' literature (but also native writers' texts that pay attention to migrations and global deterritorializations) present new social landscapes or projects and are shrinking the distance between cultural elites, between those who belong to a specific culture and those who are interlopers. Agency is at the centre of this creativity because, for Appaduraj, 'imagination' is 'a property of collectives, and not merely a faculty of the gifted individual.'[8] This particular agency can allow the construction of diasporic public spheres that 'are no longer small, marginal, or exceptional.'[9] This book's focus on the large number of literary texts authored by migrants has the double purpose of documenting and validating the public discourse that migrants have created and of giving them space in an academic debate on Italian studies. The body of work written by migrants has created contexts in which immigrants have been portrayed as agents of change, able to talk back to the limited and limiting roles assigned to migrants. Even if still marginal, these narratives of otherness mark a fundamental change in the constitutive aspects of Italian culture(s), from literature to mass media, to the changing cultural profile of Italian cities, restaurants, and stores.

Appaduraj focuses in particular on mass media because 'for migrants, both the politics of adaptation to new environments and the stimulus to move or return are deeply affected by a mass-mediated imaginary that frequently transcends national space.'[10] Film becomes therefore the ideal space in which invented homelands find a home. Films on migration analysed in chapter 3 portray localities destabilized by the presence of otherness. Film explores how the presence of this 'otherness' changes the boundaries that define the *Heim*, concepts of belonging or unbelonging, sameness and difference. In fact, film visually contextualizes subjectivities and allows a visualisation of 'the tension between cultural homogenization and cultural heterogenization.'[11] In this book the analysis of film devoted to migration issues serves the purpose of adding to the complexity of representational strategies of identity construction in migration. In fact, the gaze that follows the other in urban landscapes can be redirected, manipulated, and talked back to in film. However, the main focus of this book has remained on literature, as film is an expensive, privileged medium to which migrants do not have easy access.

Both literature and film have produced innovative representations of the directions in which the cultural Italian landscape is moving and they have performed such representations under disadvantaged conditions. Relegated to being marginal (with very few exceptions), films and literature about migration issues are often considered as a secondary, negligible, component in studies about contemporary Italy. Analysing migration culture in Italy is instead a way to open up the area study of Italian culture to (it needs to be reiterated) a global dimension. As Appaduraj argues, we must not forget in fact that 'locality itself is a historical product and that the histories through which localities emerge are eventually subject to the dynamics of the global.'[12] Studying migration culture in the context of Italian culture involves the creation of a '*site* for the examination of how locality emerges in the globalizing world.'[13] The result is an analysis of how 'global facts take local form.'[14] Migration literature becomes therefore an area of study necessary for understanding the present and future role of Italian culture in a globalizing world. In fact, both literature and film about a minor Italy highlight a specific 'glocalism,' that is, the local form that the phenomenon of global migration has taken in Italy.

My book began with a discussion of Italians abroad, of a diaspora narrated through a representation of invented homelands that make the relationship of 'here' and 'there' always impermanent. A book on contemporary migrations to Italy must first connect with the many embodiments of otherness that have marked Italian migrants since the country's unification. The protagonists of the contemporary phenomenon of a migration of return are descendants of Italians who migrated from Italy to once prosperous countries such as Argentina, but whose economic standing in the world has now changed. They return to an Italy with an accented cultural background in order to reinscribe themselves in a context with which they are at the same time familiar and unfamiliar. Though they are Italian citizens thanks to the *ius sanguinis* that allows people to inherit Italian citizenship, the subjects of a migration of return are the embodiments of complicated politics of identity, and concepts of origin, of sameness, and of difference. In this context of indeterminacy it becomes necessary to focus on what Paul Gilroy calls the 'logic of sameness and differentiation.'[15] In this logic what constitutes the 'same' reveals itself to be always changing because it contains tensions that make the same an entity that is never the same.

In an analysis of Italian contemporary multiculturalism, it is necessary to focus on strategies of relation that identify the struggle inherent in constructing meaning, specifically the meaning of difference, in culture. Concepts of talking back, of destination cultures, of a process that I have called 'recolouring,' and of a sameness that reveals its inherent difference constitute a contested terrain where relations between dominant and dominated, the native and the stranger (which are never simply a native and a stranger), must not be essentialized. The space in which the meaning of difference is constructed is a Mediterranean crossroads. The emphasis is on the ever-changing identities of a tongue of land in the middle of the Mediterranean Sea that is mapped through a complicated network of transformations. Such transformations demand multidisciplinary tools of investigation.

Studying migration culture also makes a discussion of methodology necessary. The tools employed in talking about these texts have originated from different disciplinary paradigms. However, my reluctance to talk about the aesthetic value of the literature authored by migrants is not intended to downgrade their work, but rather to present the powerful work of imagination that migrants have created in a diasporic public sphere. In addition, talking about migrants' literature while it is being written also requires a suspension of the validity of traditional aesthetical models codified in Italian canonical texts. Migrants' literature demands a revision of canons through a synthesis of disparate theoretical approaches to texts that dialogues with the local literary traditions that at the same time, they are changing.

Migration studies in Italy is a field directly connected to global multiculturalism that can only be accessed via an interdisciplinary methodology. Therefore, migration studies finds its ideal *Heim* in cultural studies. As a particular branch of Italian studies, migration studies in Italy articulates itself at a strategic crossroads in which traditional tools of literary criticism and theoretical approaches to texts meet. What is at stake is a delineation of continuity and changes in the redefinition of a cultural context. Practising cultural studies in Italian studies demands the performance of that interdisciplinary encounter that creates a process of theorization which pushes Italian studies forward in new predictable and unpredictable directions, to which process, I hope, this book has contributed.

In conclusion there is really no conclusion. This book has mapped a decade from the beginning of the 1990s to the beginning of the third millennium. As I am writing, other changes in the cultural landscape are adding to the complex set of theoretical approaches that I have employed: the Bossi-Fini law concerning preventative incarceration before expulsion has not fulfilled the expectation of the hard-liners in migration politics. In fact, after the approval of the Bossi-Fini law, undocumented immigrants arrested by the police, as established by the recent immigration laws, were later set free by judges because being an undocumented migrant is still considered a *contravvenzione*, not a crime.[16] A *contravvenzione* does not carry incarceration as a penalty. On the front page of the left-wing newspaper *Il Manifesto*, Alessandro Dal Lago wrote that the decision of the Corte Costituzionale defended human rights and the values inherent in the Italian constitution (along Habermassian lines of patriotic constitutionalism) and rejected the post-fascist/Northen League attempt to ignore founding principles of equality inherent in the constitution itself.[17] Consequently, representatives from Alleanza Nazionale and the Northern League demanded a revision of the Constitution so that undocumented immigration could be considered a crime.

The decision from the Corte Costituzionale is one of many blows directed against the Berlusconi administration, which has failed on many fronts, and is thus losing support and validity. In this specific juncture in time, new stories about being other in Italy are being published and film directors are planning new representations of stories of emigration and immigration. Paolo Virzì is adapting for the screen Melania Mazzucco's *Vita*, telling of Italians in New York at the beginning of the twentieth century. Marco Tullio Giordana, known for directing politically charged films such as *I cento passi* (*One Hundred Steps*, 2000), about the Sicilian mafia, and *La meglio gioventù* (*The Better Youth*, 2002), which traces the story of a whole generation through the turmoil of the 1960s and 1970s, is now developing a film entitled *Quando sei nato non puoi più nasconderti* (*As You Are Born, You Cannot Hide*). Inspired by a book by Maria Pace Ottieri *Quando sei nato non puoi più nasconderti: viaggio nel popolo sommerso* (*As You Are Born, You Cannot Hide: A Journey among the Undocumented People*, 2003), Giordana's film traces the life of an undocumented migrant who lands in Lampedusa and travels north, reaching the city of Milan. I find it particularly revealing that contemporary Italian film directors perform a discourse on alterity by producing films that discuss both Italian emigration and immigrations to Italy. Their work validates my own approach to Italian multiculturalism, which, I hope, will be useful to other scholars in confronting the complex issues inherent in talking about Italian multiculturalism(s) and in making otherness and other people the objects of academic investigations.

Notes

Introduction

1 Zantop, *Colonial Fantasies*, vii.
2 We often call a dialect what is actually a language. Even Italian, like Milanese, Venetian, and Piedmontese, could be called a dialect. They are all romance languages.
3 See my introduction to the edited volume *Mediterranean Crossroads* (13–42).
4 Deleuze and Guattari, *Nomadology*, 50.
5 In writing this chapter, and also this book, I felt that it was my responsibility to show the wealth of material that migrant writers have already published. That led me to decide to discuss a large number of texts in order to document the complexity of a phenomenon that opens fascinating possibilities for the future of Italian culture. Unfairly relegated to the status of a transitory phenomenon undeserving of much academic attention, migrants' literature is already an unerasable presence with which native authors are starting to dialogue. I attempted the difficult operation of privileging a few texts, but at the same time made sure that a large number of authors found critical space in this book so as attempt to present the multifaceted aspects of the processes of cultural hybridization taking place in Italy at the beginning of a new millennium.

1. Strategies of 'Talking Back'

1 Jacobson, *Whiteness of a Different Color*, 57.
2 In his short story 'La salvezza' ('Salvation'), the Algerian Italian writer Amor Dekhis treats Biffi's statement with humour. The story is about a migrant in Italy who tries to prevent his relatives from moving to Italy and

imposing on him for hospitality. He tells them that if they want to migrate to Italy they have to become Christians: 'It's a condition only recently added. They only want Christians, even better if they are Catholic. There must be a priest down there who can convert you' (111). Of course the relatives refuse to migrate on such terms and vehemently states his faith in Allah and his prophet. (All translations of quotations from novels and short stories are mine unless otherwise indicated.)

3 See Mario Pirani, 'Il diavolo e gli stranieri,' *la Repubblica*, 14 Sept. 2000, 1 and 17. See also Luigi Accattoli, 'In Vaticano la sua posizione è minoritaria,' *corriere della sera*, 14 Sept. 2000, 10, and Orazio La Rocca, 'Immigrati, Sodano [Secretary of State of the Vatican] con Biffi: 'Parole sagge sui musulmani,' *la Repubblica*, 15 Sept. 2000, 11.

4 See Michele Smargiassi, 'Accogliere gli immigrati solo se sono cattolici,' *la Repubblica*, 14 Sept. 2000, 4. Islam is Italy's second most prevalent religion, but figures reveal that such a statement is misleading: 1,280,000 Muslims live in a country, Italy, whose population amounts to about 57,000,000 people. According to *la Repubblica* of 14 Sept. 2000 (p. 5), 36.5% of immigrants are Muslim, 27.4% are Catholic, and 22.1% practise other Christian religions. The obsessive anxiety with an ongoing Islamic 'invasion' of Italy is proved irrational (but intolerance is never rational) in light of the fact that most immigrants to Italy practise a Christian religion.

5 See Aldo Fontanarosa, 'E la Lega esalta il cardinale: "Finalmente infrange un tabù,"' *la Repubblica*, 14 Sept. 2000, 4. Concerned about the interference of the Vatican in political life, politicians started to distance themselves from Cardinal Biffi's position as soon as 15 September. See *Il corriere della sera*, 15 Sept. 2000, 7.

6 See Fred L. Gardaphé, *Italian Signs, American Streets*, 1–4.

7 Balibar, 'The Nation Form: History and Ideology,' 87.

8 Ibid., 93; emphasis in the original text.

9 Ibid.

10 Ibid.

11 Ibid., 94.

12 Ibid., 96–7.

13 For a debate devoted to the construction of the identity of the foreigner in an Italian cultural context, see Domenichelli and Fasano, eds., *Lo straniero*.

14 The terms 'native' and 'immigrant' writers are highly problematic, as will become evident later on in my text. They homogenize categories that are fragmented and filled with contradictions. I am using them here because I lack alternative terms, but will problematize them in my discussions.

15 Sayad, *La double absence*.

16 Dal Lago, *Non-persone.*

17 Ward, '"Italy" in Italy.'

18 See also an unsigned article entitled 'Germania, agguato nazi: grave un operaio italiano. A Dedelow, nel Land orientale del Brandeburgo. Arrestati due ragazzi,' *la Repubblica*, 25 Aug. 1998, 17.

19 Jacobson, *Whiteness of a Different Color.*

20 Ibid., 56.

21 Ibid.

22 Ibid.

23 Ibid.

24 Ibid.

25 Malcolm X, *Malcolm X on Afro-American History,* 24; quoted by Guglielmo and Salerno, *Are Italians White?*

26 In his talk at Dartmouth College on 1 May 2003, Ballerini noted that this new history of Italian literature would include the work of Jewish intellectuals who have often been excluded from other anthologizations because the language they employ is a fusion of Italian and Hebrew. He mentioned, for instance, the writings of Judah Abravanel, better known as Leone Ebreo (1460–1523). My own discussion on internal differences within Italian culture does not deal with Jewish culture and, in particular, literature as an 'other' Italian culture. People have remarked on this absence during oral presentations of my work. The decision to leave such important issues out of my discussion has not been taken lightly. My discourse on migration focuses on twentieth-century migrations and seeks to develop the issues relating to recent migrations to Italy. Figures such as the Hungarian Italian writer Edith Bruck would fit in this time frame, but would lead me to a discussion on the Holocaust that deserves more textual space than I could devote to the subject. I apologize to the readers who consider my decision a serious lacuna in my work.

27 See Ranieri, *Oggi o dimane.*

28 Komla-Ebri, *Neyla*, 61.

29 Balibar, 'The Nation Form: History and Ideology,' 96.

30 Ibid., 96–7.

31 Ibid., 103.

32 Hargreaves, 'Resistance at the Margins,' 228–9.

33 Ibid., 232.

34 Ibid., 232–3.

35 In January 2004, in fact the agency Doctors without Borders accused Italy of human rights violations. The accusations targeted holding facilities that were nothing but cargo containers, the lack of legal assistance for immi-

grants awaiting expulsion in the holding facilities, and the use of drugs to keep the immigrants sedated, and concerned, in particular, holding facilities in Torino, Lamezia Terme, and Trapani. The dossier created by Doctors without Borders once more raised questions about the legality of such *centri di permanenza temporanea*. See Giancarlo Mola, 'Immigrati reclusi in container e drogati. L'accusa di "Medici senza frontiere": nei centri trattamento disumano,' *la Repubblica*, 27 Jan. 2004, 24.

36 Slemon, 'Unsettling the Empire.'

37 Ibid.

38 Ibid.

39 The book *Lo straniero e il nemico: materiali per l'etnografia contemporanea*, edited by Alessandro Dal Lago, has exhaustively explored the genealogy of the foreigner as enemy in the Italian historical past and present. The fear of an immigrant invasion is fuelled even by the press that defines itself as politically moderate. On 9 September 1994, *la Repubblica* displayed the first-page headline 'L'assalto degli immigrati: migliaia di clandestini sbarcano al Sud.' On page 17, two other articles reiterate the state of emergency that immigration has provoked: 'Il ritorno dei disperati: Bloccati 400 albanesi [*sic*]. Nell'ultimo mese forse un migliaio di clandestini sono sbarcati sulle coste pugliesi. È una nuova invasione,' by Domenico Castellaneta, and an unsigned, short article 'Assalto alle isole siciliane: altri 108 clandestini intercettati al largo di Pantelleria, Favignana e Lampedusa.' On the same page another short, unsigned article proclaims 'Mille nomadi a Firenze: censiti i rom. La città può ospitarne solo la metà.' Arturo Buzzolan responds with an article on the same page entitled 'Pestaggio razzista: picchiano in dieci venditore senegalese. Torino, in venti assistono senza intervenire.'

40 Carlotta Mismetti Capua, 'Vi racconto gli italiani,' *Diario*, 19 Dec. 2002, 49.

41 The Italian army was the first Western force defeated by an African army. Mussolini tried to re-establish Italy's prestige in 1935 when he invaded Ethiopia. Officially conquered in 1936, the Ethiopian resistance kept fighting against the invading Italian troops until 1941, when Italy lost all of its African colonies.

42 Marcus Garvey; quoted by Ayele Bekerie, 'African Americans and the Italo-Ethiopian War,' 117.

43 Of course there is the monumental work authored by Angelo Del Boca, and that by others such as Gian Paolo Calchi Novati at the University of Pavia. Still, Italian colonialism has only recently attracted a considerable amount of academic attention.

44 See, for instance, Nuruddin Farah, *Sardines: A Novel*.

45 Dell'Oro, *L'abbandono.*
46 Flaiano, *Tempo di uccidere.*
47 Antonaros, *Tornare a Carobèl.* See also Emanuelli, *Settimana nera.*
48 Ba, 'Nel cuore di un clandestino,' 16–22.
49 Immigrants' texts published at the beginning of the 1990s are marked by collaborations with linguistic experts. Salah Methnani worked with Mario Fortunato, Pap Khouma with Oreste Pivetta, Saidou Moussa Ba with Alessandro Micheletti, and Nassera Chohra with Alessandra Atti Di Sarro.
50 In this regard, Jenny Sharp asserts: 'Sites of resistance [are] those ruptures in the representation of ... colonialism as a civilizing mission' ('Figures of Colonial Resistance,' 99).
51 Suleri, 'The Rhetoric of English India,' 112.
52 When it was first shown, Visconti's film was highly criticized. Made in 1960, the film appeared while Italy was experiencing a large economic boom that lasted roughly from 1958 until 1963. About the film Miriam Mafai writes: 'Luchino Visconti's *Rocco and His Brothers* burst onto the scene like a bomb ... bringing to the screen the tragedy of our migrants, the uprootedness of Southern Italians in an unfriendly city, where there is no room for the traditional values of the poor families of farmers. The Pafundis are farmers from Lucania who migrated to Milan. The mother still wraps herself up in a black shawl that covers her from head to toe as if it were a chador. Her three sons will be defeated in their battle with the industrial reality of a big city. They will be defeated both when they choose the path that leads to violence, and when they choose to adapt and follow the path to integration' (Mafai, *Il sorpasso,* 74).
53 See Giovanni Maria Bellu, 'Tre Italiani su quattro con l'incubo immigrati: "Colpa loro se aumenta la criminalità,"' *la Repubblica,* 22 July 2000, 12.
54 Gardaphé, *Italian Signs, American Streets,* 1–4.
55 See Kristeva, *Strangers to Ourselves.* See also Grillo and Pratt, eds., *The Politics of Recognizing Difference.*
56 See Bhabha, ed., *Nation and Narration* and Bhabha, *The Location of Culture;* Braidotti, *Nomadic Subjects;* and Lionnet, *Autobiographical Voices* and *Postcolonial Representations.*
57 I have used the metaphor of a cultural crossroads in my introduction to the book *Mediterranean Crossroads.*
58 Taylor, 'The Politics of Recognition.'
59 Ibid., 34.
60 Ibid., 38.
61 Habermas, 'Struggles for Recognition in the Democratic Constitutional State,' 131.

62 Balibar, *Identità culturali.*
63 Appiah, 'Identity, Authenticity, Survival,' 156.
64 Ibid., 159.
65 Taylor, 'The Politics of Recognition,' 70.
66 Abate and Behrmann, *Die Germanesi.*
67 Abate, *Il ballo tondo*, 25.
68 De Mauro, 'Linguistic Variety and Linguistic Minorities,' 92.
69 Ibid., 88–9.
70 Abate, 'Bruciori,' in *Il muro dei muri*, 83.
71 Abate, 'La biondina occhispenti,' in *Il muro dei muri*, 25.
72 Abate, *Il ballo tondo*, 31.
73 Abate, 'Il cuoco d'Arbëria,' 333.
74 Ibid., 333.
75 Ottieri, 'Ancora pane e cioccolata,' *Diario*, 3 Nov. 2000, 32–5. She is also the author of a novel, *Amore nero*, and of non-fiction texts that document her interest in migration issues: *Stranieri* and *Quando sei nato non puoi più nasconderti: viaggio nel popolo sommerso.*
76 Ottieri, 'Ancora pane e cioccolata,' 32.
77 See Pugliese, *L'Italia tra migrazioni internazionali e migrazioni interne.*
78 The data was sent to me by Corrado Bonifazi, demographer at the Centro Nazionale delle Ricerche in Rome, in an electronic message dated 19 March 2002. He wrote: 'Cittadini Italiani cancellati per trasferimento residenza per l'estero. Anni 1990–1997: 1990, 48,916; 1991, 51,478; 1992, 50,226; 1993, 54,980; 1994, 59,402; 1995, 34,886; 1996, 39,017; 1997, 38,984.'
79 Andrea Casalegno, 'L''Italicità' della globalizzazione,' *Il Sole 24 Ore*, 28 March 2004, 31.
80 Clementina Sandra Ammendola, 'Immigrazione di ritorno e percorsi di cittadinanza,' in *Borderlines: Migrazioni e identità nel Novecento,*' ed. Jennifer Burns and Loredana Polezzi (Isernia: Cosmo Iannone ed., 2003), 213–23.
81 In her article 'Immigrati, via libera nuovi arrivi,' Giovanna Casadio reports that the new immigration quotas of October 2002 reserved 4000 entry visas for Argentinean citizens who have Italian ancestors (*la Repubblica*, 17 Oct. 2002, 25). The Veneto region opened an office to facilitate the migration of the Italians returning from the Argentinian province of Cordoba. Thanks to Zanussi, a factory that produces home appliances, these migrants entered Italy with a work contract. This 'progetto rientro' (project return), as it has been called, has supplied a model for other regions. Lombardy followed with a similar project that, however, is highly criticized by both the trade unions and other immigrant communities because of its emphasis on the priority given to 'blood,' that is, the Italian identity of the protagonists of

these migrations of return. See Marzio G. Mian, 'Bentornato, Argentino,' *Io donna*, 14 Dec. 2002, 114–18.

82 The best source of information on migrations of return from Argentina can be found in the *Dossier statistico immigrazione*, published by Caritas every year. In the 2002 volume, Ada Germani edited a section entitled 'Argentina: nuovo paese di emigrazione.' The data she supplies is quite revealing: 26 million Italians migrated from Italy between 1876 and 1986. Of them, 11.6% moved to Argentina. The migration of return from Argentina started in the 1950s, as post–Second World War migrations from Italy to Argentina were not as successful as previous ones. Between 1980 and 1990 applications for Italian citizenship increased. In 1988 they were 6269, became 12,493 in 1990, and peaked in 1991 with 43,451 applications. Between 1993 and 1997, 54,300 Argentinian citizens acquired Italian citizenship. In 1998, 17,000 Argentineans were granted Italian citizenship; the number increased to 20,000 in 2000. In the first two months of 2002, 17,000 Argentineans applied for Italian citizenship at the consulate in Buenos Aires. The dossier adds that currently there are about 600,000 Argentineans living abroad. 160,000 of them left the country in the last three years. See Germani, 'Argentina,' 48–54.

83 See Stella, *Schei.*

84 Habermas, 'Struggles for Recognition in the Democratic Constitutional State,' 141.

85 'Dance some break dance. / No, we don't do break dancing. / How come, you are black and you don't do any break dancing! / We do not dance break dance. / Then dance an African dance' (Khouma, *Io, venditore di elefanti*, 79).

86 Rossetti, *Schiena di vetro*, 122.

87 'Vu cumprà' is a term that has defined not only the migrant but also that niche in the Italian economy that some migrants have carved out in order to survive. In some cases, migrants have transformed themselves from undocumented street sellers without a permit into regular vendors with stalls at markets. On page 1 of *CorrierEconomia*, a section of the *Corriere della sera*, 19 June 2000, was titled 'E li chiamavano "vu cumprà."' On page 2 and 3, four additional articles explored the economic and entrepreneurial success of immigrants in the north-east of Italy; the success of a Chilean political refugee, Rodrigo Vergara, who became a translator in Italy; the economic empires of migrants who founded their own companies; and the story of how Zhou Likang acquired his considerable wealth in Italy. See Roberto Morelli, 'E il Piave mormorò: Sì allo straniero'; Roberta Scagliarini, 'Dal Cile il re dei traduttori industriali'; Cecilia Zecchinelli, 'Ecco i nuovi imprenditori d'Italia'; and Cecilia Zecchinelli, 'Il più ricco dei tanti Cinesi.'

88 Gardaphé, *Italian Signs*, 56.
89 One also cannot forget the presence of Italian communities in Egypt and in Maghreb, and in particular in Tunisia in the nineteenth and early twentieth centuries.
90 See the selection of nicknames for Italian migrants included in Paolo Rumiz, 'Noi, vecchi emigranti,' *la Repubblica*, 9 Oct. 2002, 41.
91 Rossetti, *Schiena di vetro*, 131.
92 See also the more recent novels by Pariani, *Quando Dio ballava il tango*, and Mazzucco, *Vita*. Both are well–known Italian writers who narrate Italian migration to the Americas braiding fiction with the autobiographical narratives of migration in their families. Pariani tells of a migration to Argentina. Mazzucco focuses on a migration to New York. Both texts construct family autobiographies.
93 Gnisci is the author of several texts that discuss Italian immigration literature: *Noialtri europei, Il rovescio del gioco, Slumgullion: saggi di letteratura comparata, Ascesi e decolonizzazione*, and *La letteratura italiana della migrazione*. Among the texts written in Italy on the immigrants' literature, see Ghezzi, 'La letteratura africana in Italia.'
94 See, for instance, Stella's *Quando gli Albanesi eravamo noi*.
95 Ashcroft, 'Post-Colonial Transformations and Global Culture,' 28.
96 Ibid., 29.
97 Patiño, 'Naufragio.'
98 Ibid., 205.
99 Ibid., 213.
100 Eco, *Cinque scritti morali*, 98.
101 Appiah, 'Identity, Authenticity, Survival: Multicultural Societies and Social Reproduction,' 161.

2. Minor Literature, Minor Italy

1 Abate, 'L'eredità,' 35. 'Your inheritance, *son figlio Sohn bir*, / is this treasure of blackberries *more mir e mir* / that I have on the tip of my tongue, / *këto fjalë parole Wörter* words, / these freeways of the sun: / take them, you can / *mein Sohn bir figlio mio* my son / and travel them the way you want: / I have already paid the toll.'
2 Kubati, M, 31. 'During the appetizers and the first course they / talked about me, of that East-West / South-North direction of my own journey, of my / literature degree that is completely / useless, of publishers and work ...'

3 Derrida, *Monolingualism of the Other.*
4 Ibid., 17.
5 Ibid., 36.
6 Balibar, 'The Nation Form,' 98.
7 Derrida, *Monolingualism of the Other*, 8, 23, and 14.
8 Ibid., 40.
9 Ibid., 63.
10 Ibid., 33.
11 Deleuze and Guattari, *Kafka: Toward a Minor Literature.*
12 In a recent conversation (March 2002), Salah Methnani has argued that he is actually the writer who read the book by Günter Wallraff and used it as a model. It would make my observations even more relevant if two immigrant writers, one from Tunisia, the other from Senegal, have used the same literary model in order to write their autobiographies.
13 I am thinking, of course, of Pascal D'Angelo's *Son of Italy*, Constantine Panunzio's *The Soul of an Immigrant*, and Marie Hall Ets, *Rosa, The Life of an Italian Immigrant.*
14 Wa Thiong'o, *Decolonising the Mind*, 12.
15 Ibid., 13.
16 Ibid., 15.
17 Ashcroft, 'Post-Colonial Transformation and Global Culture,' 31.
18 Spivak, *The Post-Colonial Critic*, 64.
19 Deleuze and Guattari, *Kafka*, 16.
20 Derrida, *Monolingualism of the Other*, 57.
21 Deleuze and Guattari, *Kafka*, 28.
22 Hajdari, *Ombra di cane*, 47. He is also the author of *Corpo presente* with parallel texts in Albanian and Italian, and *Antologia della pioggia* (2000), previously published in Albanian in 1990.
23 See also the case of Ridha Brahim, an immigrant from Tunisia who won the 'La Torate' award in 1998 for narrative in Friulano dialect. His 'Fûr dal timp' ('Outside Time') tells the story of a car accident. See the article by Luciano Santini, 'Fogolâr e narghilè.'
24 Ceserani, *Guida allo studio della letteratura*, 3–4.
25 The anthology was sold together with the daily newspaper *la Repubblica* as a special edition under the licence of Giulio Einaudi Editore.
26 Viano, 'Ecce Foemina,' 224.
27 Ibid.
28 Deleuze and Guattari, *Kafka*, 17.
29 Pivetta, 'Narrazioni Italiane,' 20.

30 Deleuze and Guattari, *Kafka*, 17.
31 See Angioni, *Una ignota compagnia* (1992); Lodoli, *I fannulloni* (1990); Saponaro, *Il ragazzo di Tirana* (1996); and Tadini, *La tempesta* (1993).
32 Fazel, 'Far Away from Mogadishu,' 151–2.
33 Deleuze and Guattari, *Kafka*, 17.
34 Chohra, *Volevo diventare bianca*, 132.
35 '[I thought] that they were savages and that I wanted to go back to France: it is not possible, these cannot be our relatives; they do not have chains to flush the toilet, instead of houses they live in tents like Indians, instead of light bulbs they use candles, of course, they do not have ceilings, where would they hang their chandeliers? They sleep in the middle of the road and my bed is not even soft, they do not have water taps, and, worst of all, they do not even have television sets! I cannot stay here any longer. Tomorrow I will go back to France' (ibid., 34).
36 Salem, *Con il vento nei capelli*, 138.
37 Ibid., 137.
38 Ibid., 145–6.
39 I thank my colleague Margaret Williamson for defining my work as a study on 'destination cultures.'
40 Radhakrishnan, *Diasporic Mediations*, 28.
41 See Turnaturi, *Tradimenti*.
42 Hargreaves and McKinney, 'Introduction: The Post-Colonial Problematic in Contemporary France,' 4.
43 She translated her presentation into Italian and published it in the article 'Culture unite d'Europa,' *Il Sole 24 Ore*, 13 Dec. 1998, 38.
44 Amara Lakhous made this statement on 3 November 2004 during his talk in a series of presentations by migrant writers entitled 'Scritture Migranti,' held in the Campidoglio in Rome. The series was organized by the councilwoman Franca Eckert Coen, the University 'La Sapienza' in Rome, and the cultural association 'Gianni Bosio.'
45 See Boelhower, *Immigrant Autobiography in the United States* and *Through a Glass Darkly*.
46 Sollors, *Beyond Ethnicity*, 241.
47 Hargreaves, *Voices from the North African Immigrant Community in France*, 20.
48 Another example of second-generation themes developed by first-generation migrants to Italy is Komla-Ebri's short story 'Identità trasversa.' The story begins with the words of the protagonist, Kuami, the son of a migrant to Italy: '"A me papà della tua Africa non me ne frega niente"' ('I don't give a damn about your Africa'; 89). He does not give a damn about his father's Africa and he does not want to travel back there because he is a different

black man from his father: he has grown up in Italy and his father's native land is completely foreign to him. He argues for a more flexible interpretation of colour and cultural lines than what his father has to offer.

49 Hargreaves, *Voices from the North African Immigrant Community in France*, 53.

50 See also Lamri, 'Il mio paese è il mio corpo.'

51 Lamri, 'Solo allora, sono certo, potrò capire,' 45.

52 Bartowski, *Travelers, Immigrants, Inmates*, xix.

53 Ibid., 85.

54 Ibid., 3.

55 Gangbo, *Verso la notte Bakonga*, 12.

56 Ibid., 20.

57 Ibid., 29.

58 Ibid., 51.

59 Ibid., 52–3.

60 Mika's experience as a black man in Italy is also voiced by a character in Komla-Ebri's short story 'Identità trasversa.' Kuami, the protagonist, states: 'Have you ever wondered what it meant for me when I figured out I was the only one 'of color' in a class of whites? Have you ever imagined how painful my surprise was when a stupid child called me a *negro*? I had not even realized I was different. It is not as if one gets up every morning, looks into the mirror and tells himself: Guess what, I am black! Others see you as different' ('Identità trasversa,' 91).

61 I am indebted to Guido Zebisch and his articulation of the concept of 'post ethnic' in his article 'Post-Ethnic Writing in Germany,' presented at the conference Writing Europe 2001: Migrant Cartographies.

62 Gangbo, *Verso la notte Bakonga*, 108.

63 Ibid., 135.

64 Kaplan, 'Resisting Autobiography,' 119–20.

65 Shakespeare's *Romeo and Juliet* is the inspiration for other narratives about Italian immigration. In June 2000 a version of the famous plot was performed in Turin. The Senegalese actor Modou Gueye played Romeo and a native Italian actress, Elena Cavallo, played Juliet. The conflict in the play mirrors the conflict between immigrants and local people in Turin, in particular at the market of Porta Palazzo. The performance was organized by the Teatro dell'Angolo, the Teatro Stabile, and the Teatro Grinzane Cavour. See 'L'amore di Romeo e Giulietta nell'odio di una casba urbana,' *la Repubblica*, 13 June 2000, 37. Scenes from *Romeo and Juliet* are also performed in the film on immigration *Un nero per casa* (*Black and Underfoot*), directed by Gigi Proietti in 1998. See also the film by Roberta Torre, *Sud Side Stori*, a

musical inspired both by *West Side Story* and by *Romeo and Juliet*. It takes place in Palermo; Romeo is Sicilian and Juliet is a Nigerian prostitute.

66 Gangbo, *Rometta and Giulieo*, 92.

67 Ibid., 36.

68 Ibid., 20.

69 Ibid., 165.

70 Chandra, *Media chiara e noccioline*, 77.

71 Ibid., 71.

72 Ibid., 72.

73 Ibid., 83.

74 Ibid., 82.

75 Ibid., 78.

76 Dones, *Sole bruciato*, 10.

77 Kubati, *M*, 14.

78 Dekhis, 'La salvezza,' 112.

79 I would also like to mention a web publication, *El Ghibli: Rivista online di letteratura della migrazione* (http://www.el-ghibli.provincia.bologna.it), directed by Pap Khouma. Its editorial board includes Tahar Lamri, Gabriella Ghermandi, Mia Lacomte, Raffaele Taddeo, Amara Lakhous, Kossi Komla-Ebri, Clementina Sandra Ammendola, and Ubax Cristina Ali-Farah. Another note worthy literary journal is *Sagarana* (http://www.sagarana.net/rivista/index.html), whose director, Julio Monteiro Martins, teaches Portuguese at the University of Pisa. A writer in Brazil, Martins has also published collections of short stories in Italian: *Racconti Italiani* and *La passione del vuoto*.

80 Corso Salani is also the director of the documentary *Eugen si ramona* (1989). It documents the uprising in Bucharest in 1989 where, during the revolution, he shot footage that is shown at the beginning of *Occidente*.

81 Agnieszka Czekanska, a Polish actress, plays Malvina in *Occidente*. She had collaborated with Corso Salani in his film *Gli occhi stanchi* (1996), in which she played Ewa, a Polish prostitute who crosses Europe on her trip back to Poland.

82 Salani, the director, plays the part of Alberto.

83 Inevitably, my discussion and list of anthologies and journals of migrants' writings is incomplete.

84 Armando Gnisci now organizes the European Festival of Migrant Writers.

85 In 2003, Christiana De Caldas Brito became a member of the jury for the Eks&Tra literary award, replacing Tahar Lamri.

86 In 1996 the volume *Mosaici d'inchiostro* (*Ink Mosaics*), edited by Roberta Sangiorgi, collected some of the poems and short stories submitted to the

award competition. Gëzim Hajdari resubmitted his work, winning the special medal from the President of the Republic. Another writer, Yousef Wakkas, sent his submission from prison and won the first prize, because his short story irreverently manipulated Italian language and grammar. In fact, in this volume the narrative structures became more complex and sophisticated. Anty Grah tells of a life as a prostitute in France and Clementina Sandra Ammendola attacks any theoretical approach to migrant writing that places the migrant writer in a position of inferiority. In 1997, *Memorie in valigia* (*Memories in a Suitcase*), edited by Ramberti and Sangiorgi, contained short stories whose authors started to experiment with humour, which in 2001 became the proposed topic for that year's literary award and anthology. At the 1997 edition of the award, Kossi Komla-Ebri won first prize. He continued to submit short stories in subsequent years, but also became involved in politics in his city of Erba, in Lombardy, in order to oppose the local stronghold of the Northern League party. In 2002, his left-wing coalition won the local elections and he submitted a novel entitled *Neyla* to Einaudi, a major Italian publisher located in Turin. Einaudi rejected the volume, which was finally published by the Milanese Edizioni dell'Arco in 2002 and was sold by street vendors. *Neyla* has been translated into English by Peter Pedroni and will be published by Fairleigh Dickinson University Press.

87 See the anthology *Anime in viaggio*, which collects texts from the sixth edition of the literary award originated by Eks&Tra. The name of the editor is not mentioned in the book.

88 In 2002 Eks&Tra also became a publisher of texts authored by migrants. With the support of the province of Mantua, for instance, Eks&Tra printed Yousef Wakkas's *Fogli sbarrati: viaggio surreale e reale tra carceratie migranti.*

89 Komla-Ebri's short story 'Imbarazzismi (Imbarazzi in bianco e nero)' is also the title of his book published by Arco Marna (2002). Abdel Malek Smari is the author of the novel *Fiamme in paradiso.*

90 See Beverly, 'The Margin at the Center.'

91 The Roman company Edizioni Interculturali has published volumes on migration issues in a series directed by Armando Gnisci who teaches comparative literature at the University 'La Sapienza' in Rome.

92 See Passarelli and Spinelli, *Gli stranieri in carcere.*

93 I am particularly grateful to Maria Ponce de León for generously allowing me to use the information about publishing companies founded in Roman prisons that she eloquently discussed in her dissertation titled 'Meccanismi di sopravvivenza.'

94 Di Liegro, *Immigrazione.*

95 Turnaturi, *Immaginazione sociologica e immaginazione letteraria*, 45.

3. Cinema and Migration: 'What' and 'Who' Is a Migrant?

1 Please see 'Senza patria,' a chapter in Dal Lago's *Giovani, stranieri e criminali*, 29–34. Here Dal Lago discusses statements on migrants and migration voiced by Luisa Muraro, one of the best known Italian feminists. Dal Lago reacts to Muraro's defence of the rights of a 'local population' and to the patriarchal voice of a 'left' that defends the rights of an immigrant minority.

2 Restaino and Cavarero, *Le filosofie femministe*, 158.

3 Ibid., 159.

4 Ibid., 159.

5 Ibid., 160.

6 Ibid.

7 All the quotations from *Tu che mi guardi* are taken from the English translation by Paul A. Kottman, *Relating Narratives*. Page references provided are from this translation.

8 Ibid., 161.

9 Ibid., 163.

10 See the short film *Algerie* (1995) directed by Luca Guadagnino for an interview with Rachid Benhadj, who discusses his Algerian identity in connection with Algerian politics. Benhadj is also the director of another remarkable film he made in Arabic in Algeria: *Louss – Roses des sables* (*Louss – Roses in the Desert*, 1989). A physically challenged Moussa and his sister Zineb live in the Sahara desert. Zineb works packing dates, Moussa draws, hopelessly falls in love, and cares for a rose that has bloomed in the desert. Benhadj succeeds in creating complex psychological portraits of these two characters at the margins of village life. He is also the director of the short film *L'ultima cena* (*The Last Supper*, 1995), which deals with fragments of African life in Verona, Italy.

11 See Braidotti, *Per un femminismo nomade* and *Nomadic Subjects*.

12 Ginzburg's title is inspired by Collodi's *Pinocchio* and a particular scene in which Pinocchio's big wooden eyes startle Geppetto because it seems that they are staring at him.

13 The reverse journey to Africa in the company of an Italian is also the subject of another short documentary/film. The well-known director Paolo Virzì hired Oumar Ba to appear in his comedy *Ferie d'agosto* (1996), in which, Ba played a stereotypical *vu cumprà* who helps in uncovering the hypocritical behaviour of self-proclaimed liberals. In *Il viaggio di Oumar* (1998), Virzì follows Oumar Ba back to Senegal. This documentary/film records both Oumar's autobiography and the questions that the director asks Oumar throughout the trip. Broadcast by RAI 2, the film is still an unequal collabo-

ration between native and non-native artist, but it allows Oumar Ba to achieve the visibility that leads to other projects. Ba has worked with Italian directors such as Emanuela De Marchi and Ugo Gregoretti, and with the Algerian Swiss director Mohamed Soudani. Oumar has also directed a short documentary entitled *Conversazione* that was made to celebrate the end of apartheid in South Africa. The film was shot in the suburbs of Milan.

14 Kottman, *Relating Narratives*, 4.

15 Ibid., 36.

16 Ibid.

17 Fraire, 'La linea d'ombra,' 29.

18 Ibid., 29.

19 Ashcroft, 'Post-Colonial Transformations and Global Culture,' 28.

20 Kottman, *Relating Narratives*, 99.

21 The quotation is from an interview with Rachid Benhadj by Maria Pia Fusco in her article 'Intolleranza, un male che conosco,' *la Repubblica*, 9 Aug. 1998, 43. *Mirka* was produced by the Italian film company Filmart in collaboration with France and Spain and, unexpectedly, according to the director, attracted the attention of actors such as Vanessa Redgrave (Kalsan) and Gérard Depardieu (Strix). Its director of photography is the Oscar-winning Vittorio Storaro.

22 Kottman, *Relating Narratives*, 88.

23 Hargreaves and McKinney, 'Introduction,' 6.

24 Marco Bellocchio protested against RAI because the company kept the films without broadcasting them until July 1999. They were shown on the second channel starting at 11:10 p.m. and therefore had a limited audience. See 'Su RaiDue "Un altro paese nei miei occhi": Bellocchio-Freccero film con polemica,' *la Repubblica*, 1 July 1999, 53 (no author indicated).

25 RAI 3 has also been broadcasting a very boring, at times grotesque, multi-ethnic talent/quiz show entitled *Pacem in Terris* (1999). See King and Woods, eds., *Media and Migration*.

26 Chambers, *Migrancy, Culture, Identity*, 5.

27 Eastern European women are at the centre of many Italian films. Carlo Mazzacurati's *Vesna va veloce* (*Vesna Moves Fast*, 1996) portrays the stereotypical prostitute that seems to inhabit the contemporary Italian imaginary. Vesna, who is twenty, arrives in Italy from the Czech Republic. An Italian man falls in love with her and tries to 'save' her. Although the cover of the film-video defines the plot as being influenced by both Truffaut and De Sica, the film fails to create anything but another stereotype about eastern women, about women, and about prostitution. The short black-and-white film *Cuori spezzati* (*Broken Hearts*, 1997) is the story of Mirosh and Lule.

Directed by Federico Bruno, the film is a homage to neorealism and tells of the exploitation of Albanian children like Mirosh, who is used as a window-washer, a beggar, and a male prostitute by unscrupulous adults. Lule is a girl sold on the prostitution market who befriends Mirosh while they are both on the boat that takes them from Albania to Italy. Both are undocumented migrants and Mirosh becomes a victim of the violence witnessed by Lule.

28 Cavarero, 'Who Engenders Politics?' 95.

29 Ibid., 96.

30 Ibid., 97.

31 Ibid., 97.

32 Ibid., 99.

33 Ibid., 100.

34 Ibid., 102.

35 Ibid., 102.

36 Ibid., 103.

37 Ibid., 103.

38 Ibid.

39 In *Pressions* (1999), the director Sanvi Panau portrays the irrational behaviour of the sixty-year-old wife of a French politician, who obsessively screams at Africans she sees in the streets. Represented as a mad woman's chant in Panau's short film, the demand that immigrants 'go back to their own country' achieves through repetition a metaphorical representation of the irrational demands made by an aggressive majority.

40 Cavarero, 'Who Engenders Politics?' 107.

41 Ibid., 110.

42 Ibid., 110.

43 Ibid., 111.

44 Directed by Davide Del Boca, this documentary contains several interviews with Pap Khouma, with southern Italians living in Milan, who see African street vendors as unfair competition, with Antonio Golini, an expert in demographics, and with Nicoletta Gandes, district attorney in Milan.

45 Cavarero, 'Who Engenders Politics?' 106.

46 Ba has also collaborated as an actor and writer on the documentary *Bataaxal* (*La lettera*, 1997), directed by Luca Lucini. It starts with Ba reading a letter addressed to his mother about his experience as a migrant in Milan. It develops into an exploration of the reasons why Senegalese people have no choice but migration to improve the economic condition of their families.

47 Cross-cultural film projects are particularly relevant to my discourse on Italian migration culture and the construction of a destination culture that

does not respect national boundaries. Of particular note is a film directed by Fatih Akin, who is Turkish German, entitled *Solino* (2002), the name of a village in Puglia. The film narrates the migration of a family from the Italian south to Hamburg where they open a pizzeria. The story of an Italian migration is told by a Turkish German director who ventriloquizes other migrations through the experiences of Rosa, Romano, Gigi, and Giancarlo. The narrative spans twenty years (1964–84) and documents the changing relationship between children and parents in an Italian family in Hamburg. Dialogues between Romano and his sons are particularly revealing. Romano speaks in Italian and his children answer in German, which is the language the brothers use to communicate with each other. If they revert to Italian, their accent is marked by their familiarity with German. Gigi returns to Italy in his twenties and performs a migration of return that his brother Giancarlo vehemently refuses. Returning means for Gigi to give up his dreams as a filmmaker that his brother will be able to fulfil. Returning here involves a mutilation rather than a reconnection with mythical roots. (I thank Alessandro Fabrizi for pointing me in the direction of this film and for helping me acquire a copy of it.)

48 On this subject, Mulvay writes: 'As a Wolof, Sembene came from an oral tradition in which the *griot* functioned as poet and storyteller. As the son of a fisherman, he was self-educated ... Sembene's cinema is more the product of popular, Senegalese traditions and his films are directed towards the cultural needs of the Senegalese people through the specific possibilities offered by the cinema ... Sembene's commitment to promoting and transforming traditional culture [is] to using the cultural developments of Western society in the interests of Africa. Sembene was more interested in finding a dialectical relationship between the two cultures than in an uncritical nostalgia for pre-colonial pure African-ness' ('Xala,' 517).

49 Mulvay, 'Xala,' 518.

50 Kachru, 'The Alchemy of English,' 319.

51 Another film made thanks to an Italian, Swiss, and French financial collaboration, Silvio Soldini's *Brucio nel vento* (2001), is based on the novel *Yesterday* by the Czech author Agota Kristof. Distributed internationally in French with English subtitles, the film contains a poetic narrative about displacement and self-identification through newly acquired languages. The protagonist is a young boy, Tobias, the son of the village prostitute. He witnesses the comings and goings of his mother's clients and of one in particular – Dalibor, the village teacher who also becomes Tobias's teacher. Once he discovers that Dalibor is his biological father, Tobias stabs both his mother and his father while they are sleeping, then he runs away from his

Czech village. Arrested for vagrancy, he ends his childhood in a reformatory. After leaving the juvenile detention house, Tobias Horvath abandons his legal name to become Dalibor Liska, who moves to Switzerland and works in a factory that makes semi-manufactured parts for watches. He becomes a migrant who produces the traditional and stereotypical Swiss product: watches. However, he only makes parts of a watch, never a whole one. Dalibor remarks on the fragmented nature of his work, which is also a powerful metaphor for the fragmented nature of his life in Switzerland, where he can only establish temporary relationships with other people. Dalibor spends his free time writing poetic prose with a pencil. His narratives are only pencilled in. They are fragile lifelines that can be easily erased. He writes in French, as it is the language of 'here,' he says, the language in which he is scripting his daily existence. However, French gradually looses its predominance in the film as more and more Czech characters start to populate Dalibor's life, including Line. Line, or Caroline, is his ideal woman. He met her in school in the village. She was the schoolteacher's daughter and therefore Tobias/Dalibor's half-sister. Dalibor meets her again because Line, her husband Kristof, and their baby daughter temporarily migrate to the same place, which always remains unnamed in the film, where Dalibor lives. Kristof is a researcher at the university and Line works in the watch factory where Dalibor also works. Locations remain unnamed throughout the film. First there is a Czech village, then a somewhere that is in Switzerland, vaguely outlined by the French that people speak. Every location can only be temporary. As Line and Dalibor fall in love, the location needs to be changed. In fact, when Line decides to leave her husband, she stabs him in self-defence. Dalibor and Line escape to another country that is never named but is still recognizable. In fact, Dalibor tells of his work with fishermen, while Line listens to language-acquisition tapes in Italian. It is a new language of the 'here' that can script the relative happy ending of Dalibor and Line's story. Soldini's ending betrays Agota Kristof's original narrative. Soldini, in fact, makes room for the development of Line, the female character. Kristof's novel focuses on the dramatic life of the male character and scripts a punitive ending. Soldini makes his film revolve around both characters and allows them to survive through a new linguistic resurrection.

52 On 21 October 2002, 35 European satellite networks (in Italy 'Tele+ bianco,' at 11:00 pm) broadcasted a program of short documentaries and interviews devoted to migration. Ba and Soudani's idea of constructing a European film project directly connects to this more recent attempt to discuss migration from a European point of view, treating it as an issue that concerns the

states that compose Europe, beyond individual national and linguistic borders. *Le luci di Brindisi* (*Brindisi's Lights*) is the title of the program, which originated from an idea of Jorge Semprun, a Spanish intellectual who migrated to France during the Spanish Civil War. He was a communist, a resistance fighter, and a prisoner at Büchenwald, but also the minister of culture in Spain from 1988 to 1991. The idea for a European program that debates the issues of migrants in Europe comes, therefore, from a man who has experienced migration, marginalization, and persecution. The first segment in the program, titled 'La lettera,' tells the story of an Albanian boy in Italy who writes to his friends back in Albania. He fills his narrative about Italy with information about the glamour of living in the West, but then tears his letter into pieces because it is filled with lies. Another segment tells of the lives of migrants in Bologna who cannot find a place to live and are repeatedly evicted from temporary lodgings. The protagonists of other segments include an African man who was born rich, but abandoned by his parents becomes poor, lives in the streets, but then emerges as a writer (this story resembles the life of Jadelin Mabiala Gangbo). Another segment tells the story of a Tamil family who collects films made in India. There are also interviews with 12 immigrants who have found employment as cultural mediators and describe the intolerance that immigrants experience in Europe. A reportage piece narrates the experiences of an Algerian journalist who lives with the immigrants in Marseilles and experiences with them the frustrating search for a job, a house, and legal documentation, and what it means to be a *sans papier.* Another report tells of Swedish Nazi skinheads and their threatening and nostalgic demonstrations. A final report documents the ways in which undocumented migrants reach Europe. The directors of the short films and the documentaries/reports include Pascal Catougno, Said Bakthaoui, Gilles Bavon, Amedeo Ricucci, Nicola Zamperini, Patrice del Mazery, Mathias Quincé, and Paul Moreira.

53 See Parati, 'Living in Translation, Thinking with an Accent,' 280–6.

54 Cavarero, *A più voci*, 8.

55 Ibid., 11.

56 Ibid., 14.

57 Ibid., 10.

58 Ibid., 13.

59 Tarr, 'French Cinema and Post-Colonial Minorities,' 69.

60 Ibid.

61 The Tunisian Mohsen Melliti wrote *Pantanella: canto lungo la strada* in 1992. Originally written in Arabic, the novel was translated into Italian by Monica Ruocco and became public only in Italian, while the Arabic version was

never published. In 1995 Melliti wrote his second novel, *I bambini delle rose*, in Italian without any mediating intervention on the part of an Italian expert. See also the article by Luca Fontana, 'Il ritorno dei marocchiani' ('The Return of the Morokkians'), *Diario*, 15 Sept. 2000, 22–9. The journalist follows migrants who travel back to Morocco for summer vacation and justifies his article by stating that 'Sappiamo tutto degli extracomunitari che arrivano in Italia cercando lavoro. Poco, invece, conosciamo delle loro vite private e dei mondi da cui provengono' ('We know everything about the migrants who arrive in Italy looking for work. We know very little instead about their private lives and the cultures they come from'; 22).

62 A number of short films and documentaries have been devoted to migration issues. Unfortunately short films are not well distributed and therefore reach a small number of people. I would like to mention a few that are relevant to this discussion on representations of migration and migrants. *Io sono invisibile* (*I Am Invisible*, 2000) was written by Mustapha Chati and Anna Passatore and directed by Tonino Curagi and Anna Gorio. It begins by supplying figures concerning migrations to Italy: in 1998 there were 300,000 undocumented migrants in Italy; in 1999, following a *sanatoria* (amnesty), the number decreased to 113,000. It also stresses that in 2000 the amount of 182 billion lire was spent to patrol the coast of Italy and stop people from entering the country. These figures are followed by individual stories of undocumented migrants: young men from Morocco, Katarina from Ukraine, and Agata from Brazil. The short film eloquently juxtaposes 'whatness' to 'whoness' and ends with images taken from a cemetery. On gravestones inscribed with 'sconosciuto di sesso maschile' or 'femminile' (unknown, male or female) the anonymity of numbers is translated into the nameless death of undocumented migrants.

Transsexual like Agata, Fernanda Farias de Albuquerque is the subject of a 1997 short film *Le strade di Princesa: ritratto di un trans molto speciale* (*Princesa's Streets: Portrait of a Very Special Transsexual*). The director, Stefano Consiglio, interviews Princesa in prison (guilty of attempted murder) following the success of her autobiography *Princesa*, written in collaboration with Maurizio Jannelli. *Pane Egiziano* (*Egyptian Bread*, 1997), directed by Laura Qualia, tells of an Egyptian man's bureaucratic odyssey to obtain a licence to open a pizzeria in Milan. The story points to the paradox that a traditional Italian dish is now made by Egyptians in many pizzerias and portrays a migrant's difficult path to independence as embodied in his own pizza parlor. The documentary *Ragazzi fuori* (*Boys Outside*, 2000) deals with teenagers who live at the margin of society in Turin. Directed by Aurelio Grimaldi, the film documents the lives of both native and non-native young adults, in particular a young man from Tirana who came to Italy attracted by the representation of the country he saw on television and found himself confronting a very different reality. *Clandestini in città* (*Undocumented in the City*, 1992), directed by Marcello Bivona, is the story of a friendship between Alì and two native Italians, Lallo and Rosa, and of Alì's realization that the dreams that motivated his migration cannot become reality. Bivona is also the director of *Ritorno a Tunisi* (*Back to Tunis*, 1998), which documents the history of the Italian community in Tunisia in the first half of the twentieth century. A particular fragment of the history of Italian migration to northern Africa, it is also the story of Bivona's family.

63 Bhabha, 'On the Irremovable Strangeness of Being Different,' 34.

64 Ibid.

65 The COE or Centro Orientamento Educazione has been one of the promoters of the annual African Film Festival that takes place in March in Milan. Its collection of films draws an interesting parallel between Italian and European films on migration issues. For instance, Jean Marie Teno's *Clando* (1996), informed by the problems of undocumented migrants in Germany, is in dialogue with films such as *Clandestini in città* and Maderna's *Jahilia*. The link with international and European filmmaking, in particular, is evident in Theo Eshetu's work. Of Ethiopian origin, Eshetu was born and educated in England. He has been living and working in Italy since 1982. In his *Il sangue non è acqua fresca* (*Blood Is Not Fresh Water*, 1998), Eshetu traces his nomadism back to Ethiopia, where he interviews his grandfather and constructs a narrative about Italian colonialism.

66 Taghmaoui is known to American audiences for his roles in *The Good Thief* (2003), *The Three Kings* (1999), and *Hideous Kinky* (1999), respectively directed by Neil Jordan, David O. Russell, and Gilles MacKinnon.

67 The controversy provoked by this film is summarized in the article by Als Ob, 'Razzismo (vero e falso) in tv,' *Il Sole 24 Ore*, 13 Dec. 1998, 30. The author of the article reports on the outrage that the film raised and recognizes the limitations of Proietti's *Un nero per casa*. However, his point is that there are much more dangerous forms of racism that are considered acceptable: calling Rom people 'nomads,' talking about 'invasions' of migrants, and creating television programs in which people publicly cheer the murderer of an Albanian accused of theft. The film received a positive review in the article by Turrioni, 'A me gli occhi, please,' which is mainly about Proietti's career as a film director.

68 Other recent Italian films have proposed the stereotypical representation of the migrant as 'maid.' See *Cominciò tutto per caso* (*Everything Began by Chance*, 1993) directed by Umberto Marino. In this film Marilu is a Philip-

pine woman who works for an Italian family. She falls in love with a local Italian plumber and their relationship flourishes with the help of Stefania, the woman who employs Marilu. The plot of *L'altra donna* (*The Other Woman*, 1980), directed by Peter del Monte, revolves around Olga, a middle-class woman with a son. She is separated and employs an Ethiopian, Regina, who works as her maid. Olga grows less insecure thanks to her friendship with Regina, but Olga is also the only one benefiting from such a relationship.

69 In discussing the representations of Albania and Albanians in contemporary films in Italian, it is relevant to mention the work of Matteo Garrone. His 1997 *Terra di mezzo* (*The Land In-between*) is divided in three episodes: 'Silhouette' is a non-stereotypical portrayal of Nigerian prostitutes who work outside of Rome (see Anais Ginori, 'Nigeria, la città delle prostitute dove tornano le "italiane,"' *la Repubblica*, 13 Nov. 2002, 13). 'Self-Service' is the story of an Egyptian man who has worked the night shift at a Roman gas station for twelve years. 'Euglen e Gertian' is the story of two Albanian young men who are hired to perform underpaid odd jobs. Under different names, they are also the subject of a feature film entitled *Ospiti* (*Guests*) that Garrone directed in 1998. Gherti and Ghini, two Albanian cousins, live in Rome and try to hold on to their jobs as well as their dignity. They encounter Italians who for different reasons inhabit the margins of Italian society: an old man whose wife has gone mad and a photographer who stammers. Garrone works with non-professional actors and contributes to the complex discussion on difference in contemporary Italy by confronting the issues faced by young immigrant men.

70 For a recent article on the history of Italian/Albanian relations, see Mai, 'La costruzione culturale dell'Italia in Albania e viceversa,' 77–93.

71 Fanon, *Les damnés de la terre*.

72 American audiences are familiar with Thandie Newton from a number of commercial films, including *Interview with a Vampire: The Vampire Chronicles* (Neil Jordan, 1994), *Beloved* (Jonathan Demme, 1998), *Mission Impossible II* (John Woo, 2000), *The Truth about Charlie* (Jonathan Demme, 2002), and *Shade* (Damian Nieman, 2003).

73 Lasdun, *The Siege and Other Stories*.

74 Peploe is known for a number of films: *Triumph of Love* (2002), *Rough Magic* (1995), and *High Season* (1988).

75 Cavarero, 'Who Engenders Politics?' 102.

76 Ibid., 103.

77 Ibid., 105.

78 Ibid., 102.

79 There are a number of films that I have not included in my discussion and they deserve mention.

Michele Placido's *Pummarò* (1990) is the story of Kwaku, a young doctor from Ghana who comes to Italy in search of his brother. The plot is similar to the story in Saidou Moussa Ba and Alessandro Micheletti's *La promessa di Hamadi*, but Placido's film contains a romantic plot absent in the novel.

Giovanna Gagliardo's *Caldo soffocante* (*Sweltering Heat*, 1991) tells an unsettling story of a search for the 'other.' Christine, a French woman, finds documents belonging to an African woman and tries to find their elusive owner. *Teste rasate* (*Shaved Heads*, 1993), directed by Claudio Fragasso, investigates the phenomenon of neo-Nazism among young men in Italy and episodes of racially motivated violence.

Silvio Soldini's *Un'anima divisa in due* (*A Soul Split in Two*, 1993), which won the Golden Lion prize at the Venice Film Festival in 1993, tells of the irreconcilable differences between Pietro and Pabe. Pabe is a Rom woman who feels trapped in the conformity of a love relationship with Pietro. Pietro, a native Italian, finds with Pabe the courage to transgress, but maintains his position of power as a man and a native Italian. A traditional happy ending cannot take place and Pabe leaves Pietro. Soldini is a well-known Italian director whose filmography includes *L'aria serena dell'ovest* (*The Serene Air of the West*, 1990), *Le acrobate* (*The Acrobat Women*, 1997), *Pane e tulipani* (*Bread and Tulips*, 2000) which achieved international success, and *Agata e la tempesta* (*Agatha and the Storm*, 2004). In 2001 he made *Brucio nel vento* (*Burning in the Wind*), a story of migration from eastern Europe to Switzerland.

Stefano Reali's *Verso Nord* (*To the North*, 2003) tells of the journey of a Moroccan child who travels through Italy with an Albanian killer and an Italian male nurse who has let himself be corrupted by easy money. The two adults accompany him on a journey to Switzerland where the child has to join the family that has literally 'bought' him. Edmond and Saimir are the protagonists of Francesco Munzi's *Saimir* (2004). They are a father and a fifteen-year-old son who migrated from Albania to Italy. They are close, but find it very difficult to communicate openly with each other. In order to make money quickly and guarantee a decent future for his son, Edmond works in people-trafficking. Saimir is a teenager who has problems fitting in among his peers and with the girl he has a crush on. When he discovers that his father is involved in an underage prostitute ring, he sets out on a journey of personal redemption that will redefine his space of belonging.

For a discussion of some of these films see Parati, 'Intellectual Witnesses of Exile,' 205–24.

4. The Laws of Migration

1 Bodei, *Il noi diviso*, 54. 'Next to imaginary countries, there are also real ones.'
2 Vattimo, *Nichilismo ed emancipazione*, 152. The stability of the law depends on a chain of interpretations that have embodied it in history.'
3 Cavarero, 'Who Engenders Politics?' 95.
4 Ibid., 96.
5 Ibid., 97.
6 Ibid., 98.
7 Mafai, *Il sorpasso*, 23.
8 Ibid., 23.
9 Ibid., 25. See also Alasia, *Milano, Corea. Inchiesta sugli immigrati*. The book was originally published in 1960 and expanded in the 1975 volume.
10 *Corriere della Sera*, 27 April 2002, 9. Other data from the same newspaper issue indicate that Great Britain in 2002 had more than one million undocumented migrants, Ireland a meager 10,000, Belgium 90,000, Germany between 500,000 and one and a half million, France 400,000, and Greece about one million.
11 Only 3.4% of migrants from Romania choose Italy as their destination; most still prefer to move to Germany.
12 Sri Lanka is followed by Poland, Peru, India, Nigeria, Ghana, Macedonia, Brazil, and Russia (Bonifazi, 'Dimensioni e caratteri dell'immigrazione straniera'). In October 2002 the Caritas organization presented in Rome its new dossier about immigration (cf. *Dossier Immigrazione*). It states that Albanians have become the largest group of migrant workers in Italy, followed by migrants from Morocco, Romania, Switzerland, the former Yugoslavia, Tunisia, Senegal, China, and Poland. Together they make up 17.5% of the workforce in Italy. Caritas also expressed its condemnation of the Bossi-Fini immigration laws. See also Giovanna Casadio, 'Immigrati, legge da bocciare,' *la Repubblica*, 24 Oct. 2002, 23.
13 Meneghel Bellencin, 'Donne ed emigrazione.'
14 See Andall, *Gender, Migration and Domestic Service*.
15 The presence of Chinese people in Italy dates back to the 1920s and 1930s, when they arrived from France and England and managed to carve out a space even under Mussolini's fascist dictatorship.
16 On this topic, refer to the article by Brusa, 'L'impatto dei fenomeni immigratori.'
17 Lombardy hosts 400,000 migrants, 80% of them concentrated around Milan.

It is estimated that in this region there are between 72,000 and 101,000 undocumented migrants.

18 Rotondi, 'Immigrazione, multicultura e nuovi processi di territorializzazione.'

19 Papotti, 'I paesaggi etnici.' For a historical perspective on the relationship between urban space and foreigners, see Calabi and Lanaro, eds., *La città italiana e i luoghi degli stranieri.*

20 Augé, *Nonluoghi.*

21 Ibid., 109.

22 Young, *Colonial Desire*, 30.

23 Subtitled *Caratteristiche e tendenze, differenze regionali e processi di territorializzazione nella nuova società multiculturale*) (Characteristics and Tendencies, Regional Differences, and Processes of Territorialization in the New Multicultural Society). See also the article by Giancarlo Mola, 'Ottanta sindaci del Nordest a lezione di immigrazione,' *La Repubblica*, 22 Oct. 2002, 24.

24 In his book *Homo sacer. Il potere sovrano e la nuda vita*, Giorgio Agamben reminds us that the category of rights belongs to people who are citizens, that is, it belongs to a specific national juridical system. Decrees that protect non-citizens can easily be erased in emergencies such as wars. Thus, the rights of non-citizens are only temporary.

25 Giovanna Casadio, 'Più difficile espellere i clandestini: dopo l'ordine del questore, due giorni per il sì del magistrato,' *la Repubblica*, 29 Mar. 2002, 21.

26 Marco Nese, 'Sì agli stranieri nell'Esercito, penso a una brigata di albanesi,' *Corriere della Sera*, 22 Feb. 2002, 1, 9.

27 See the unsigned article 'Indigeni reclutati per anni in Africa,' *Corriere della Sera*, 22 Feb. 2002, 9. It reads: 'Ascari' era il nome dato dagli esploratori o dai carovanieri dell'Africa Orientale a indigeni armati incaricati di proteggerli. Nel XVII secolo sono i soldati di un corpo di fanteria marocchina. Tra il XIX e il XX secolo sono i soldati indigeni delle truppe coloniali tedesche (reclutati nell'Africa Orientale e Sudoccitentale tra il 1890 e il 1918) e italiane (arruolati in Eritrea, Somalia e Libia tra il 1877 e il 1941).' 'Ascari was the name that explorers and caravan guides in eastern Africa gave to natives hired and armed to protect them. In the 17th century, that's the name for a regiment of Moroccan infantry soldiers. Between the 19th and the 20th century, it's the name for African soldiers serving among German colonial troops (enlisted in eastern and south-western Africa) and Italian colonial troops (enlisted in Eritrea, Somalia, and Lybia between 1877 and 1841).'

28 Gian Antonio Stella, 'Quando "criminale" era il marchio affibbiato ai nostri emigranti,' *Corriere della Sera*, 22 Feb. 2002, 1, 9.

29 Komla-Ebri, 'Identità trasversa,' 96. The patriarchal rhetoric of male bread-winning in this quotation may even appeal to post-fascists and Northern Leaguers, who could also understand the eloquent metaphor that Komla-Ebri employs.

30 See Dal Lago, *Giovani, stranieri e criminali*, 125–8.

31 The Bossi-Fini bill proposed sanctions against human traffickers: up to 12 years in prison and a fine of 15,000 euros for each smuggled person.

32 Unfortunately, even Italian intellectuals have embraced the possibility of employing the armed forces in solving immigration issues. Gianni Vattimo has surprisingly written: 'Lotta agli scafisti e ai loro prezzi, facciamo lavorare la nostra marina mercantile, anche a costo di far fuoco sui battelli contrabbandieri.' ('Let's fight against people-smugglers and their high prices. Let's make our merchant marine work even if it means shooting at people-smugglers' boat.') Vattimo is guilty of embracing the idea of migrants as 'whats' that could be sacrificed in order to fight the smuggling of those migrant 'goods.' Opening fire on a boat transporting undocumented migrants means killing people that a campaign against illegal smugglers is supposedly protecting. Another potential scenario also comes to mind: immigrants enlisted in the armed forces opening fire on other immigrants. The post-fascists and the Northern Leaguers would wholeheartedly endorse such a strategic measure to defend the nation against undocumented immigration. Vattimo, *Nichilismo ed emanicpazione*, 114.

33 Established by the Turco-Napolitano law of 1998, these centres have been endorsed by the Bossi-Fini law, which promotes the addition of others in allowing for special funding that could facilitate their construction. The first of these centres was established in 1998 in Trapani, Sicily. Their long-standing substandard living conditions have created revolts among the inmates. Articles of outrage about the centres have been published, in particular, by the newspaper *Il Manifesto*, which has openly named them 'new concentration camps.' See, for instance, Erri De Luca, 'Campi di infamia,' *Il Manifesto*, 30 Nov. 2002, 1.

34 The article continues on page 17. See also Ezio Vallarolo, 'A Torino in corteo contro i nuovi lager,' *Il Manifesto*, 30 Nov. 2002, 7.

35 There have been five *sanatorie* or amnesties since 1986. In her article 'Il lavoro degli immigrati tra divieti e sanatorie,' *la Repubblica*, 16 Oct. 2002, Giovanna Zincone stresses the problematic nature of the amnesties and states that: 'Le sanatorie, in tutti i campi, funzionano se si presentano come

una tantum, come evento straordinario, altrimenti alimentano la convinzione che sia giusto e utile non rispettare le regole' ('In any context, *sanatorie* work if they take place *una tantum*, that is, as an extraordinary event, otherwise they strengthen some people's conviction that it is right and useful not to respect the rules'; 17).

36 Elio Pagnotta, 'Alla Calabria il record (27.8%) del lavoro nero,' *Il Sole 24 Ore*, 1 Mar. 2002, 17.

37 Barbara Fiammeri, 'Immigrati, primo sì alle nuove regole,' *Il Sole 24 Ore*, 1 Mar. 2002, 17. For an analysis of domestic work and immigrant women in Italy, see Andall, *Gender, Migration and Domestic Service*; Cortesi, 'Mercato del lavoro e mobilità della popolazione'; Ghilardi, 'Donne e immigrazione'; and Raffaele, 'Le immigrate extracomunitarie in Italia.'

38 Maristella Iervasi, 'Sull'immigrazione il governo sa solo seminare panico,' *L'Unità*, 31 Mar. 2002, 10. There is some poetic justice in having an immigration law named after 'Turco' (Turkish) and 'Napolitano' (Neapolitan) – an ironic commentary on the relationship between Italian immigration history and the process of law-making.

39 She is referring to Article 10 of the Italian constitution: 'The foreigner who is deprived in his own country of democratic freedom guaranteed by the Italian constitution has the right to receive asylum in the territory of the Republic according to the conditions established by the law.'

40 Bourdieu expresses a similar opinion on the rhetoric of left-wing parties in France: 'Their vote catching demagogy is based on the assumption that "public opinion" is hostile to "immigration," to foreigners, to any kind of opening of the frontiers. The verdict of the "pollsters" – the modern day astrologers – and the advice of the spin-doctors who make up for their lack of competence with conviction, urge them to strive to "win votes from le Pen"' (Bourdieu, *Acts of Resistance*, 17).

41 The author of the front-page article is not indicated. 'Immigrati, legge sbagliata: la Chiesa boccia il governo. Nuova tragedia: morti 6 clandestini,' *la Repubblica*, 12 Mar. 2002, 1.

42 Lello Parise, 'Clandestini, un'altra strage: sei morti in mare. Scajola: Centri di accoglienza all'estero,' *la Repubblica*, 12 Mar. 2002, 2.

43 Ibid.

44 Marco Politi, 'Attacco di [Cardinal] Ruini al governo: "Immigrati, legge sbagliata,"' *la Repubblica*, 12 Mar. 2002, 3.

45 *Famiglia Cristiana* has for decades been one of the most widely read publications in Italy. Its articles, columns, and inserts cater to wide-ranging audiences. The magazine is particularly relevant to migration studies because it frequently contains articles on migration data and immigration laws and

provides an irreplaceable source of information regarding the Catholic church's position on immigration.

46 Anfossi, 'I "boat people" e la legge di Bossi,' 47.

47 Anfossi, 'Uomini o topi,' 44.

48 See also *Dossier immigrazione*. This book was sold together with an issue of *Famiglia Cristiana*, 11 May 2003.

49 Anfossi, 'Uomini o topi,' 44.

50 Anfossi, 'I "boat people" e la legge di Bossi,' 46.

51 In October 2002 Fernando Prodomo, the *pubblico ministero* (prosecuting attorney) of Florence, questioned the constitutional legitimacy of the Bossi-Fini law. According to Prodomo the law goes against articles 2, 3, and 37 of the Italian constitution, which means that it violates the article that protects human rights (#2), the article that guarantees equal rights for citizens (#3), and the article that sees incarceration as rehabilitation of the prisoner (#37). See Franca Selvatici, '"Legge Bossi-Fini incostituzionale." Un pm vuol ricorrere alla Consulta,' *la Repubblica*, 27 Oct. 2002, 23. In November 2002 Alessandro Nencini, a Florentine judge, declared that the arrest of any undocumented migrant prescribed by a section of the Bossi-Fini laws goes against articles 3, 13, 27, and 97 of the Italian constitution. He added that the administrative arrest of undocumented migrants 'restricts individual freedom' and 'violates constitutional principles of reasonableness.' See the short article (no author indicated) entitled 'La Bossi-Fini viola la Costituzione,' *la Repubblica*, 19 Nov. 2002, 24.

52 On 12 November 2002, *la Repubblica*, other newspapers, and television news reported that about 600,000 undocumented migrants had handed in the forms to document themselves and regularize their employment. About 360,000 applicants worked as COLF and *badanti*. The remaining 240,000 applicants generically labelled themselves as 'lavoratori subordinati' (employed in a variety of positions). Although Bossi and Fini reject the name *sanatoria*, with such a large number of applicants this is definitely a major amnesty. The applications divided according to regions were: 122,000 in Lombardy; 78,000 in Lazio; 60,000 in Veneto; 54,000 in Piedmont; 46,000 in Emilio Romania; 45,000 in Tuscany; 42,000 in Campania; 15,000 in Sicily; 14,000 in Liguria; 5900 in Puglia; 1200 in Sardinia; and 700 in Val D'Aosta. Previous amnesties were much smaller. In 1986, there were 120,000 applications; they increased in 1990 (Martelli law) to 215,000; there were 244,000 applicants after the Dini decree of 1995 and the number increased by 217,000 in 1998, following the Turco-Napolitano law. See Giancarlo Mola, 'Immigrati, la carica dei 600,000,' *la Repubblica*, 12 Nov. 2002, 12–13. Another article published by *la Repubblica* a day later pushed the number of applica-

tions to 700,000. See Giancarlo Mola, 'Immigrati, giallo sui numeri: verso le 700mila domande,' *la Repubblica*, 13 Nov. 2002, 22. See also Giovanna Casadio and Giancarlo Mola, 'Immigrati, sanatoria per 700mila,' *la Repubblica*, 14 Nov. 2002, 14. This article stated that 340,258 applicants were made by COLF and *badanti* and 356,501 were from other workers. The article estimated that before the regularizations allowed by the Bossi-Fini law there were 1,464,589 documented migrants in Italy. The figure could increase to 2,161,348 with the amnesty that followed the Bossi-Fini law, as about 696,759 migrants could take advantage of the regularization process in 2002. In November 2002 the Northern League protested a section of the law: undocumented migrants who reported to the police that their employers refused to regularize their position could obtain a stay permit for six months in order to follow the bureaucratic *iter* of their action. The Northern League supported the deportation of such migrants.

53 See Giovanna Casadio, 'Immigrati, sul posto fisso resa dei conti nel governo,' *la Repubblica*, 6 Sept. 2002, 22. See also Casadio, 'Braccio di ferro sugli immigrati: passa il decreto sulla emersione,' *la Repubblica*, 7 Sept. 2002, 9; and Gerardo Pelosi, 'Sanatoria, porta stretta ai dipendenti,' *Il Sole 24 Ore*, 8 Sept. 2002, 17.

54 See Luca Fazzo, 'Raccolto di mele a rischio: la Lega vuole i polacchi,' *la Repubblica*, 14 Sept. 2002, 24. See also Luca Fazzo, 'Ed ecco a voi un esempio di perché servono gli immigrati,' *Il Venerdì di Repubblica*, 4 Oct. 2002, 54–6.

55 The *sanatoria* originating from the Bossi-Fini law documented 640,000 people. There were 107,493 applications for documentation approved in Rome; of these Romanians were the largest group of applicants (46,000), followed by Ukranians (11,000), and Poles (8200). See Giovanna Vitale, 'Immigrati: la carica dei centomila,' *la Repubblica*, 18 Feb. 2004, iv. See also Marco Ludovico, 'Meno sbarchi: 640,000 in regola,' *Il Sole 24 Ore*, 4 Jan. 2004, 10.

56 See Attilio Bolzoni, 'Le mille vittime senza nome nel grande cimitero del mare,' and Michela Giuffrida, 'Sicilia, annegano 14 clandestini,' *la Repubblica*, 23 Sept. 2002, 8, 9. The article by Bolzoni also includes data: 16,139 undocumented people reached the coasts of Sicily, Puglia, and Calabria between January and August 2002. This indicates an increase of almost 4000 people from the same period of 2001, but a decrease from the year 2000, when 18,452 reached the Italian coast as undocumented migrants. See also Claudia Fusani and Michela Giuffrida, 'Sbarchi, accordo con la Tunisia: controlli severi in cambio di soldi, mezzi e quote di immigrati,' *la Repubblica*, 25 Sept. 2002, 20, and on the following page, Attilio Bolzoni and Francesco Viviano, 'I mercanti dei "nuovi schiavi": ecco chi sono e come si organizzano,' *la Repubblica*, 25 Sept. 2002, 21.

57 Unsigned article, '"I pedalò vanno bene per recuperare i cadaveri." Botta e risposta del premier sulla lotta agli sbarchi,' *La Stampa*, 28 Sept. 2002, 19. See also Fusani, '"I cadaveri degli immigrati? Li raccogliamo con i pedalò,"' *la Repubblica*, 28 Sept. 2002, 5.

58 This anachronistic attempt to bestow visible power on the Church could be explained by provisions in the Bossi-Fini law that interfered with the Church's role in migration. This new law removed the possibility of 'sponsoring' a migrant, whereas previously an Italian citizen could sponsor the citizen of another country, who would then legally work for the sponsor in Italy. Because of its missionary work all over the globe, the Catholic church often functioned as mediator in selecting the migrant. Previous laws allowed 15,000 sponsored migrants a year to enter Italy as documented workers. This new Bossi-Fini regulation could potentially invalidate the Church's direct influence on migration. In an attempt to contain the potential consequences of such a decision on state and church relations, the administration could have considered allowing a visible presence of the Catholic church in education, a diplomatic gesture to appease the Church. Such a regression in the separation between Church and State also invites other explanations and speculations.

59 See Giancarlo Mola, 'Crocefisso obbligatorio in aula: "Nessun decreto del governo,"' *la Repubblica*, 27 Sept. 2002, 24.

60 Ilaria Conti, 'Miss Africa 2002: una corona per Tessy,' *la Repubblica*, 23 Sept. 2002, 1.

61 Anfossi, 'I "boat people" e la legge di Bossi,' 47.

62 This concerted dialogue or circularity is part of a structure in which 'la questione non può essere limitata a un mito contemporaneo alimentato dai mezzi d'informazione di massa, ma riguarda l'atteggiamento di chiusura della nostra società verso gli stranieri e le diverse pratiche sociali con cui i migranti sono esclusi e trasformati in nemici della società' ('the issue cannot be considered only as a contemporary myth kept alive by the mass media, but rather it concerns our society's exclusion of foreigners. It concerns social practices that serve to marginalize migrants and turn them into enemies of society'; Dal Lago, *Non-persone*, 9).

63 See an unsigned article 'Voto agli immigrati: ecco la proposta di An,' *La Repubblica*, 16 Oct. 2003, at http://www.repubblica.it/2003/j/sezioni/politica/immigrazione2/pdielle/pdielle.html. See also another unsigned article, 'D'Alema: merito a Fini, ma la proposta l'avevamo presentata prima noi,' *L'Unità*, 16 Oct. 2003, at www.unita.it/index.asp?topic_tipo=&topic_id=29739.

64 In 2004 individual cities organized elections for representatives of immi-

grants to the city council. The representatives would not have the right to vote, but would voice concerns coming from the immigrants and their communities. In Rome, 32,771 immigrants were eligible to elect representatives, a process that the mayor of Rome, Walter Veltroni, interpreted as a transition in the transformation of immigrants into electors. See Veltroni, 'Da immigrati a elettori,' *la Repubblica*, 3 Feb. 2004, 1, 17. See also the unsigned article 'Stranieri, è già campagna elettorale,' *la Repubblica*, 3 Feb. 2004, iii. And Miriam Mafai, 'Immigrati: un segnale di civiltà,' *la Repubblica*, 30 Mar. 2004, i and vii.

65 Christensen, 'Leaving the Back Door Open.'

66 Ibid., 4.

67 Ibid., 4.

68 Ibid., 5.

69 Ibid., 5. Having been an 'alien' myself, I feel uncomfortable in using such a term that frequently appears in the quotations. For the sake of correctness, however, I need to leave the usage as is.

70 Ibid., 6.

71 Ibid.

72 On 9 June 2000, the conservative newspaper *Il Giornale* published a number of articles signed by experts on the issue of migration. The contribution from the philosopher Stefano Zecchi employs a medical language that has its roots in an interpretation of migration as a contaminating agent. Even when he tries to support the inevitability of cultural cohabitation, Zecchi writes: 'In order to have a constructive integration it is necessary that the original stem, that is the one on which the graft is made, be healthy, and that it is a quality graft. Then a balance is achieved that permits a better interaction between two or more cultures. At times generating a new one. One fears integration when one's own culture is considered fragile, decadent. It is a justified fear because what is weak is swept away. Recent studies on globalization have underlined that the planet is not heading in the direction of homogenity of cultures. Only strong and vital traditions will survive. Weak traditions will be overtaken by the river of history' (7). The medical language employed in talking about multiculturalism establishes a paradigm of survival to an external attack that should be feared as it will test the 'strength' or 'weakness' of the body of a nation that could be wiped away by a History (history with a capital letter, constructed on exclusion) that euthanizes or wipes away the weak. According to Zecchi, that process is unchangeable.

73 Christiana De Caldas Brito's 'Io, polpastrello 5.423' is posted on the website http://digilander.libero.it/vocidalsilenzio/leggebossi.thm, devoted to

migrants' writings and news. It is also one of the short stories in Gnisci and Moll, eds., *Diaspore europee & lettere migranti*, 46–9.

74 Zecchi, *Il Giornale*, 9 June 2000, 7.

75 Christensen, 'Leaving the Back Door Open,' 7.

76 Ibid., 7.

77 Palanca, *Guida al pianeta immigrazione*, 55.

78 Ibid.

79 Christensen, 'Leaving the Back Door Open,' 10.

80 Ibid.

81 There are approximately 11 newspapers for migrants written by migrants in Rome. Beside the ones mentioned in the text of this chapter, others include: *Afrofootball*, *Africa*, and *AfricaWeb*. They can be purchased in a selected number of newstands concentrated in the areas where migrants live. There are also journals, such as *Terre di mezzo: il giornale di strada*, that have been 'visible' for a number of years. *Terre di mezzo* is structured as a publishing venture that benefits migrants who sell the paper at street corners in Italy's major cities. A percentage of the sales goes to the seller. This monthly journal follows the issues that concern migrants and publishes articles authored by native and non-native Italians.

82 In the United States, the beginning of the twentieth century was characterized by a proliferation of local newspapers in Italian. Later, the Italian/American newspapers were published in English. See Danky and Wiegand, *Print Culture in a Diverse America*.

83 Christensen, 'Leaving the Back Door Open,' 10.

84 The first Republic roughly started with the victory of the republicans against the monarchy in the post–Second World War referendum. It ended at the beginning of the 1990s, when investigations against corruption and the collapse of the Berlin Wall (1989) proclaimed the demise of the historical parties that had dominated the Italian political life. In the second Republic, the two largest parties, previously the *Democrazia Cristiana* (DC) and the *Partito Comunista Italiano* (PCI), fragmented themselves into smaller political parties.

85 Christensen, 'Leaving the Back Door Open,' 11.

86 Ibid., 17.

87 Dal Lago, *Non-persone*, 8.

88 Andrea Monorchio (the *ragioniere generale dello Stato*) stressed that 'Italy needs at least 50,000 immigrants a year because in the next decades the Italian population will be less numerous and older' ('Monorchio: Abbiamo bisogno di 50,000 immigrati l'anno,' *la Repubblica*, 14 Feb. 1997, 7). See also Eugenio Fatigante, 'Inps, Ossigeno dagli immigrati,' *Avvenire*, 1 Aug. 2002,

18. The article supplies data concerning the amount of money that immigrants pay into the national pension plan, which finances the pensions of an increasing number of native Italians.

89 In 'Immigrati, una buona legge,' Guido Bolaffi expressed his enthusiasm for the 1998 Turco-Napolitano law because this bill not only focuses on quotas and the fight against people smugglers, it also guarantees immigrants 'legalmente presenti un percorso chiaro e sicuro di accessi ai diritti sociali e civili indispensabili per consentire loro di non rimanere nella condizione di eterni stranieri anziché di nuovi cittadini' ('It also guarantees that immigrants 'who are documented [can], following clear directives, take advantage of their social and civil rights which are necessary to allow migrants to become new citizens instead of remaining in the condition of eternal foreigners"; *la Repubblica*, 20 Nov. 1997, 13). Articles 26 and 27 allowed family reunification if the parent in Italy could provide adequate housing and sufficient money to support the family. Article 35 extended to immigrant minors the obligation to attend school and established Italian language classes that adults could attend. Article 30 even stipulated the right to health services for both documented and undocumented migrants. In order to help with the shortage of health workers, article 34 established a national exam for immigrant nurses who could then practise in Italy. Articles 19 and 23 established that the employer had to guarantee lodging. People and associations could sponsor a person if they accepted responsibility for that person's lodging, expenses, and health insurance. The figure of the sponsor, an important component in the Turco-Napolitano law and strongly supported by every volunteer association, disappeared in 2002 in the Bossi-Fini law.

90 Dal Lago, *Non-persone*, 8. According to article 12 of the law, immigrants could be kept in these camps for only 30 days. However, this does not take account of the slow pace of Italian justice.

91 Brusa, 'La legge italiana del Marzo 1998,' 47.

92 See Tesfahuney, 'Mobility, Racism, and Geopolitics.'

93 Bolaffi, *Una politica per gli immigrati*, 69. Since 1993, Bolaffi has been the head of the department of social affairs of the Presidenza del Consiglio dei Ministri. Since 1996 he has represented Italy on the International Network 'Metropolis' and in the Institute for Migration Policies in Washington, DC.

94 Haider went on an official visit to Italy in December 2000. As governor of Carinthia, he donated a Christmas tree to the Pope. Demonstrations against him were organized in Rome.

95 Bolaffi, *I confini del patto*, viii.

96 Ibid.

97 Bourdieu, *Acts of Resistance*, 22.

98 Jules-Rosette, *Black Paris*, 148.

99 See also the debate published in *PMLA* on the value of literature as an educational tool: David F. Bell, 'Why Major in Literature – What Can We Tell Our Students?' In the context of migration studies and migrants' literature, it is particularly useful to quote Bell: 'To be deprived of literature means to be deprived of a chance to play with and test the paradigms of knowledge of a given period in a manner that is not simply mimetic. At its best, such play can outstrip those paradigms, provoke discoveries, and make connections that cannot easily be made in a laboratory or in everyday life' (489).

100 Coombe, 'Contingent Articulations,' 22.

101 Ibid., 35.

102 Bourdieu has stated that 'one of the major functions of the adjective "clandestine" which fastidious souls concerned with their progressive image link with the term "immigrant" is surely to create a verbal and mental identification between the undetected crossing of frontiers by people and the necessarily fraudulent and therefore clandestine smuggling of objects that are forbidden (on both sides of the frontier) such as drugs or weapons. This is a criminal confusion which causes the people concerned to be thought of as criminals' (Bourdieu, *Acts of Resistance*, 16–17).

103 See also Wakkas, *Fogli sbarrati.*

104 I am borrowing and paraphrasing the concept of 'breaking and entering' from Gardaphé, *Italian Signs, American Streets*, 1–4.

105 I cannot devote much space in this book to a discussion of the definition of the stranger, and so have placed bibliographical references in notes in various chapters. In the context of a discussion on legal and literary issues concerning immigrants, Ceserani's definition of the stranger is particularly useful. He argues for a need to analyse the 'meccanismi ideologici che presiedono all'idea collettiva di "straniero" e alla formazione dello stereotipo nell'immaginario delle varie comunità umane' ('ideological mechanisms that dominate a collective idea of 'foreigner' and the construction of stereotypes in the imaginary of various human communities'; *Lo straniero*, 20).

106 Bourdieu, *Acts of Resistance*, 17.

107 Binder and Weisberg, *Literary Criticism of Law*, 18.

108 Ibid., 18.

109 Ibid., 23.

110 Fish, *Doing What Comes Naturally*, 86.

111 Ibid., 97.

112 Ibid.

113 Ashcroft, 'Post-Colonial Transformation and Global Culture,' 29.

114 Bourdieu, *Acts of Resistance*, 16.

115 Derrida and Vattimo have also co-edited a volume entitled *Diritto, giustizia e interpretazione*.

116 Vattimo, *Nichilismo ed emancipazione*, 65.

117 Ibid., 57.

118 Ibid., 72.

119 Ibid., 139.

120 Ibid.

121 Ibid., 147.

122 Ibid., 151.

123 See Balbo and Manconi, *I razzismi possibili* and *I razzismi reali*.

124 I need to bring into the discussion another example: In the winter of 2004, the region of Tuscany attempted to develop a 'soft' practice of infibulation that would halt the risky practice in unsanitary conditions. The proposal was that the doctors would appease traditional demands by incising a hole in a young woman's clitoris, thereby limiting the mutilation. This would have been performed in a public hospital with public funding. It would have been a way to legalize violence against women, financed with public funding. Such an alternative, while it was motivated by an attempt to save women's lives, naively believed that a tradition could be changed and that men would have accepted this symbolic mutilation, a procedure that nevertheless would have remained a mutilation. Predictably, Aidos and other women's associations vehemently protested the legalization of any kind of infibulation in a democratic Italy. See Michele Bocci, 'La via italiana all'infibulazione,' *la Repubblica*, 21 Jan. 2004, 23. See also Bocci, 'L'infibulazione è sempre barbarie,' *La Repubblica*, 22 Jan. 2004, 26, and Maria Novella De Luca, 'Aiuteremo le donne immigrate a respingere l'infibulazione,' *la Repubblica*, 27 Feb. 2004, 30.

125 Vattimo, *Nichilismo ed emancipazione*, 114.

126 Kymlicka, *Multicultural Citizenship*, 153; original emphasis.

127 See Chambers and Kymlicka, eds., *Alternative Conceptions of Civil Society*. See also Kymlicka, ed., *The Rights of Minority Cultures*.

128 Cole, *The New Racism in Europe*, 2.

129 Ibid., 2.

130 Ibid., 130.

131 See, for instance, Kroeber and Kluckhohn, *Il concetto di cultura*.

132 Bourdieu, *Acts of Resistance*, 123–4; original emphasis.

133 See Fortunato and Methnani, *Immigrato*, 29, 39.

134 Delle Donne, *Convivenza civile e xenofobia*, 7.

135 Ida Magli, 'Islam e Occidente, sintesi impossibile,' *Il Giornale*, 9 June 2000, 6.

136 Bourdieu, *Acts of Resistance*, 19.

137 Ibid., 9.

138 Balibar, 'Is There a Neo-Racism?' 20.

139 Ibid., 21.

140 Carlini, ed., *La terra in faccia*, 84–91. The life narrative is anonymous.

141 In his article 'Immigrazione: nuova legge, ma quale politica?' Livi Bacci summarizes the restrictive laws that want to turn Europe into a fortress. According to Livi Bacci, undocumented migrants in Spain were subject to a fine; in 2002 they were immediately expelled. The two years required for permanent residence in Spain have now turned into five. Five years are also required for a permanent residence card in Holland, which has programmatically increased the number of expulsions. Holland is even considering a possible revision of the Schengen treaty. In Denmark a migrant used to obtain a permanent residence card after three years, whereas seven years are now required. Only migrants who are 24 and older, and have at least 7000 Euros in a bank, may apply for family reunification. Like Spain and Holland, Denmark expels undocumented migrants and has created more restrictive laws concerning political and humanitarian asylum. This decision, writes Livi Bacci, has alarmed Sweden because it will increase the number of applications for political asylum to the Scandinavian country. In 2001 even the labour majority in Great Britain considered practising the immediate expulsion of a person whose application for political asylum has been rejected. That expulsion procedure would be performed by the police, rather than a civil authority. Livi Bacci finds that the German approach to immigration laws is the only one that has a logistical plan and pays attention to possible future development in migratory movements. The 2002 German law welcomes work-related immigration by offering a permanent work permit to highly qualified workers, and creates a 'point' system for the admisssion of foreign workers. It also establishes a federal office that develops a program of integration for the 5.4 million migrants that arrived in Germany between 1990 and 2001 (*Il Mulino*, 403 [Sept.–Oct. 2002], 904).

142 See Kymlicka, *Multicultural Citizenship*.

Conclusion

1 Fallaci, *La forza della ragione*, 50–1. 'Look, today's invasion of Europe is nothing but another aspect of that expansionism. It is more deceitful though,

more treacherous. It is not the many Kara Mustafa, Lala Mustafa, Ali Pasha, and Suleiman the Magnificent and janissaries that characterize [such an invasion]. It is the immigrants who settle in our homes, who have no respect for our laws and impose their ideas, their customs, and their God on us. Do you know how many of them live on the European continent, that is, in the area that spans from the Atlantic coast to the Ural mountains? About fifty-three million.'

2 Ibid., 52.

3 Andrea Tarquini, 'Qui ci vuole un euro-islam,' *la Repubblica*, 29 May 2004, 67–70.

4 Ibid., 70.

5 Appaduraj, *Modernity at Large*, 38.

6 Ibid., 4.

7 Ibid., 6.

8 Ibid., 8.

9 Ibid., 10.

10 Ibid., 5.

11 Ibid., 32.

12 Ibid., 18.

13 Ibid., 18; original emphasis.

14 Ibid., 18.

15 Gilroy, 'Roots and Routs,' 26.

16 In July 2004 the Corte Costituzionale demanded the revision of two article of the Bossi-Fini law: Article 13, comma 5-bis, established the immediate expulsion of an undocumented migrant without allowing the migrant the right to defend himself; article 14, comma *quinquies*, declared that if the undocumented migrant did not leave Italy within five days from the date of the expulsion order, the migrant would be arrested and put in jail. See Miriam Mafai, 'Quando si cavalca la tolleranza zero,' *la Repubblica*, 16 July 2004, 1, 15. The same issue of *la Repubblica* also contained a number of other articles on the decision of the Corte Costituzionale: Liana Milella, 'Immigrati, bocciata la Bossi-Fini,' 2; Giovanna Casadio, 'La Lega: sentenza politica cambiamo la Costituzione,' 2; Claudia Fusani, 'Pisanu: "Subito il decreto per modificare la legge,"' 3; Luca Fazzo, '"Era tutta una grande finzione per noi giudici è un sollievo,"' 3.

17 Alessandro Dal Lago, 'La falla,' *Il manifesto*, 16 July 2004, 1.

Bibliography

Abate, Carmine. *Il ballo tondo.* Genoa: Marietti, 1991; Rome: Fazi Editore, 2000.
– 'Il cuoco d'Arbëria.' *Nuovi argomenti* 10 (Apr.–June 2000): 331–6.
– 'L'eredità.' In *Parole di sabbia*, ed. Francesco Argento, Alberto Melandri, and Paolo Trabucco, 35. S. Eustachio di Mercato S. Severino, Salerno: Il Grappolo, 2002.
– *La festa del ritorno.* Milan: Mondadori, 2004.
– *La moto di Scanderbeg.* Rome: Fazi Editore, 1999.
– *Il muro dei muri.* Lecce: AARGO, 1993.
– *Tra due mari.* Milan: Mondadori, 2002.
Abate, Carmine, and Meike Behrmann. *Die Germanesi: Geschichte und Leben einer süditalienischen Dorfgemeinschaft und ihrer Emigranten.* Frankfurt: Campus, 1984. Trans. under the title *I Germanesi: storia e vita di una comunità calabrese e dei suoi emigranti.* Cosenza: Pellegrini, 1986.
Agamben, Giorgio. *Homo sacer. Il potere sovrano e la nuda vita.* Turin: Einaudi, 1995.
Akin, Fatih, dir. *Solino.* 2002.
Alasia, Franco. *Milano, Corea. Inchiesta sugli immigrati.* 1960. Reprint, Milan: Feltrinelli, 1975.
Ammendola, Clementina Sandra. 'Immigrazione de ritorno e percorsi di cittadinanza.' In *Borderlines: Migrazioni e identità nel Novecento*, ed. Jennifer Burns and Loredana Polezzi, 213–23. Isernia: Cosmo Iannone ed., 2003.
Andall, Jacqueline. *Gender, Migration and Domestic Service: The Politics of Black Women in Italy.* Burlington, Vt.: Ashgate, 2000.
Anfossi, Francesco. 'I "boat people" e la legge di Bossi.' *Famiglia Cristiana* 31 (2002): 46–7.
– 'Uomini o topi: l'Italia di fronte al dramma dei boat-people.' *Famiglia Cristiana* 31 (2002): 44–5.

Angioni, Giulio. *Una ignota compagnia*. Milan: Feltrinelli, 1992.
Anime in viaggio. Rome: ADN Kronos, 2001.
Antonaros, Alfredo. *Tornare a Carobèl*. Milan: Feltrinelli, 1984.
Appaduraj, Arjun. *Modernity at Large: Cultural Dimensions of Globalization*. Minneapolis: Minnesota University Press, 1996.
Appiah, Anthony. 'Identity, Authenticity, Survival: Multicultural Societies and Social Reproduction.' In *Multiculturalism: Examining the Politics of Recognition*, ed. Amy Guttman, 149–63. Princeton: Princeton University Press, 1994.
Argento, Francesco, Alberto Melandri, and Paolo Trabucco, eds. *Parole di sabbia*. S. Eustachio di Mercato S. Severino, Salerno: Il Grappolo, 2002.
Ashcroft, Bill. 'Post-Colonial Transformation and Global Culture.' In *Post-modernism and Postcolonialism*, ed. Silvia Albertazzi and Donatella Possamai, 17–32. Padua: Poligrafo, 2002.
Augé, Marc. *Nonluoghi: introduzione ad un'antropologia della surmodernità*. Rome: Eleuthera, 1993.
Avvenire. 1 Aug. 2002.
Ba, Saidou Moussa. 'Nel cuore di un clandestino.' *Italian Studies in Southern Africa. Margins at the Centre: African Italian Voices* 8, no. 2 (1995): 16–22.
Balbo, Laura, and Luigi Manconi. *I razzismi possibili*. Milan: Feltrinelli, 1990.
– *I razzismi reali*. Milan: Feltrinelli, 1992.
Balibar, Étienne. *Identità culturali*. Milan: Franco Angeli, 1991.
– 'Is There a Neo-Racism?' In *Race, Nation, Class: Ambiguous Identities*, ed. Étienne Balibar and Immanuel Wallerstein, 17–28. London: Verso, 1991.
– 'The Nation Form: History and Ideology,' In *Race, Nation, Class*, 86–106.
Barolini, Helen. *Umbertina*. New York: The Feminist Press, 1999.
Bartowski, Frances. *Travelers, Immigrants, Inmates: Essays in Estrangement*. Minneapolis: University of Minnesota Press, 1995.
Bekerie, Ayele. 'African Americans and the Italo-Ethiopian War,' In *Revisioning Italy: National Identity and Global Culture*, ed. Beverly Allean and Mary Russo, 116–33. Minneapolis: University of Minnesota Press, 1997.
Bell, David F. 'Why Major in Literature – What Can We Tell Our Students?' PMLA 117.3 (May 2002): 487–521.
Benhadj, Rachid, dir. *L'albero dei destini sospesi*. 1997.
– *Louss – Roses des sables*. 1989.
– *Mirka*. 1999.
– *L'ultima cena*. 1995.
Beverly, John. 'The Margin at the Center: On Testimonio (Testimonial Narrative).' In *De/Colonizing the Subject: The Politics of Gender in Women's Autobiography*, ed. Sidonie Smith and Julia Wattson, 91–114. Minneapolis: University of Minnesota Press, 1992.

Bhabha, Homi. *The Location of Culture.* London: Routledge, 1994.
– 'On the Irremovable Strangeness of Being Different.' *PMLA* 113.1 (Jan 1998): 34–9.
Bhabha, Homi, ed. *Nation and Narration.* London: Routledge, 1991.
Binder, Guyora, and Robert Weisberg. *Literary Criticism of Law.* Princeton: Princeton University Press, 2000.
Bodei, Remo. *Il noi diviso: ethos e idee dell'Italia repubblicana.* Turin: Einaudi, 1998.
Boelhower, William. *Immigrant Autobiography in the United States: Four Versions of the Italian American Self.* Verona: Essedue Edizioni, 1982.
– *Through a Glass Darkly: Ethnic Semiosis in American Literature.* New York: Oxford University Press, 1987.
Bolaffi, Guido. *I confini del patto: il governo dell'immigrazione in Italia.* Turin: Einaudi, 2001.
– *Una politica per gli immigrati.* Bologna: Mulino, 1996.
Bonifazi, Corrado. 'Dimensioni e caratteri dell'immigrazione straniera attraverso i dati della statistica ufficiale.' Paper presented at the conference Mobilità geografica in Italia: Università degli Studi di Trieste, 14–17 Mar. 2002.
– *L'immigrazione straniera in Italia.* Bologna: Mulino, 1998.
Bouchane, Mohamed. *Chiamatemi Alì.* Milan: Leonardo, 1990.
Bourdieu, Pierre. *Acts of Resistance: Against the New Myths of Our Time.* Trans. Richard Nice. Cambridge, Eng.: Polity Press, 1998.
Braidotti, Rosi. *Nomadic Subjects: Embodiment and Sexual Difference in Contemporary Feminist Theory.* New York: Columbia University Press, 1994.
– *Per un femminismo nomade.* Viterbo: Stampa Alternativa, 1996.
Brito, Christiana De Caldas. 'Ana de Jesus.' In *Le voci dell'arcobaleno,* ed. Roberta Sangiorgi, 59–61. Santarcangelo di Romagna: Fara Editore, 1995.
– 'Io, polpastrello 5.423.' In *Diaspore europee & lettere migranti,* ed. Armando Gnisci and Nora Moll, 46–9. Rome: Edizioni Interculturali, 2002. Also at web site: http://digilander.libero.it/vocidalsilenzio/leggebossi.html.
Bruno, Federico, dir. *Cuori spezzati.* 1997.
Brusa, Carlo. 'L'impatto dei fenomeni immigratori nei "luoghi" dell'Italia postmoderna. Problemi di metodo e casi di studio,' Paper presented at the conference Mobilità geografica in Italia, Università degli Studi di Trieste, Mar. 14–17, 2002.
– 'La legge italiana del marzo 1998 sulla disciplina dell'immigrazione e le "geografie" della cittadinanza e dell'esclusione.' In *Immigrazione e multicultura nell'Italia di oggi: la cittadinanza e l'esclusione, la 'frontiera adriatica' e gli altri luoghi dell'immigrazione, la società e la scuola,* ed. Carlo Brusa, vol. 2: 41–58. Milan: Franco Angeli, 1999.

Calabi, Donatella, and Paola Lanaro, eds. *La città italiana e i luoghi degli stranieri, XIV–XVII secolo.* Rome: Laterza, 1998.

Carlini, Giuliano, ed. *La terra in faccia: gli immigrati raccontano.* Rome: Ediesse, 1991.

Cavarero, Adriana. *A più voci: filosofia dell'espressione vocale.* Milan: Feltrinelli, 2003.

– *Tu che mi guardi, tu che mi racconti: filosofia della narrazione.* Milan: Feltrinelli, 1997. Trans. Paul A. Kottman as *Relating Narratives: Storytelling and Selfhood.* London: Routledge, 2000.

– 'Who Engenders Politics?' In *Italian Feminist Theory and Practice*, ed. Graziella Parati and Rebecca West, 88–103. Madison, NJ: Fairleigh Dickinson University Press, 2002.

Ceserani, Remo. *Guida allo studio della letteratura.* Rome: Laterza, 2002.

– *Lo straniero.* Rome: Laterza, 1998.

Chambers, Ian. *Migrancy, Culture, Identity.* London: Routledge, 1994.

Chambers, Simone, and Will Kymlicka, eds. *Alternative Conceptions of Civil Society.* Princeton: Princeton University Press, 2001.

Chandra, Viola. *Media chiara e noccioline.* Rome: DeriveApprodi, 2001.

Chohra, Nassera. *Volevo diventare bianca.* Ed. Alessandra Atti di Sarro. Rome: E/O, 1993.

Christensen, David. 'Leaving the Back Door Open: Italy's Response to Illegal Immigration.' *Georgetown Immigration Law Journal*, Spring 1997. Electronic article: 11 Geo. Immigr. L.J. 461.

Cole, Jeffrey. *The New Racism in Europe: A Sicilian Ethnography.* Cambridge: Cambridge University Press, 1997.

Collodi, Carlo. *Pinocchio.* Firenze: Vallechi, 1955.

Coombe, Rosemary. 'Contingent Articulations: A Critical Cultural Studies of Law.' In *Law in the Domains of Culture*, ed. Austin Sarat and Thomas Kearns, 21–64. Ann Arbor: University of Michigan Press, 1998.

Corriere della Sera, 14 Sept. 2000; 22 Feb. 2002.

Cortesi, Gisella. 'Mercato del lavoro e mobilità della popolazione: il ruolo delle donne immigrate in Italia.' In *Donne e geografia. Studi, ricerche, problemi,* ed. Gisella Cortesi and Maria Luisa Gentileschi, 107–16. Milan: Angeli, 1996.

Corti, Maria. 'Culture unite d'Europa.' In *Il sole 24 Ore*, 13 Dec. 1998, 38.

Dal Lago, Alessandro. *Giovani, stranieri e criminali.* Rome: Manifestolibri, 2001.

– *Non-persone: l'esclusione dei migranti in una società globale.* Milan: Feltrinelli, 1999.

Dal Lago, Alessandro, ed. *Lo straniero e il nemico: materiali per l'etnografia contemporanea.* Genoa: Costa and Nolan, 1998.

D'Angelo, Pascal. *Son of Italy.* New York: Macmillan, 1924.

Danky, James Philip, and Wayne A. Wiegand. *Print Culture in a Diverse America.* Urbana: University of Illinois Press, 1998.
De Albuquerque, Farias Fernanda. *Princesa.* Ed. Maurizio Iannelli. Rome: Sensibili alle Foglie, 1994.
Dekhis, Amor. 'La salvezza.' In *Matriciana/Cuscus: storie di integrazione,* ed. Giulio Mozzi and Marina Bastianello, 99–113. Padua: Poligrafo, 2002.
Del Boca, Davide, dir. *Stranieri tra noi.* 1989.
Deleuze, Gilles, and Felix Guattari. *Kafka: Toward a Minor Literature.* Trans. Dana Polan. Minneapolis: University of Minnesota Press, 1993.
– *Nomadology: The War Machine.* Trans. Brian Massumi. New York: Semiotext(e), 1986.
Delle Donne, Marcella. *Convivenza civile e xenofobia.* Milan: Feltrinelli, 2000.
del Monte, Peter, dir. *L'altra donna.* 1980.
De Mauro, Tullio. 'Linguistic Variety and Linguistic Minorities.' In *Italian Cultural Studies: An Introduction,* ed. David Forgacs and Robert Lumley, 88–101. Oxford: Oxford University Press, 1996.
Dell'Oro, Erminia. *L'abbandono.* Turin: Einaudi, 1991.
Demme, Jonathan, dir. *Beloved.* 1998.
– *The Truth About Charlie.* 2002.
Derrida, Jaques. *Forza di legge. Il 'fondamento mistico dell'autorità.'* Turin: Bollati Boringhieri, 2003.
– *Monolingualism of the Other; or, the Prosthesis of Origin.* Trans. Patrick Mensah. Stanford: Stanford University Press, 1998.
Derrida, Jacques, and Gianni Vattimo, eds. *Diritto, giustizia e interpretazione.* Rome: Laterza, 1998.
De Sica, Vittorio, dir. *Miracolo a Milano.* 1951.
Diario, 15 Sept. 2000; 19 Dec. 2002.
Di Liegro, Luigi. *Immigrazione: un punto di vista.* Rome: Sensibili alle foglie, 1997.
Domenichelli, Mario, and Pino Fasano, eds. *Lo straniero.* Vols. 1 and 2. Rome: Bulzoni, 1997.
Dones, Elvira. *Sole bruciato.* Milan: Feltrinelli, 2001.
Dossier immigrazione: la nuova Italia multietnica. Milan: San Paolo, 2003.
Eco, Umberto. *Cinque scritti morali.* Milan: Bompiani, 1997.
Emanuelli, Enrico. *Settimana nera.* Milan: Mondadori, 1963.
Ets, Marie Hall. *Rosa: The Life of an Italian Immigrant.* Minneapolis: University of Minnesota Press, 1970.
Fallaci, Oriana. *La forza della ragione.* New York: Rizzoli International, 2004.
Faloppa, Federico. *Lessico e alterità: la formulazione del 'diverso.'* Alessandria: Edizioni dell'Orso, 2000.

Famiglia Cristiana. 31 Mar. 2002.
Fanon, Franz. *Les damnés de la terre*. Paris: François Maspero, 1974.
Farah, Nuruddin. *Sardines: A Novel*. London: Allison and Busby, 1981.
Fazel, Shirin Ramzanali. 'Far Away from Mogadishu.' Trans. Nathalie Hester. In *Mediterranean Crossroads: Migration Literature in Italy*, ed. Graziella Parati, 146–58. Madison, NJ: Fairleigh Dickinson University Press.
– *Lontano da Mogadiscio*. Rome: Datanews, 1994.
Fish, Stanley. *Doing What Comes Naturally: Change, Rhetoric, and the Practice of Theory in Literary and Legal Studies*. Durham: Duke University Press, 1989.
Flaiano, Ennio. *Tempo di uccidere*. Milan: Mondadori, 1993.
Fortunato, Mario, and Salah Methnani. *Immigrato*. Rome: Theoria, 1990.
Fragasso, Claudio, dir. *Teste rasate*. 1993.
Fraire, Manuela. 'La linea d'ombra.' In *Tra nostalgia e trasformazione*, ed. Centro Documentazione Donna, 28–34. Florence: Libreria delle donne, 1986.
Gagliardo, Giovanna, dir. *Caldo soffocante*. 1991.
Gangbo, Jadelin Mabiala. *Rometta e Giulieo*. Milan: Feltrinelli, 2001.
– *Verso la notte Bakonga*. Milan: Lupetti e Fabiani, 1999.
Gangbo, Jadelin Mabiala, and Piersandro Pallavicini, eds. *L'Africa secondo noi*. Milan: Arco, 2002.
Gardaphé, Fred L. *Italian Signs, American Streets: The Evolution of Italian American Narrative*. Durham: Duke University Press, 1996.
Garrone, Matteo, dir. *Terra di mezzo*. 1997.
Guadagnino, Luca, dir. *Algerie*. 1995.
Germani, Ana. 'Argentina: nuovo paese di emigrazione.' In *Caritas. Dossier statistico immigrazione*, 48–54. Rome: Caritas, 2002.
Ghezzi, Carla. 'La letteratura africana in Italia: un caso a parte.' *Africa: Rivista trimestrale di studi e documentazione dell'istituto Italo-Africano*, June 1992, 275–86.
Ghilardi, C. 'Donne e immigrazione: storie di vita tra conflitto e integrazione.' In *Immigrazione e multicultura nell'Italia di oggi: il territorio, i problemi, la didattica*, ed. Carlo Brusa, 182–92. Milan: FrancoAngeli, 1997.
Gilroy, Paul. 'Roots and Routes: Black Identity as an Outernational Project.' In *Racial and Ethnic Identity: Psychological Development and Creative Expression*, ed. H.W. Harris et al., 15–30. London: Routledge, 1995.
Ginzburg, Carlo. *Occhiacci di legno. Nove riflessioni sulla distanza*. Milan: Feltrinelli, 1998. Trans. Martin Ryle and Kate Soper as *Wooden Eyes: Nine Reflections on Distance*. London: Verso, 2002.
Giordana, Marco Tullio, dir. *I cento passi*. 2000.
– *La meglio gioventù*. 2002.
Il Giornale. 9 June 2000.

Gnisci, Armando. *Ascesi e decolonizzazione.* Rome: Lithos, 1996.
– *La letteratura italiana della migrazione*. Rome: Lilith, 1998.
– *Noialtri europei.* Rome: Bulzoni, 1991.
– *Il rovescio del gioco.* Rome: Sovera, 1993.
– *Slumgullion: saggi di letteratura comparata.* Rome: Sovera, 1994.
Gnisci, Armando, and Nora Moll, eds. *Diaspore europee & lettere migranti.* Rome: Interculturali, 2002.
Grillo, Ralph, and Jeff Pratt, eds. *The Politics of Recognizing Difference: Multiculturalism Italian-Style.* Aldershot, Eng.: Ashgate, 2002.
Guccini, Francesco, and Loriano Macchiavelli. *Macaronì: romanzo di santi e delinquenti.* Milan: Mondadori, 1997.
Guglielmo, Jennifer, and Salvatore Salerno. *Are Italians White? How Race Is Made in America.* New York: Routledge, 2003.
Guttman, Amy, ed. *Multiculturalism: Examining the Politics of Recognition.* Princeton: Princeton University Press, 1994.
Habermas, Jürgen. 'Struggles for Recognition in the Democratic Constitutional State.' Trans. Shierry Weber Nicholsen. In *Multiculturalism: Examining the Politics of Recognition*, ed. Amy Gutmann, 107–48. Princeton: Princeton University Press, 1994.
Hajdari, Gëzim. *Antologia della pioggia.* Rimini: Fara, 2000.
– *Corpo presente.* Tirana, Albania: Botimet Dritëro, 1999.
– *Ombra di cane.* Frosinone: Dismisuratesti, 1993.
Hargreaves, Alec. 'Resistance at the Margins: Writers of Maghrebi Immigrant Origin in France.' In *Post-Colonial Cultures in France*, ed. Alec Hargreaves and Mark McKinney, 226–39. London: Routledge, 1997.
– *Voices from the North African Immigrant Community in France: Immigration and Identity in Beur Fiction*. Providence: Berg, 1991.
Hargreaves, Alec, and Mark McKinney. 'Introduction: The Post-Colonial Problematic in Contemporary France.' In *Post-Colonial Cultures in France*, ed. Hargreaves and McKinney, 3–25.
Hodzic, Jadranka. 'L'altra parte dell'Adriatico.' In *Mosaici d'inchiostro*, 45–47. Santarcangelo di Romagna: Fara, 1996.
Ibba, Alberto, and Raffaele Taddeo, eds. *La lingua strappata: testimonianze e letteratura migranti.* Milan: Leoncavallo Libri, 1999.
Io Donna. 14 Dec. 2002.
Itab, Hassan, and Renato Curcio. *La tana della iena.* Rome: Sensibili alle Foglie, 1991.
Jacobson, Matthew Frye. *Whiteness of a Different Color: European Immigrants and the Alchemy of Race.* Cambridge, Mass.: Harvard University Press, 1998.
Jordan, Neil, dir. *Interview with a Vampire: The Vampire Chronicles*. 1994.

Jules-Rosette, Benetta. *Black Paris: The African Writers' Landscape*. Urbana: University of Illinois Press, 1998.
Kachru, Braj. 'The Alchemy of English.' In *The Routledge Language and Cultural Theory Reader*, ed. Lucy Burke, Tony Crowley, and Alan Girvin, 317–29. London: Routledge, 2000.
Kaplan, Caren. 'Resisting Autobiography: Out-Law Genres and Transnational Feminist Subjects.' In *De/Colonizing the Subject: The Politics of Gender in Women's Autobiography*, ed. Sidonie Smith and Julia Watson, 115–38. Minneapolis: University of Minnesota Press, 1993.
Khouma, Pap. *Io, venditore di elefanti*. Milan: Garzanti, 1990.
King, Russell, and Nancy Woods, eds. *Media and Migration: Constructions of Mobility and Difference*. London: Routledge, 2001.
Komla-Ebri, Kossi. 'Identità trasversa.' In *Parole di sabbia*, ed. Francesco Argento, Alberto Melandri, and Paolo Trabucco, 89–97. S. Eustachio di Mercato S. Severino, Salerno: Il Grappolo, 2002.
– *Imbarazzismi* (Imbarazzi in bianco e nero). Milan: Arco Marna, 2002.
– *Neyla: un incontro, due mondi*. Milan: Arco, 2002.
Kramer, Stanley, dir. *Guess Who's Coming to Dinner*. 1967.
Kristeva, Julia. Strangers to Ourselves. New York: Columbia University Press, 1991.
Kristof, Agota. *Yesterday*. London: Secker and Warburg, 1997.
Kroeber, Alfred, and Clyde Kluckhohn. *Il concetto di cultura*. Bologna: Mulino, 1972.
Kubati, Ron. *M*. Nardò, Lecce: Besa, 2002.
– *Va e non torna*. Nardò, Lecce: Besa, 2000.
Kymlicka, Will. *Multicultural Citizenship: A Liberal Theory of Minority Rights*. Oxford: Clarendon Press, 1995.
Kymlicka, Will, ed. *The Rights of Minority Cultures*. Oxford: Oxford University Press, 1995.
Laboratorio paroleMOLEste, eds. *Piovono storie: romanzo collettivo*. Ravenna: Fernandel, 2002.
Lamri, Tahar. 'Il mio paese è il mio corpo.' In *Da qui verso casa*, ed. Davide Bregola, 83–95. Rome: Interculturali, 2002.
– 'Il pellegrinaggio della voce.' In *Parole di sabbia*, ed. Francesco Argento, Alberto Melandri, and Paolo Trabucco, 60–70. S. Eustachio di Mercato S. Severino, Salerno: Il Grappolo, 2002.
– 'Solo allora, sono certo, potrò capire.' In *Le voci dell'arcobaleno*, ed. Roberta Sangiorgi, 43–58. Santarcangelo di Romagna: Fara, 1995.
Lasdun, James. *The Siege and Other Stories*. London: Vintage, 1999. Trans. Daniela Guglielmino and Laura Noulian as *L'assedio*. Milan: Garzanti, 1999.

Lionnet, Françoise. *Autobiographical Voices: Race, Gender, Self Portraiture.* Ithaca: Cornell University Press, 1989.
– *Postcolonial Representations: Women, Literature, Identity.* Ithaca: Cornell University Press, 1995.
Livi Bacci, Massimo. 'Immigrazione: nuova legge, ma quale politica?' *Il Mulino* 403 (Sept.–Oct. 2002): 903–8.
Lodoli, Marco. *I fannulloni.* Turin: Einaudi, 1990.
Mafai, Miriam. *Il sorpasso: gli straordinari anni del miracolo economico, 1958–1963.* Milan: Mondadori, 1997.
Mai, Nicola. 'La costruzione culturale dell'Italia in Albania e viceversa: strategie di resistenza e politiche di auto-definizione nel passaggio dal colonialismo al post-colonialismo.' *Modern Italy: Journal of the Association for the Study of Modern Italy* 8 (May 2003): 77–93.
Malcolm X. *Malcolm X on Afro-American History.* New York: Pathfinder Press, 1970.
Il Manifesto. 30 Nov. 2002.
Marino, Umberto, dir. *Cominciò tutto per caso.* 1993.
Martins, Julio Monteiro. *La passione del vuoto.* Nardò, Lecce: Besa Editrice, 2003.
– *Racconti Italiani.* Nardò, Lecce: Besa Editrice, 2000.
Mazzucco, Melania. *Vita.* Milan: Rizzoli, 2003.
Mellitti, Mohsen. *I bambini delle rose.* Rome: Edizioni Lavoro, 1995.
– *Pantanella: canto lungo la strada.* Trans. Monica Ruocco. Rome: Edizioni Lavoro, 1992.
Memmi, Albert. *Racism.* Minneapolis: University of Minnesota Press, 2000.
Meneghel Bellencin, Giovanna. 'Donne ed emigrazione: un'esperienza vissuta.' Paper presented at the conference Mobilità geografica in Italia, Università degli Studi di Trieste, 14–17 Mar. 2002.
Micheletti, Alessandro, and Saidou Moussa Ba. *La memoria di A.* Novara: DeAgostini, 1995.
Mozzi, Giulio, and Marina Bastianello, eds. *Matriciana/Cuscus: storie di integrazione.* Padua: Poligrafo, 2002.
Mulvay, Laura. 'Xala, Ousmane Sembene 1976: The Carapace That Failed.' In *Colonial Discourse and Post-Colonial Theory: A Reader,* ed. Patrick Williams and Laura Chrisman, 517–34. New York: Columbia University Press, 1994.
Munzi, Francesco, dir. *Saimir.* 2004
Nieman, Damian, dir. *Shade.* 2003
Ottieri, Maria Pace. *Amore nero.* Milan: Mondadori, 1984.
– *Quando sei nato non puoi più nasconderti: viaggio nel popolo sommerso.* Rome: Nottetempo, 2003.
– *Stranieri: un atlante di voci* (Foreigners: A Map of Voices). Milan: Rizzoli, 1997.

Palanca, Vaifra. *Guida al pianeta immigrazione.* Rome: Riuniti, 1999.
Panau, Sanvi, dir. *Pressions.* 1999.
Panunzio, Constantine. *The Soul of an Immigrant.* New York: Macmillan, 1921.
Papotti, Davide. 'I paesaggi etnici dell'immigrazione straniera in Italia.' In *Studi in onore di Giovanna Brunetta,* ed. Mauro Varotto and Marcello Zunica, 151–66. Padua: Università degli Studi, Dipartimento di Geografia, 2002.
Parati, Graziella. 'Intellectual Witnesses of Exile.' In *L'esilio come certezza: la ricerca d'identità culturale in Italia dalla rivoluzione francese ai giorni nostri,* ed. Andrea Ciccarelli and Paolo Giordano, 205–24. West Lafayette, Ind.: Bordighera, 1998.
– 'Living in Translation, Thinking with an Accent.' *Romance Languages Annual* 8 (1996): 280–6.
Parati, Graziella, ed. *Mediterranean Crossroads: Migration Literature in Italy.* Madison, NJ: Fairleigh Dickinson University Press, 1999.
– *Italian Studies in Southern Africa. Margins at the Centre: African Italian Voices* 8, no. 2 (1995).
Pariani, Laura. *Quando Dio ballava il tango.* Milan: Rizzoli, 2002.
Passarelli, Della, and Antonio Spinelli. *Gli stranieri in carcere: Dossier 94.* Rome: Sinnos, 1994.
Patiño, Martha Elvira. 'Naufragio.' In *Parole oltre i confini,* ed. Roberta Sangiorgi and Alessandro Ramberti, 203–13. Santarcangelo di Romagna: Fara, 1999.
Pivetta, Oreste. 'Narrazioni Italiane.' *Tuttestorie: racconti letture trame di donne* 2 (1994): 20–3.
Placido, Michele, dir. *Pummarò.* 1990.
Poletti, Syria. *Gente con me.* Venice: Marsilio, 1998.
Ponce de León, Maria. 'Meccanismi di sopravvivenza: letteratura carceraria contemporanea in Italia, poesia, narrativa e teatro 1970–1997.' PhD diss., Northwestern University, 1998.
Proietti, Gigi, dir. *Un nero per casa.* 1998.
Pugliese, Enrico. *L'Italia tra migrazioni internazionali e migrazioni interne.* Bologna: Mulino, 2002.
Radhakrishnan, Rajagopalan. *Diasporic Mediations: Between Home and Location.* Minneapolis: University of Minnesota Press, 1996.
Raffaele, Giovanni. 'Le immigrate extracomunitarie in Italia.' *Studi Emigrazione* 29, no. 106 (1992): 194–225.
Ramberti, Alessandro, and Roberta Sangiorgi, eds. *Memorie in valigia.* Sant' Arcangelo di Romagna: Fara Editore, 1997.
Ranieri, Massimo. *Oggi o dimane.* Sony Music, 2001.
Reali, Stefano, dir. *Verso Nord.* 2003.

La Repubblica. 14 Feb.–20 Nov. 1997, 9–25 Aug. 1998, 1 July 1999, 22 July–15 Sept. 2000, 12 Mar.–19 Nov. 2002, 10 Oct. 2003, 21 Jan–30 Mar. 2004.

Restaino, Franco, and Adriana Cavarero. *Le filosofie femministe*. Torino: Paravia Scriptorium, 1999.

Righini Ricci, Giovanna. *Le scapole dell'angelo*. Milan: Mondadori, 1973.

Rossetti, Raul. *Schiena di vetro*. Turin: Einaudi, 1989.

Rotondi, Graziano. 'Immigrazione, multicultura e nuovi processi di territorializzazione: Il caso veneto nel contesto nazionale.' Paper presented at the conference Mobilità geografica in Italia, Università degli Studi di Trieste, 14–17 Mar. 2002.

Salani, Corso, dir. *Eugen si ramona*. 1989.

– *Gli occhi stanchi*. 1996.

Salem, Salwa. *Con il vento nei capelli: vita di una donna palestinese*. Ed. Laura Maritano. Florence: Giunti, 1993.

Sangiorgi, Roberta, ed. *Il doppio sguardo: culture allo specchio*. Rome: ADN Kronos, 2002.

– *Mosaici d'inchiostro*. Santarcangelo di Romagna: Fara, 1996.

– *Le voci dell'arcobaleno*. Santarcangelo di Romagna: Fara, 1995.

Sangiorgi, Roberta, and Alessandro Ramberti, eds. *Destini sospesi di volti in cammino*. Santarcangelo di Romagna: Fara, 1998.

– *Parole oltre i confini*. Santarcangelo di Romagna: Fara, 1999.

Santini, Luciano. 'Fogolâr e narghilè.' *Famiglia Cristiana* 49 (1998): 90–2.

Saponaro, Giorgio. *Il ragazzo di Tirana*. Florence: Giunti, 1996.

Sayad, Abdelmalek. *La double absence: Des illusions de l'émigré aux souffrances de l'immigré*. Paris: Seuil, 1999.

Segre, Cesare, and Carlo Ossola. *Poesia italiana: Novecento I and II*. Vols. 5 and 6. Rome: Gruppo Editoriale l'Espresso, 2004.

Sharp, Jenny. 'Figures of Colonial Resistance.' In *The Post-Colonial Studies Reader*, ed. Bill Ashcroft, Gareth Griffiths, and Helen Tiffin, 99–103. London: Routledge, 1995.

Slemon, Stephen. 'Unsettling the Empire: Resistance Theory for the Second World.' *World Literature Written in English* 30, no. 2 (1990): 99–103.

Smari, Abdel Malek. *Fiamme in paradiso*. Milan: Saggiatore, 2000.

Soldini, Silvio, dir. *Le acrobate*. 1997.

– *Agata e la tempesta*. 2004.

– *Un'anima divisa in due*. 1993.

– *Brucio nel vento*. 2001.

– *L'aria serena dell'ovest*. 1990.

– *Pane e tulipani*. 2000.

Il Sole 24 Ore. 13 Dec. 1998, 1 Mar.–8 Sept. 2002, 4 Jan.–28 Mar. 2004.

Sollors, Werner. *Beyond Ethnicity: Consent and Descent in American Culture*. New York: Oxford University Press, 1986.

Soudani, Mohamed, dir. *Waalo fendo: La, où la terre gèle*. Script by Saidou Moussa Ba. 1997.

Spivak, Gayatri Chakravorty. *The Post-Colonial Critic: Interviews, Strategies, Dialogues*. Ed. Sarah Harasym. New York: Routledge, 1990.

La Stampa. 28 Sept. 2002.

Stella, Gian Antonio. *Quando gli Albanesi eravamo noi*. Milan: Rizzoli, 2002.

– *Schei: dal boom alla rivolta. Il mitico Nordest*. Milan: Baldini e Castoldi, 1996.

Suleri, Sara. 'The Rhetoric of English India.' In *The Post-Colonial Studies Reader*, ed. Bill Ashcroft, Gareth Griffiths, and Helen Tiffin, 111–13. London: Routledge, 1995.

Tadini, Emilio. *La tempesta*. Turin: Einaudi, 1993.

Tarr, Carrie. 'French Cinema and Post-Colonial Minorities.' In *Post-Colonial Cultures in France*, ed. Alec Hargreaves and Mark McKinney, 59–83. London: Routledge, 1997.

Taylor, Charles. 'The Politics of Recognition.' In *Multiculturalism: Examining the Politics of Recognition*, ed. Amy Gutmann, 25–73. Princeton: Princeton University Press, 1994.

Tesfahuney, Mekonnen. 'Mobility, Racism, and Geopolitics.' *Political Geography* 17, no. 5 (1998): 499–515.

Torre, Roberta, dir. *Sud Side Stori*. 2000.

Turnaturi, Gabriella. *Immaginazione sociologica e immaginazione letteraria*. Rome: Laterza, 2003.

– *Tradimenti: imprevedibilità nelle relazioni umane*. Milan: Feltrinelli, 2002.

Turrioni, Maurizio. 'A me gli occhi, please.' *Famiglia Cristiana* 47 (1998): 34–7.

L'Unità. 31 Mar. 2002; 16 Oct. 2003.

Vattimo, Gianni. *Nichilismo ed emancipazione: etica, politica, diritto*. Milan: Garzanti, 2003.

Il venerdì di Repubblica, 4 Oct. 2002.

Viano, Maurizio.'Ecce Foemina.' *Annali d'Italianistica* 4 (1986): 224.

Wakkas, Yousef. *Fogli sbarrati: viaggio surreale e reale tra carcerati e migranti*. Rimini: Eks&Tra, 2002.

Ward, David. '"Italy" in Italy: Old Metaphors and New Racisms in the 1990s.' In *Revisioning Italy: National Identity and Global Culture*, ed. Beverly Allen and Mary Russo, 81–97. Minneapolis: University of Minnesota Press, 1997.

Wa Thiong'o, Ngugi. *Decolonising the Mind: The Politics of Language in African Literature*. Portsmouth, NH: Heinemann, 1986.

Woo, John, dir. *Mission Impossible II*. 2000.

Young, Robert J.C. *Colonial Desire: Hybridity in Theory, Culture, and Race.* London: Routledge, 1995.

Zantop, Susanne. *Colonial Fantasies: Conquest, Family, and Nation in Precolonial Germany, 1770–1870.* Durham: Duke University Press, 1997.

Zebisch, Guido. 'Post-Ethnic Writing in Germany.' Paper presented at the conference Writing Europe 2001: Migrant Cartographies, University of Leiden and Amsterdam, 22–4 Mar. 2001.

Index